Multilayered Security and Privacy Protection in Car-to-X Networks

Hagen Stübing

Multilayered Security and Privacy Protection in Car-to-X Networks

Solutions from Application down to Physical Layer

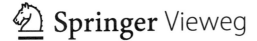
Springer Vieweg

Hagen Stübing
Darmstadt, Germany

Darmstädter Dissertation

D17

ISBN 978-3-658-02530-4   ISBN 978-3-658-02531-1 (eBook)
DOI 10.1007/978-3-658-02531-1

The Deutsche Nationalbibliothek lists this publication in the Deutsche Nationalbibliografie;
detailed bibliographic data are available in the Internet at http://dnb.d-nb.de.

Library of Congress Control Number: 2013938288

Springer Vieweg
© Springer Fachmedien Wiesbaden 2013

Printed on acid-free paper

Springer Vieweg is a brand of Springer DE.
Springer DE is part of Springer Science+Business Media.
www.springer-vieweg.de

Acknowledgments

First and foremost, I would like to express my gratitude to my supervisor and great mentor Professor Sorin A. Huss. I have been amazingly fortunate to have an advisor, who gave me the freedom to explore different exciting ideas at once, while always guiding me with the right scientific advice. I appreciate his openness especially for unconventional ideas and for giving my work direction. He has always been available to advise and to support me during my studies.

I am glad to have won Professor Frank Kargl as a further referee. He is considered to be a leading expert in the field of ITS security and privacy and I enjoyed working with him on a secure and privacy-friendly C2X communication within the Car2Car Communication Consortium. Thanks for his interest and agreement to supervise this work.

The financial support of the Adam Opel AG is gratefully acknowledged, and I would like to thank my colleagues at the Advanced Engineering Department for their continuous support during the last four years. Special thanks go to Harald Berninger and Steffen Knapp for reviewing parts of this thesis and for giving me great feedback during my studies. Further thanks go to Bernd Büchs for being a helping hand during the experimentation phase and for providing me with the latest Dilbert strips every morning.

I am very thankful to Professor Katzenbeisser and the Security Engineering Group at CASED Darmstadt for giving me advice on appropriate verification methods and tools, which was very helpful to round off this work.

Another group of people I would like to thank are the members of the Working Group Security of the Car2Car Communication Consortium. It was a true pleasure working with each of you, and I am especially thankful for the very constructive and always friendly working spirit inside our Task Force PKI. I am sure that our work bears fruit and this exciting Car2Car technology will become reality in the coming years.

Moreover I wanted to thank Jonas Firl and Attila Jaeger for the inspiring discussions we had, including, but not limited to technical and academical issues only. Thank you for at least trying to debate and solve all the world's largest political and economical problems at once. I enjoyed our little talks and it was always a pleasure working with you. Besides that, thanks for the excellent review of this work.

Thanks to Professor Abdulhadi Shoufan for improving my academic writing skills and for being a personal role model to me over the years. Further thanks go to Tom Assmuth, Alexander Biedermann, Gregor Molter, Maria Tiedemann, and Marc Stöttinger. You brightened up my university stays during the week. At Opel this part belongs to my Ph.D. colleagues Gerald Schmidt, Thomas Schramm, Oliver Jung, Rami Zarife and Thomas Streubel. Thanks to you all.

I owe my loving thanks to my enchanting girlfriend Kathrin, my brother, my grandparents, my aunts, my uncles, and my cousins, which have all been a constant source of love, support and strength all these years. Without their encouragement and understanding it would have been impossible for me to finish this work.

Lastly, and most importantly, I wish to thank my parents, Brigitte and Hartmut Stübing. To them I dedicate this thesis.

Besten Dank! May you all benefit from a secure and privacy-friendly Car2Car Communication in the near future!

Zusammenfassung

Die Car-to-X (C2X) Kommunikation gilt als eine der vielversprechendsten Technologien zur aktiven Unfall- und Stauvermeidung. Fahrzeuge tauschen dabei unter sich, sowie mit Infrastruktureinrichtungen aktuelle Mobilitätsdaten sowie Meldungen zu möglichen Gefahren aus. Eigens für die C2X Kommunikation wurde der WLAN Standard 802.11p entwickelt, der die Verbindung aller Teilnehmer im Ad-hoc Modus mit Kommunikationsreichweiten bis zu mehreren hundert Metern erlaubt. In der C2X-Kommunikation versenden Fahrzeuge mehrmals in der Sekunde ihre eigenen Mobilitätsdaten, wie Position, Geschwindigkeit und Fahrtrichtung in Form von sogenannten Cooperative Awareness Messages (CAMs). Diese Nachrichten können von umliegenden Fahrzeugen ausgewertet werden, um den Fahrer vor mögliche Kollisionen rechtzeitig zu warnen. Detektiert das Fahrzeug besondere Verkehrsereignisse, wie beispielsweise Glatteis, ein Stauende oder Hindernisse auf der Fahrbahn, werden Dezentralized Environment Notification Messages (DENMs) generiert und über mehrere Fahrzeuge via Multi-hop Kommunikation im relevanten Gebiet verteilt.

Damit sich die C2X-Kommunikation erfolgreich etablieren kann, muss der Anwender von der Sicherheit des Systems überzeugt und der Schutz seiner Privatsphäre sichergestellt sein. Die aktuelle Sicherheitslösung sieht vor, die Nachrichtenintegrität sowie Sender Authentizität mittels digitaler Signaturen und Zertifikate sicherzustellen. Die zugrundeliegende Public Key Infrastruktur (PKI) wird momentan vom Car2Car Communication Consortium (C2C-CC) entwickelt und von der ETSI (European Telecommunications Standards Institute) standardisiert. In dieser Arbeit wird der aktuelle Entwicklungsstand hinsichtlich der PKI Gesamtarchitektur sowie zugehörige Protokolle detailliert vorgestellt.

Die Absicherung der C2X-Kommunikation über Kryptographie stellt eine notwendige, wenn auch nicht völlig ausreichende Maßnahme zur Verifikation von empfangenen Nachrichten dar. So könnte zum Beispiel ein Angreifer mit fortgeschrittenen Kenntnissen versuchen, über das interne Fahrzeugnetz Zugriff auf geheime Schlüssel zu erhalten, um damit gefälschte Nachrichten zu signieren. Ein Angreifer am Straßenrand, der an beliebigen Positionen z.B. Vollbremsungen simuliert, stellt eine erstzunehmende Gefahr für alle Verkehrsbeteiligten dar. Auch ein Vortäuschen von Fahrzeugen auf Kollisionskurs an nicht einsehbaren Kreuzungen kann zu einer Fehleinschätzung und Fehlwarnung der Applikation auf Empfängerseite führen, was unvorhersehbare Ausweichmanöver des Fahrers zur Folge haben kann. Ein solcher Angreifer ist mittels kryptographischer Verfahren nicht zu detektieren und erfordert komplementäre Techniken basierend auf einer Analyse des Nachrichteninhaltes.

In dieser Arbeit wird ein mehrstufiges Überprüfungsverfahren von C2X-Nachrichten vorgeschlagen. In der ersten Stufe werden die in einer Nachricht enthaltenen Mobilitätsdaten bezüglich physikalischer Rahmenbedingungen bewertet. Ist diese erfolgreich abgeschlossen, wird diese Nachricht in Bezug auf alle zuvor erhaltenen Nachrichten analysiert. Dabei wird ein geeignetes Mobilitätmodell verwendet, um vorhergesagte Mobilitätsdaten mit tatsächlich erhaltenen Daten abzugleichen und auf Plausibilität zu überprüfen. Das angewandte Mobilitätmodell wurde in laufenden Feldtests implementiert und hat sich in den meisten Situationen als zuverlässiger Schätzer für die Bewegungsprädiktion herausgestellt. In hoch dynamischen Verkehrssituation, wie beispielsweise plötzlichen Überholvorgängen oder abrupten Bremsvorgängen, ist das Mobilitätsmodell jedoch zu träge. Der spontan auftretende laterale bzw. longitudinale Versatz zwischen zwei aufeinanderfolgenden Nachrichten führt zu einer inkorrekten Prädiktion und in Folge dessen zu einer fehlerhaften Evaluation der Nachricht. In einer dritten Verifikationsstufe kommt daher in dieser Arbeit ein Verfahren zur Manövererkennung mittels Hidden Markov Models zum Einsatz, mit Hilfe dessen die zweite Verifikationsstufe entsprechend kalibriert werden kann. Das entwickelte Verifikations-Framework wurde vollständig in Fahrzeugen implementiert und auf seine Wirksamkeit hin untersucht.

Während bei der Datenauthentizität und Plausibilität auf zuvor beschriebene Verfahren zurückgegriffen werden kann, ist die effektive Sicherstellung des Datenschutzes Gegenstand laufender Forschung. Durch das Anhängen eines eindeutigen Zertifikates an jede versendete CAM Nachricht, ist es möglich, die aktuelle Position und Identität eines Fahrzeugs eindeutig festzustellen. Darüber hinaus erlaubt die hohe räumliche und zeitliche Auflösung der enthaltenen Positionsdaten eine genaue Analyse des Fahrverhaltens. Der Schutz der Privatsphäre ist nicht nur aus rechtlichen Hintergründen zwingend erforderlich, sondern stellt vielmehr eine Grundbedingung für die Akzeptanz der Technologie in der Bevölkerung dar.

Um die Nachverfolgung von Fahrzeugen durch mögliche Angreifer zu erschweren, hat sich das C2C-CC auf ein einfaches Verfahren basierend auf einer Pseudonymisierung geeinigt. Dabei wechselt ein Fahrzeug nach bestimmten Zeitabständen alle statischen Merkmale innerhalb einer Nachricht. Diese einfache Form der Pseudonymisierung bietet lediglich Schutz gegenüber schwachen Angreifern, die nur lokal Zugriff auf versendete Nachrichten haben. Mehrere Untersuchungen, die innerhalb verschiedener Forschungsprojekte angestellt wurden, haben ergeben, dass ein Angreifer, der unmittelbar einen Pseudonymwechsel beobachtet, diesen aufgrund des räumlichen und zeitlichen Zusammenhangs in den meisten Fällen wieder auflösen kann. Der Ansatz der Pseudonymisierung stellt somit lediglich eine Grundabsicherung dar, die um entsprechende Maßnahmen zu effektiven Schutz der Privatsphäre gegenüber einem globalen Angreifer erweitert werden muss.

In dieser Arbeit wurde ein dezentrales Privacy-Protokoll entwickelt, welches es Teilnehmern ermöglicht, zyklisch einen geheimen Gruppenschlüssel zu bestimmen. Zur Berechnung des Gruppenschlüssels wurden zwei alternative Ansätze untersucht. Nach einem ersten Ansatz werden Schlüsselfragmente von jedem Teilnehmer einzeln erzeugt und in verschlüsselter Form an alle anderen Teilnehmer versendet. Der gemeinsame Gruppenschlüssel berechnet sich dann aus einer Konkatenation aller Fragmente. Für das zweite Verfahren wurde ein n-party Diffie-Helman Verfahren auf das hoch dynamische C2X-Umfeld übertragen. Ein gemeinsamer geheimer Gruppenschlüssel erlaubt es Gruppenmitgliedern, gleichzeitig authentifizierbare Nachrichten zu senden, ohne die eigene Identität preiszugeben. Das beschriebene Protokoll erzeugt damit eine dynamische Mix Zone, innerhalb dessen Fahrzeuge sich vermischen und somit ihr Pseudonym wechseln können, ohne das ein Angreifer den Wechsel zuordnen kann. Um die minimal notwendige Gruppendauer zu bestimmen, wurde das Protokoll vollständig implementiert und mit neuesten Verkehrs- und Kommunikationssimulatoren evaluiert. Ein Referenzangreifer wurde modelliert und der Grad der Anonymität in Abhängigkeit von der Gruppendauer und der Verkehrsdichte untersucht. Es konnte gezeigt werden, das das beschriebene Verfahren die Verfolgbarkeit einzelner Fahrzeuge deutlich im Vergleich zur einfachen Pseudonymisierung verringert.

Auf physikalischer Schicht wird das oben beschriebene Privacy-Protokoll durch den neuarti-
gen Ansatz des Secure C2X Beamforming wirkungsvoll unterstützt. Die C2X-Kommunikation
basiert momentan noch auf Antennen, die ein omni-direktionales Feld für das Senden und
Empfangen aufweisen. Dadurch können auch unerwünschte Parteien am Straßenrand in das
Kommunikationsfeld eingebunden werden. Um böswillige Angreifer daran zu hindern, die
Verkehrssicherheit durch verfälschte Nachrichten zu gefährden oder die Privatsphäre der
Fahrer durch den Empfang ihrer Daten zu verletzen, ist eine Technik erforderlich, die in der
Lage ist, sowohl das Sende- als auch das Empfangsfeld der Antenne zu adaptieren.

Die Entwicklung des Secure C2X Beamforming Ansatzes geht auf eine Analyse der verschiedenen C2X-Applikationen und den damit verbundenen Nachrichten zurück. Vergleicht
man das Ausbreitungsgebiet einer Nachricht mit dessen tatsächlichen Relevanzbereich, stellt
man fest, dass für keine C2X-Applikation ein omni-direktionales Antennenfeld zwingend
erforderlich ist. Ziel des Secure C2X Beamforming ist es daher, mittels eines geeigneten
Antennensystems das Sendefeld so zu formen, dass es mit dem tatsächlichen Relevanzbereich der Nachricht übereinstimmt. Um ein solches Antennensystem zu definieren, wurde ein
tool-gestützter Designablauf vorgestellt. Eine dedizierte Metrik soll es Antennenentwicklern
ermöglichen, verschiedene Ausbreitungs-Charakteristiken bezüglich deren Sicherheitseigen-
schaften quantitativ zu untersuchen. Der beschriebene Designablauf wurde beispielhaft auf
ein generisches Antennenarray Model, sowie auf ein bereits bestehendes Antennensystem
aus laufenden Feldtests angewandt.

Die vorgestellten Ansätze und Konzepte sind innerhalb des ITS-Referenzmodelles (einem auf
das C2X-Szenario angepassten ISO/OSI Modell) auf verschiedenen Schichten angesiedelt.
Die Verfahren bauen aufeinander auf und sind so abgestimmt, dass diese sich gegenseitig
in ihrer Wirksamkeit unterstützen. So ermöglichen zum Beispiel Zertifikate und Signaturen, die auf *Applikations-Schicht* erzeugt werden auf *Netzwerk-Schicht* Gruppenteilnehmer
innerhalb des Privacy-Protokolls zu authentifizieren und sichere Kommunikationskanäle aus-
zubilden. Die Plausibilitätsprüfung ist auf der sogenannten *Facility-Schicht*, einer eigenen
C2X-Schicht zwischen Netzwerk und Applikationsschicht, angesiedelt und ermöglicht es,
nicht vertrauenswürdige Teilnehmer von der Gruppenbildung auszuschließen. Auf der *phy-
sikalischen Schicht* werden darüber liegende Verfahren wirkungsvoll durch eine Reduzierung
des Sendefeldes auf die tatsächlichen Adressaten einer Nachricht unterstützt. Im speziellen
für das Privacy-Protokoll ist es daher auch möglich, während der Gruppenbildungsphase ex-
plizit nur Gruppenmitglieder in die Kommunikation einzubeziehen. Dadurch bekommt ein
möglicher Angreifer reduzierte Kenntnisse über die tatsächliche Gruppenzusammensetzung,
was die Nachverfolgbarkeit innerhalb der Gruppe zusätzlich erschwert.

Abbreviations

ACC	Adaptive Cruise Control
AES	Advanced Encryption Standard
AOA	Angle of Arrival
ART	Acceptance Range Threshold
ASIC	Application-Specific Integrated Circuit
AT	Acceptance Threshold
AU	Application Unit
BER	Bit Error Rate
BN	Bayesian Network
BSA	Basic Set of Applications
C2C	Car-to-Car
C2C-CC	Car2Car Communication Consortium
C2CGE	Car2Car Group Establishment
C2I	Car-to-Infrastructure
C2X	Car-to-X
CA	Certification Authority
CAM	Cooperative Awareness Message
CAN	Controller Area Network
CCH	Control Channel
CCU	Communication Control Unit
CRL	Certificate Revocation List
CSMA	Carrier Sense Multiple Access
DA	Dissemination Area
DECT	Digital Enhanced Cordless Telecommunications
DENM	Decentralized Environment Notification Message
DH	Diffie-Hellman
DIAMANT	Dynamische Informationen und Anwendungen zur Mobilitätssicherung mit Adaptiven Netzwerken und Telematik-Infrastruktur
DoS	Denial-of-Service
ECC	Elliptic Curve Cryptography
ECDSA	Elliptic Curve Digital Signature Algorithmus
EEBL	Emergency Electronic Break Light
EIRP	Equivalent Isotropically Radiated Power
ESC	Electronic Stability Control
ETSI	European Telecommunication Standards Institute
EU	European Union
FGSV	Forschungsgesellschaft für Straßen - und Verkehrswesen
FNR	False Negative Rate
FOT	Field Operational Trials
FPR	False Positive Rate

GBC	Geographically-Scoped Broadcast
GLOSA	Green Light Optimal Speed Advisory
GPS	Global Positioning System
GSM	Global System for Mobile Communications
HMAC	Hash-based Message Authentication Code
HMI	Human Machine Interface
HMM	Hidden Markov Models
HPP	Hacker's Profiling Project
I2C	Infrastructure-to-Car
ICS	ITS Central Stations
ICW	Intersection Collision Warning
ID	Identifier
IEEE	Institute of Electrical and Electronics Engineers
IP	Internet Protocol
ITS	Intelligent Transportation System
IVS	ITS Vehicle Station
KF	Kalman Filter
LAN	Local Area Network
LBS	Location Based Services
LDM	Local Dynamic Map
Lidar	Light Detection and Ranging
LIN	Local Interconnect Network
LOS	Line Of Side
LTC	Long Term Certificate
LTCA	Long Term Certification Authority
LTL	Linear Temporal Logic
MAC	Media Access Controlm
MDM	Minimum Distance Moved
MDT	Maximum Density Threshold
MGT	Mobility Grade Threshold
MoG	Mixture of Gaussian
MTR	Maximum Tracking Round
NIST	National Institute of Standards and Technology
NoW	Network on Wheels
OBD	On Board Diagnosis
OSGi	Open Services Gateway initiative
PC	Pseudonym Certificate
PCA	Pseudonym Certification Authority
PDF	Probability Density Function
PET	Privacy Enhancing Technologies
PKI	Public Key Infrastructure
POI	Point of Interest notification
PRECIOSA	Privacy Enabled Capability in Co-operative Systems and Safety Applications
PreDriveC2X	Preparation for Driving Implementation and Evaluation of C2X communication technology
PRESERVE	Preparing Secure Vehicle-to-X Communication Systems

PVD	Probe Vehicle Data
Radar	Radio Detection and Ranging
RCA	Root Certification Authority
ROC	Receiver Operating Characteristic
RSA	Rivest, Shamir und Adleman
RSSI	Received Signal Strength Indicator
RSU	Road-Side Unit
SAE	Society of Automotive Engineers
SAM	Service Announcement Message
SCBM	Secure C2X Beamforming Metric
SCH	Service Channel
SHA	Secure Hash Algorithm
SHB	Single-Hop Broadcast
SIM	Subscriber Identity Module
sim^{TD}	Sichere Intelligente Mobilitt - Testfeld Deutschland
SLOW	Silence at Low Speeds
SM	Security Module
SMP	Security Module Provider
SNR	Signal-to-Noise Ratio
SPAT	Signal Phase And Timing Message
SVGP	Secure VANET Group Protocol
TCS	Traction Control System
TDMA	Time Division Multiple Access
TOA	Time of Arrival
TRM	Tamper-Resistant Module
TSB	Topologically-Scoped Broadcast
TTC	Time to Collision
TTL	Time-To-Live
UC	Use Case
UMTS	Universal Mobile Telecommunications System
UTC	Coordinated Universal Time
VEBAS	Vehicle Behavior Analysis and Evaluation Scheme
VIN	Vehicle Identification Number
VPN	Virtual Private Network
VSimRTI	V2X Simulation Runtime Infrastructure
WLAN	Wireless Local Area Network
WPA	Wi-Fi Protected Access

Contents

1 Introduction

Car-to-X communication is considered as a key technology towards enhancing road safety and traffic efficiency. The term *Car-to-X (C2X)* communication refers both to the *Car-to-Car* (C2C) communication defining information exchange among vehicles and to the *Car-to-Infrastructure (C2I)* communication, which includes *Road-Side Units (RSU)*. Compared to other, centralized networks like, e.g., mobile telephony, this communication technology is characterized by its decentralized organization, letting participants communicate in an ad-hoc mode via broadcast messages.

As an open and decentralized system, C2X communication will be exposed to a variety of privacy and security threats. On the one hand, not every driver will wish to identify her- or himself while driving some vehicle. In order to yield a certain customer acceptance, the tracking of vehicles and inferring of sensitive user data has to be impeded. On the other hand, a manipulated message indicating a false emergency brake signal, for instance, may lead to tremendous consequences. In order to thwart such attacks, a comprehensive integration of security and privacy techniques into every C2X architecture is necessary or, in fact, a fundamental prerequisite for a successful deployment.

1.1 Motivation

In the scope of the current work towards a reference architecture for *Intelligent Transport Systems (ITS)*, the *European Telecommunication Standards Institute (ETSI)* has defined a dedicated protocol reference model for ITS applications. As depicted in Figure 1.1 this reference architecture is basically derived from the ISO/OSI reference model [1], complemented by a so called *facility layer*; an intermediate layer, which provides supporting services to the applications above. Furthermore, the ETSI has recognized the criticality of security issues in C2X communication and settled it together with management tasks, as a cross-layer in the ITS reference model. This arrangement reflects the necessity of considering security aspects on all layers of the reference model, i.e., from the application layer down to the access technologies on the physical layer. It goes without saying, that this requirement not only applies for security. In the same way the topic of driver's privacy is equally important to current standardization activities. Bringing together the apparently contradicting requirements of a trustable source on the one hand and anonymity of the sender on the other, is considered as an ongoing challenge, not restricted to the C2X domain, only.

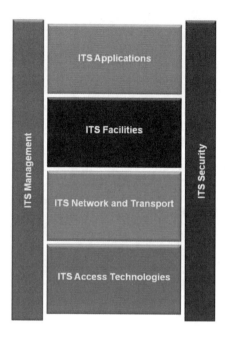

Figure 1.1: ITS reference model [2]

This work is motivated by the need for comprehensive covering of the ITS reference model with appropriated security and privacy solutions, as demanded by ETSI standards. Towards this objective, in this thesis, the following topics are discussed and open questions are answered:

1. Cryptography provides several methods to support data confidentiality, integrity, and authentication. The IEEE 1609.2 standard was especially developed with respect to communications in wireless vehicular networks [3]. With the main focus on cryptographic techniques this standard proposes digital signatures to authenticate exchanged C2X messages, while the keys, used to generate the signatures, are certified by trusted *Certification Authorities (CA)*. With respect to solutions based on asymmetric cryptography the following question is pending:

   How does the infrastructural backend has to be composed in order to support message authenticity based on asymmetric cryptography?

2. Even the strongest cryptographic measures become inadequate, if an adversary may acquire valid cryptographic credentials by compromising the vehicles C2X unit. Such a strong attacker is not detectable via cryptography anymore and represents a severe threat to the overall C2X system. This leads to the following problem formulation:

How can honest vehicles detect malicious insider nodes, without relying on cryptography?

3. Privacy is a further cornerstone for the successful deployment of the C2X technology in the market. However, the broadcast nature of C2X communication makes it extremely difficult to apply conventional encryption techniques. By linking the C2X privacy problem directly to the driver's anonymity state, approaches based on pseudonymization may be applied. However, while being a feasible solution against local adversaries, this approach turned out to be ineffective towards a strong global adversary, which has access to the majority of the messages exchanged within the network. Hence, respective measures are required to cope with stronger adversaries, leading to the following task assignment:

How can privacy be effectively ensured towards a global adversary, without the need of encrypting exchanged messages?

4. Known attempts from literature for privacy protection, are all based on an obfuscation of identifiers included inside C2X messages. Up to now, no approaches have been presented, which would aim at reducing the unnecessary distribution of messages in the first place. Hence, on a physical layer, methods are required, which *tackle the root* of the privacy problem, i.e., the extensive dissemination of messages beyond what is required by safety applications. From this, the following working question can be derived:

What are possible techniques for enhancing privacy already during the transmission of C2X messages and how can these enhancements be quantified?

Solutions, which attempt to answer these four stated questions, have to be found in compliance with general security and privacy objectives. Furthermore each solution cannot be seen in isolation from each other. Meaning that a security policy followed on higher abstraction layers shall be also taken into account on lower layers, too. In the same way, a privacy solution applied on lower layers shall not be disabled by revealing the driver's identity on upper layers.

1.2 Contributions

Towards the paramount objective of covering the entire ITS reference model with security and privacy solutions, four different aspects of the C2X system are studied, related to the four open questions, stated in the previous section. Found solutions and approaches may be directly associated to the different ITS layers as illustrated in Figure 1.2. In more detail, this thesis is providing the following contributions:

Public Key Infrastructure The Car-to-X communication technology is currently evolving from a pure research topic towards a first deployment by means of large scale field testing. Regarding security, this implies a high demand for detailed specifications on how cryptographic protection measures may be realized in practice. Within several projects and consortium work, the author of this thesis has contributed significantly to the development of a European *Public Key Infrastructure (PKI)*.

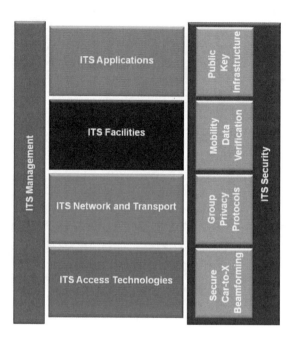

Figure 1.2: Allocation of security and privacy solutions to ITS reference model layers

(a) Within the project PreDriveC2X (Preparation for Driving Implementation and Evaluation of C2X communication technology) the author of this thesis has developed a
classification scheme for rating the trustworthiness of certificates. The scheme has
been presented first in [4] and is further refined in the context of this thesis.

(b) With the clear objective of preparing a roll-out of the system in the near future,
the Working Group Security (WG SEC) of the Car2Car Communication Consortium
(C2C-CC) has created a Task Force PKI. This group aims at establishing a first PKI
architecture including dedicated protocols for certificate management. The task force
thereby, includes experts from automobile manufacturers, suppliers as well as from
research institutes. The author of this thesis has decisively participated in the joint
specification and development of this PKI. Conceptual results from this collaboration
have been specified in [5] and an excerpt can be found in [6]. In the context of this
thesis, the advocated protocols and processes are further detailed by means of sequence
diagrams and pseudocode notations.

Mobility Data Verification Complementary security solutions based on message content
verification, promise efficient protection at a low computational complexity. In context of
this thesis, for the first time, a module for vehicle behavior analysis has been designed and
fully integrated into a C2X system. By deploying a Kalman Filter based approach, the entire

trajectory is taken into account, rather than evaluating single messages without considering the dependency between them.

(a) The development of a mobility verification framework has been initiated by the author of this thesis and has been further developed and implemented together by the first three authors listed in *Stübing et al.* [7] in the context of the project sim^{TD} [8], [9], [10], [11]. In this thesis the advocated verification flow is recalled and extended by means of additional measures for a more accurate prediciton of a vehicle's trajectory.

(b) For handling of vehicles in the near communication field, the mobility verification framework is further extended by applying a cross-verification via a vehicle's local Radar sensor as developed jointly by the first three authors listed in *Jaeger et al.* [12]. In this thesis the approach for matching Radar data to C2X messages is further extended to cover the more general case.

(c) In order to overcome the inertia of the Kalman Filter in case of dynamic traffic situations, the author of this thesis came up with the idea of using a maneuver recognition component based on *Hidden Markov Models (HMMs)* as developed by *Firl et al.* [13]. The basic concept has been continuously improved by the first two authors listed in *Stübing et al.* [14], [15], [16] and is recalled in this thesis. As a further contribution, in this thesis, the final verification framework is described, including all developed verification stages.

The mobility verification framework has been fully implemented on test vehicles and results were found through direct experimentation.

Group Privacy Protocols Up to now, only few approaches exist, for ensuring privacy towards a powerful global adversary. In this thesis, a novel approach for creating decentralized Mix Zones is presented, based on group keys.

(a) For dynamic and decentralized group establishment, this thesis contributes two possible group establishment protocols. The first protocol has been fully specified by the author of this thesis in *Stübing et al.* in [17] and enables group participants to create a common group key by means of exchanged key fragments. For the second protocol, presented in *Stübing et al.* [18], a n-party Diffie-Hellman protocol is transferred to the vehicular domain. The group establishment scheme has been proven for correctness via formal verification by means of a dedicated model checker.

(b) A global passive adversary has been modeled and simulations have been carried out to evaluate the obtained privacy enhancements with respect to this attacker model.

Secure Car-to-X Beamforming Considering the previous contributions, security and privacy have been addressed on the upper three layers of the ITS reference architecture, so far (see Figure 1.2). In order to complete the coverage of the reference architecture, a novel technique denoted as *Secure Car-to-X Beamforming* is presented, which enhances the privacy and security on the physical layer by means of radiation pattern control.

(a) In order to enable a system designer in specifying security compliant radiation patterns, in this thesis, a dedicated design methodology is presented. Each step in the design flow is supported by respective simulation tools for quick visual alignment to the stated requirements.

(b) As case study, two beamforming concepts are explored. In the context of the studies performed in *Stübing et al.* [19], [20], [21], [22] for the first time the feasibility of antenna arrays in C2X communication has been investigated. The second case study aims at specifying a Secure C2X Beamforming algorithm for an already existing antenna apparatus deployed within currently running *Field Operational Trials (FOTs)*. Besides the algorithm specification, this thesis also gives evidence on how this novel concept may be integrated into a vehicle's internal architecture.

(c) Another significant contribution of this part of the thesis consists of a quantitative evaluation of different beamforming algorithms. For this purpose a dedicated metric is defined, by which a system designer may compare the achieved patterns against the application requirements (see also *Stübing et al.* [23], [24]).

Note that the different contributions are highly related to each other. For instance, the certificates provided by the PKI ensure on application layer that vehicles may be authenticated also on network layer, which represents an essential prerequisite for establishing a common group key. Furthermore, detecting the position of malicious stations via mobility verification on the facility layer provides the basis for excluding those stations via Secure C2X Beamforming on the physical layer. In the same way, beamforming may be applied in principle, for directive distribution of key fragments to group members during the group establishment phase of the advocated privacy protocols.

The contributed concepts and approaches have been worked out and implemented in cooperation by the authors listed on the respective publications. Besides already published results, in this thesis additional concepts have been developed, which are highlighted respectively. Text passages or single phrases, which are taken literally out of any of the referenced own publications represent an original work done by the author of this thesis.

1.3 Outline

The structure of this thesis directly reflects the layered architecture model according to Figure 1.2. Hence, every layer is addressed by a separate chapter, describing dedicated security and privacy solutions. Apart from the general system description at the beginning of this thesis at Chapter 2, all chapters are structured similarly, which facilitates reading and comparison between the different concepts. Accordingly, all chapters begin with a motivational part. The different solutions are either motivated by a concrete type of attack, which might threaten the system. Or, the motivation is based on general benefits that can be obtained when applying the advocated approach. Apart from Chapter 2 for all chapters, related work is surveyed and assessed. In this thesis, related work is considered to comprise general technical background, as well as other research carried out in this field. The subsequent chapters are problem specific and contain a description of the advocated approach including an evaluation part and a brief summary closing each chapter.

From application down to physical layer, this thesis is structured as follows:

To begin with, in Chapter 2 the fundamentals of Car-to-X communication in terms of architectural composition and applications are stated. In order to get an idea about how the overall C2X network might look like in the future, in this thesis, the sim^{TD} system architecture is taken as reference. For the set of *Day-One* applications, an analysis regarding the communication type and involved messages is provided. This analysis builds the basis for deriving application related security and privacy requirements in later parts of this thesis.

In Chapter 3, a PKI is outlined, which includes state-of-the-art protection techniques as well as additional organizational concepts. This chapter also puts a different view on the motivation for having security and privacy in C2X communication in general. By analyzing the true background and actual motives of certain attacks, a very likely attacker type is identified.

As a complementary solution to cryptography, in Chapter 4 a mobility verification framework is presented. The core of this chapter is constituted of three subsections, one for every increment added in the context of this thesis. A presentation of the near-series implementation and carried-out experiments further complement this chapter.

One layer below, on Network Layer, a privacy protocol is presented in Chapter 5, which aims at creating dynamic Mix Zones in a cooperative way. Two group establishment protocols are specified and proven for formal correctness. Evaluations with state-of-the-art simulators have been carried out to evaluate privacy enhancements of the proposed protocol in presence of a global passive adversary.

In Chapter 6, the physical countermeasures based on a novel approach for Secure C2X Beamforming is introduced. Driven by a dedicated design flow, two beamforming algorithms are developed. In the evaluation part of this chapter, a novel metric for assessing security in C2X is proposed and is applied to both algorithms exemplary.

Chapter 7 concludes this thesis. Since the achieved results have been already summarized in respective subchapters, in this part a more general conclusion is drawn and perspectives regarding the expected timeframe for deployment of the presented concepts is given.

The Annex includes two further topics, which are equally important, but did not fit into the overall structure of this thesis. The first Annex A deals with an additional proposal for a situation based privacy protocol. Within the second Annex B, it is discussed how privacy issues are reflected by the current legislation in this field. In order to yield a comprehensive view on all aspects of C2X security and privacy, it is recommended to interested readers to have also a look at this part of the thesis.

2

Car-to-X Communication: System Architecture and Applications

Modern vehicles include a multitude of highly sophisticated technologies for providing active safety. Driver assistance systems like *Adaptive Cruise Control (ACC)*, *Active Braking*, *Night Vision* or *Pedestrian Recognition* are only some examples, which are devoted for enhancing future road safety. Basically, all these systems rely their actions on information received from their local sensors, which are primarily Sonar, Radar, Lidar, or Camera. For detecting vehicles in the direct proximity, *Park Assistant Systems* use ultrasonic sensors, which possess a limited measurement range about 4 m. For detection of more distant vehicles or pedestrians, camera-based object detection algorithms are deployed. With today's automotive cameras, a reliable detection can be achieved up to a total distance of 80 m. In contrast, Long-range Radar or Lidar possess very promising transmission ranges up to 200 m, which enables, e.g., active braking even at high speeds. Compared to Radar, a Lidar-based system can also be deployed to detect heavy rain or snowfall, which delivers valuable input for dynamically calibrating the sensitivity threshold of the *Electronic Stability Control* (ESC) or *Traction Control System* (TCS).

Nevertheless, these sensors generally monitor only the direct proximity of a vehicle, and do not share their collected information with other vehicles. Thus, sensing is restricted to the line of sight, leaving out hidden and unrecognized but possibly relevant vehicles or other obstacles. Furthermore, since Radar and Lidar are still expensive, car manufacturers are expected to offer this sort of safety technology only to buyers of luxury cars in the near future.

The Car-to-X technology offers new possibilities for enhancing active safety and traffic efficiency at a large scale. In Figure 2.1 the extended driver horizon by means of Car-to-X, in comparison to the limited range of local sensors is visualized. Using C2X communication, warnings of potential risky situations are no longer limited to local detection only. Instead, a dangerous situation is detected once and then forwarded via several hops, such that approaching vehicle drivers may react in time and adapt their driving behavior accordingly.

C2X communication is based on the IEEE 802.11p standard and enables time critical safety applications at very low data transmission delay. In this context, the European Commission has initiated the allocation of the 30 MHz spectrum, from 5.875 to 5.905 GHz exclusively

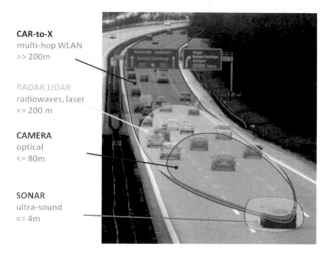

Figure 2.1: Vehicle sensor range comparison

for safety-related communications. Currently developed chipsets allow communications between stations in ad-hoc mode without the necessity of a permanent infrastructure connection. According to the European profile [25] of 802.11p, three channels with 10 MHz each, are assigned. More details on the physical layer properties will be given in Chapter 6.

In the following section the underlying system architecture of the Car-to-X technology is presented exemplarily by means of the architecture developed within the German field operational trial sim^{TD} [26], which is considered to be very close to the ETSI ITS reference architecture [2] and the communication scenario as envisioned by the C2C-CC [27]. The architecture is described in terms of involved components and communication between them. The presented system has been designed within work package WP 2.1 of the sim^{TD} project [8]. As a leading member of this work package, the author of this thesis has made substantial contributions to the design of the overall architecture [28], [8], [9], [29], [11], [30], [7].

In the second part of this chapter the C2X message types and routing algorithms as specified by sim^{TD} and the ETSI standardization body are outlined. Subsequently, the general benefits of Car-to-X applications for road safety, traffic efficiency and driver convenience are discussed.

2.1 C2X System Architecture

In the recent 20 years a significant reduction of road fatalities of almost 50% inside the European Union has been observed [31]. To a great degree this is due to the introduction of strict road safety polices defined by the European Commission Road Safety. Among others, these policies include a harmonization of penalties in the member states as well as a tightening of laws regarding working conditions of vehicles and drivers. Besides regulatory measures, several major technical achievements in the area of passive and active safety have decreased the consequences of accidents or even avoided them in the first place.

However, despite this promising trend, the evolution stills lacks behind the ambitious targets of the European Commission Road Safety. Whereas the first white paper of the European commission in 2001 had its main focus on safety and security of transport [32], in the latest white paper from 2010, sustainability has grown further in importance. Accordingly, by the year 2050 a reduction of 60% of carbon emission on the roads is aspired [33]. On a technical level, cooperative Intelligent Transport Systems (ITS) networks based on C2X communication are considered as a key technology to achieve the next major breakthrough towards a strong improvement of active safety (see Section 2.2.1) and traffic efficiency (see Section 2.2.2).

In the German research project sim^{TD} [26],[30] the Car-to-X communication is shifting from a pure research topic towards a first deployment of such a system. In sim^{TD} partners from the automotive domain, the telecommunication domain, the federal state government, several universities and research institutes have gathered to validate technologies and applications for C2X communication in a setup that is representative for a realistic deployment scenario. For that purpose about 120 controlled vehicles with hired drivers are responsible for creating certain traffic situations where applications may be tested and validated. About 100 RSUs and two traffic authorities are involved to forward messages between the different ITS domains. The traffic centers are mainly responsible for smoothing the traffic flow and reducing the traffic congestion as much as possible.

2.1.1 Components and Communication Channels

The comprehensive and seamless networking of vehicles and infrastructure represents a significant technological and organizational challenge. The sim^{TD} architecture as presented by *Stübing et al.* [30] is complex, as many different protocols and data formats are required and many stakeholders are involved. Figure 2.2 shows the system architecture from the perspective of the different components and domains as well as their interactions. In general, the system architecture is composed of two domains. In particular, these are the

- *Vehicle domain*, which comprises the hardware and software for the vehicular subsystem, and the
- *Infrastructure domain*, comprising the subsystems relevant for the infrastructure services.

The vehicles themselves are able to communicate with each other using dedicated short range communication technology based on IEEE 802.11p. Therefore, they are equipped with so-called *ITS vehicle stations (IVS)*, which deploy the ITS applications on respective hardware. The sim^{TD} scenario further includes RSUs, which are also integrated in the vehicular network and, thus, are able to communicate with an IVS. A RSU can be connected to traffic light switches in order to control traffic signs in urban scenarios. Moreover, the RSUs are connected to the infrastructure domain in order to provide connectivity from vehicles to backend services.

Besides 802.11p ad-hoc communication, as a key technology, vehicles are equipped with cellular communication hardware in order to have IP-based access to backend services and to route safety-related messages over long distances. If available, vehicles may use IEEE 802.11b/g for IP based connections via hotspots in inner city scenarios.

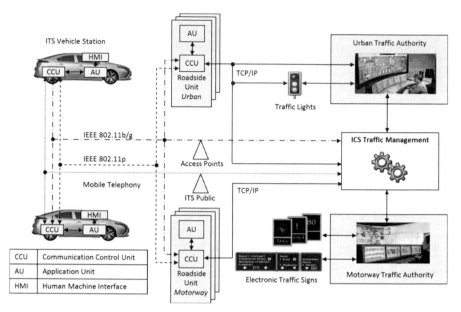

Figure 2.2: Car-to-X system architecture and communication links

A C2X system architecture, like the one deployed in sim^{TD}, may include different *ITS Central Stations (ICS)*, each responsible for a different type of road network. For instance, in sim^{TD} the *Hessian State Office for Road and Traffic Affairs* takes care of the motorways and rural roads whereas the *City of Frankfurt* covers the urban road network inside the test area.

Communication paths in sim^{TD} are vulnerable towards various attacks against security and driver's privacy. In order to prevent corruptive messages to sabotage the network, all transmitted messages have to pass various security checks. This also includes functionalities to impede tracking of vehicles in sim^{TD}. A detailed description of the entire C2X security architecture will be given in Section 3.5.3.

An IVS is comprised of the *Communication Control Unit (CCU)* and the *Application Unit (AU)*. The components implemented on the CCU handle all communication from the physical up to the network layer. This includes the implementation of respective sender/receiver modules for each communication channel, as well as techniques for channel access and congestion control on top of it. Applications that require low latency are also running on the CCU. Beside the data derived from external communication, the CCU also provides the AU with internal vehicle data observed via the *CAN (Controller Area Network)* bus. The vehicle AU hosts the C2X applications, outlined in Section 2.2.

2.1.2 Forwarding Types

Besides message generation and evaluation, the timely and directed distribution of information represents an important aspect of vehicular networks. The previously described system architecture interconnects vehicles and infrastructure to a comprehensive communication network, where information may be routed between several instances over long distances. Forwarding of C2X messages has been described in [27], [34] and successfully implemented in sim^{TD} [35]. In the following the basic forwarding types are recalled:

- **Unicast**: Unicast messages are sent from one sender node to exactly one predefined receiver node. Depending on the distance, the message is either transmitted directly, or forwarded via multiple hops. Typically this type of addressing is used for C2I communication between vehicles and RSUs.

- **Topologically-Scoped Broadcast (TSB)**: The Topologically-Scoped Broadcast represents a special type of flooding algorithm, where the sender limits the dissipation scope by defining a *Time-To-Live (TTL)* counter. For most implementations like in sim^{TD} the TTL is defined as a maximum hop count, which is decremented by every forwarder before the message is broadcasted again [35]. Experiences from previous FOTs yielded that this type of forwarding may lead to congestion very quickly and therefore should be used very rarely.

- **Single-Hop Broadcast (SHB)**: For Single-Hop Broadcast the TTL value is set to one, which limits the distribution of messages to the direct neighborhood. For most safety applications, which do not require multi hop, this represents the preferred addressing type.

- **Geographically-Scoped Broadcast (GBC)**: The so called *geocast* is the appropriate addressing type, in case messages are associated to a geographical validity. Geographical regions may be either defined as a circular area given a center point A and radius r. Or, the region is defined by a rectangular area, given two points A and B and a height value h. If the vehicle is located outside the dissemination area the message is forwarded via *directed flooding*. Hence, always the node closest to the defined area is broadcasting the message. Having reached the destination area, the message is distributed using TSB.

For forwarding of message between vehicles, every vehicle maintains a *Neighborhood Table*, which is built upon frequently sent CAM messages and includes the mobility status of all vehicles in direct communication stage. It should be noted that forwarding algorithms are not restricted to the vehicular ad-hoc domain, only. If available, a vehicle may also use a cellular link or any other infrastructure-based communication to forward the message to its destination.

2.1.3 Message Types

For safety and traffic efficiency related information exchange as well as for service announcements, the ETSI ITS standardization group has specified respective message sets. In Figure 2.3 the general C2X message format is illustrated. Besides the application payload, further information for network and facility layer is attached to every message. On network layer the sender ID, position, speed and heading are included, together with the current timestamp. In the following the tuple, consisting of position, speed and heading is denoted as *mobility data*. For forwarding of messages, addressing details and a geographical region are attached. On facility layer, additional information for evaluating and prefiltering of messages is added. For instance, by indicating the event type (CauseCode), messages can

C2X Network Header		C2X Message Payload	
Network Layer Data		Facility Layer Data	
		Generic Information	Concrete Message Information
Sender´s ID, position, speed, direction, timestamp etc.	Addressing details for distribution and forwarding algorithms	CauseCode, ActionId, cancellationFlag, generationTime, validityDuration	• Cooperative Awareness Message (CAM) • Decentralized Environment Notification Message (DENM)

Figure 2.3: General C2X message format

easily be associated to respective applications. Furthermore. the actionID is added for referencing different subsequent messages to the same event. Parameters for generation time and validity duration are necessary to manage the message storage on the vehicle.

The previous data fields are all common for different message types. In the following a brief description of the individual message types is given. A more detailed specification can be found in [36]. [37]. [35] and [38].:

- **Cooperative Awareness Message (CAM)**: Using CAMs, surrounding vehicles are informed about the host vehicle's presence. The term *host vehicle* is used in this thesis to denote the reference vehicle. These messages are used to build up the Neighborhood Table and posses a generic structure. For each ITS station. i.e., basic vehicle, emergency vehicle, public transport vehicle, or RSU, an obligatory profile is chosen. This includes a list of tagged values like, e.g., vehicle type, dimensions, status of exterior lights and acceleration with respective confidence values. Depending on the situation also further safety parameters like crash status or emergency braking signals are transmitted. The list of optional tagged values is still under discussion and includes. e.g.. the number of occupants or the current door status.

- **Decentralized Environment Notification Message (DENM)**: DENMs are event based messages. Data elements for *content type* and *subtype* allow a fine grained addressing of respective applications. For DENMs, a destination area and location reference can be specified. The destination area is relevant for forwarding via GBC. The location reference refers to the geographical validity of the hazard and is defined as a circle, rectangle or as a trace. which consists of waypoints leading to the respective traffic situation.

- **Signal Phase And Timing Message (SPAT)**: In order to enable optimized flow control on traffic light intersections. RSUs frequently broadcast the remaining green light phase for each lane. SPAT data may be further combined with messages describing the topology of the intersection for more precise referencing.

- **Service Announcement Message (SAM)**: Services offered by RSUs are broadcasted via SAMs. The exact specification of SAMs is currently still an active work item of the ETSI standardization group. Note that these messages are not saftey-related and consequently. will be sent on channels other than the three channels allocated in the G5A band (see Section 6.2.1 for further details on the channel allocation).

2.2 Car-to-X Applications and Use Cases

With respect to the customers benefits, the wide range of different Car-to-X applications and use cases may be grouped into three major categories: *road safety-related, traffic efficiency-oriented* and *service-oriented*. In recent years, field operational trials have specified, implemented and examined almost the entire spectrum of applications [39], [40], [41]. Based on the obtained results from these projects, ETSI had consolidated the different views and then defined the *Basic Set of Applications (BSA)* [42]. Each application and use case has been selected with respect to a set of criteria, including economical, organizational, and legal requirements. Due to its near-series alignment the BSA is taken as reference in this thesis. In the following a brief summary of functionality and benefits of each use case is given, including the respective communication type and involved messages according to the specifications given in [39], [40], [41].

2.2.1 Cooperative Road Safety

In this work, a special focus is set on safety-related applications, since these are considered as the main driving force for the deployment of the Car-to-X technology. Assuming a sufficient penetration rate of C2X-equipped vehicles and infrastructure these applications possess a great potential for reducing road fatalities and damages caused by traffic accidents. According to the author's opinion, during a first deployment phase, the driver will be assisted by advisory information, given by means of optical, acoustical or haptic warnings via the vehicle's *HMI (Human Machine Interface)*. Gradually, the technology will become more mature as the data reliability and trustworthiness is enhanced, and the vehicle will automatically intervene and initiate an automatic braking or evasive maneuver to avoid upcoming accidents.

Use Case	Description	Comm. Type			Message Type			
		C2C	C2I	I2C	CAM	DENM	SPAT	SAM
Emergency Vehicle Warning	CAMs include data fields for indicating a 'Siren in Use' and 'Light Bar In Use' [36], which are set by emergency vehicles to receive prioritized flow control at traffic lights. Other vehicles determine the trajectory of the emergency vehicle and inform the driver about its position and driving direction. DENMs are forwarded to inform vehicles outside the direct communication range.	■	■		■	■	■	■

Use Case	Description	Comm. Type			Message Type			
		C2C	C2I	I2C	CAM	DENM	SPAT	SAM
Slow Vehicle Indication	Based on frequently sent mobility data, the host vehicle continously determines the relative distance and velocity to the vehicle driving ahead. Depending on the remaining *Time-to-Collision (TTC)*, the driver is warned.	■			■			
Intersection Collision Warning (ICW)	By monitoring the kinematic status of all vehicles entering an intersection, future paths are predicted and drivers are warned of imminent lateral collisions.	■			■			
Motorcycle Approaching Indication	A large number of accidents involving motorcycles happen at intersections with other vehicles. As vulnerable users, motorcyclists benefit from frequently sent CAMs, which are used to directly warn vehicle drivers of an approaching motorcycle.	■			■			
Emergency Electronic Brake Lights (EEBL)	By observing the deceleration, speed and brake signals, via the local CAN bus, a sharp braking is detected and a DENM is propagated. On the receiver side, the relevance is checked and a warning is given.	■				■		
Wrong Way Driving Warning	RSUs, located on one way streets or motorway exits monitor passing vehicles via CAMs to detect wrong way drivers. Upon detection, the wrong way driver as well as affected vehicles are warned via DENMs.		■	■		■		
Stationary Vehicle	A post crash notification or car break down warning is distributed via DENMs and includes sensor information, necessary for other vehicles to assess the situation.	■				■		

Use Case	Description	Comm. Type			Message Type			
		C2C	C2I	I2C	CAM	DENM	SPAT	SAM
Traffic Condition Warning	If, for a certain road type, the host vehicle's speed is decreasing below a given threshold, a traffic jam is detected, and a DENM is propagated. On infrastructure side this information is aggregated and resent to the vehicles inside the relevant area. Note that for traffic jam detection, recent FOTs [26] take into account additional traffic parameters, like, e.g., the vehicle density or the relative speed between vehicles.	■	■	■	■	■		
Signal Violation Warning	CAMs of oncoming vehicles are observed by RSUs at traffic lights in order to detect signal violations and to warn drivers.		■	■	■	■		
Roadwork Warning	Mobile RSUs inform passing vehicles about a roadwork and related information.		■			■		
Collision Risk Warning	CAMs allow a precise assessment of the mobility of surrounding vehicles, which enables various different lateral and longitudinal collision avoidance applications	■			■			
Decentralized Floating Car Data	While traveling along the road, vehicles are collecting data via their local sensors, to detect events like, e.g., slippery roads, fog, heavy rain or a traffic jam. In case of a hazard, the affected geographical region is distributed via DENMs. Collected Probes are sent as *Probe Vehicle Data (PVD)* via RSUs to an ITS central station, which accumulates the data. RSUs announce this service via SAMs.	■	■	■	■	■		■

Table 2.1: Application class Active Road Safety

2.2.2 Cooperative Traffic Efficiency

Car-to-X communication offers new possibilities for traffic assessment and control. Conventional traffic assessment on highways or traffic light intersections is often done by using inductor loops for detecting the vehicle density in certain areas. This technology is not only cost intensive, but it is also limited in its application. In contrast, monitoring the traffic flow via frequently sent CAM messages is far less complex and more scalable. C2I Projects like DIAMANT have shown that with a C2X penetration rate of 5 out of 1.000 vehicles a traffic jam may be determined accurately enough [43]. On the other hand, the Car-to-X technology also enhances traffic control opportunities for road authorities. Today, road authorities rely only upon variable traffic sign bridges or TMC (Traffic Message Channel) for delivering traffic and travel information to the driver. Using the C2X technology, individualized information and warnings may be directly given to each driver via the vehicle's HMI.

Use Case	Description	Comm. Type			Message Type			
		C2C	C2I	I2C	CAM	DENM	SPAT	SAM
Green Light Optimal Speed Advisory (GLOSA)	Using frequently broadcasted SPAT messages, vehicles may adapt their driving behavior at traffic light intersections. By doing so, unnecessary stops or accelerations are reduced and thus, less carbon is emitted.			X			X	
Traffic Information & Enhanced Route Guidance	Traffic information including potential traffic jams or hazards is aggregated on infrastructure side and then relayed via local RSUs. Vehicles equipped with navigation systems may take this information into account for calculating an optimized route.			X		X		
In-vehicle Signage	C2X-equipped traffic signs on the road side broadcast contextual traffic information like, e.g., speed limits, stop signs, or pedestrian crossings. By showing this information directly on a vehicle's HMI, visibility is enhanced and warnings may be given to the driver if a traffic sign is violated.			X		X		

Table 2.2: Application class Cooperative Traffic Efficiency

2.2.3 Cooperative Local Services

Besides safety and traffic efficiency applications the dedicated frequency spectrum offers additional channels, which are aimed for commercial oriented services. These services are considered as a further key aspect for pushing the C2X technology into the market and by this achieving the required penetration rate.

Use Case	Description	Comm. Type			Message Type			
		C2C	C2I	I2C	CAM	DENM	SPAT	SAM
Point of Interest Notification (POI)	Local peculiarities like, e.g., touristic sights, restaurants or electric charging points are broadcasted by RSUs. Upon request, a point-to-point connection may be established to the vehicle and more detailed information is transmitted. If available, the POI is illustrated to the driver on a digital map.		■			■		■
Automatic Access Control & Parking Management	For automatically granting access to controlled areas like, e.g., private parking zones the vehicle may be localized via CAMs. A mutual identification takes place and the vehicle requests access via dedicated C2X channels.		■		■			■
ITS Local Electronic Commerce	Previously described use cases may be combined with payment services, to enable electronic tolling on highways or public parking.		■		■			■
Media Downloading	A RSU, which is connected to the internet may serve as an access point for downloading multimedia content to vehicles.			■	■			■

Table 2.3: Application class Cooperative Local Services

Application Layer Security: Public Key Infrastructure

Despite all benefits the Car-to-X applications are contributing to active safety and traffic efficiency, the exchanged messages are highly vulnerable towards several possible attacks. Especially applications, such as Emergency Electronic Break Light (EEBL) require instant driver reaction and therefore have to be reliable by all means. Forged warning messages do not only lead to a low acceptance of the Car-to-X technology by the customer, but may also have severe consequences for road safety. Hence, comprehensive security measures are strongly required. Furthermore, due to the broadcast nature of frequently sent C2X messages, attacks on the driver's privacy are relatively easy to mount, which establishes the need for sophisticated *Privacy Enhancing Technologies (PETs)*.

To begin with, a survey over security and privacy solutions for vehicular ad-hoc networks is given. The described concepts thereby include the state-of-the-art approach, as currently deployed by field operational trials and standardization works. Personal contributions of the author are highlighted within the respective sections. A major part of this chapter is dedicated to the presentation of the PKI, which was developed by the C2C-CC and is now being standardized by ETSI.

This introductory chapter of the thesis is structured as follows: First the threat potential for C2X communication is analyzed in Section 3.1. Based on this analysis the security and privacy objectives are derived in Section 3.2. In Section 3.3 and 3.4 the components of the basic security and privacy solutions are presented, respectively. The PKI architecture and required mainentance protocols are detailed in Section 3.5. Finally, in Section 3.6, the respective solutions are mapped to the previously stated objectives. By doing this, open issues are identified, which sets the stage for the following chapters.

3.1 Motivation

In the following section, a separate motivation for security and privacy in C2X communication is given. While security is related to a secure receiving of messages, privacy is more related to the sending of personal data. However, in the course of this thesis, some of the presented technical solutions are beneficial for both aspects. Meaning, that some countermeasure, applied to enhance the driver's privacy, may also have a positive effect on the security of the system, and vice versa.

3.1.1 Security Motivation

In the context of the *Network on Wheels (NoW)* [44] project and particularly during the preparation phase of the sim^{TD} FOT a comprehensive attack analysis on C2X communication has been performed [9]. Possible attacks have been modeled in terms of attack trees and are then formally evaluated with respect to their implied risk on the overall system. A threat, vulnerability and risk analysis also provides the basis for the security standardization work of ETSI [45].

However, the necessity for introducing strong security measures is not only motivated by the multitude of attacks and derived sub attacks that are possible in principle. Moreover, the overall risk is primarily determined by the incentive of an attacker for actually performing the described attacks on the system. Since the C2X technology is still evolving, no empirical data is available yet, which would allow a profiling of different C2X attackers. Therefore, in this thesis the most likely attackers are identified via a comparison with other communication domains and argumentative reasoning. To the best of the author's knowledge this is the first attempt for profiling the psychological background of C2X attackers, so far.

Within the *Hacker's Profiling Project* (HPP) [46], [47] a thorough analysis has been carried out on the different motives and backgrounds behind todays cyber crimes. A psychological profile has been prepared, categorizing each attacker according to its criticality. The variety of possible attackers thereby ranges from rather low skilled *Script Kiddies* up to highly skilled industrial spies or governmental agencies.

The wireless broadcast nature and safety focus of the C2X technology, however, may attract attackers with a completely different profile as identified up to now. Also the underlying risk assessment may differ for C2X. For instance, the risk for industrial espionage, as one of the most critical attacks in today's communication domains, seems to be rather unlikely in C2X, considering a fixed message content exchanged within CAMs and DENMs. In contrast, the Script Kiddies, so far rated as rather harmless, may be assigned to a more critical profile, if it can be assumed that they are able to modify or forge safety related messages without unreasonably great efforts and expenses. In the following, different profiles for C2X attackers are stated and listed according to their estimated impact on the safety of the C2X system.

- **Researcher**: Disclosing vulnerabilities of systems by performing various attacks, promises high reputation for researchers working in this field. Especially, if the system is intensively used by society and the applied attacks have a significant impact on its functionality. Thus, for example in *Molter et al.* [48] considerable design flaws have been revealed within *DECT (Digital Enhanced Cordless Telecommunications)* devices, used for wireless telecommunication. In the automotive domain *Koscher et al.* [49], have shown how a malicious attacker may forge messages within a vehicle's internal network, causing the vehicle to perform sudden full brakes or stopping the engine. All these research works have in common, that experiments have been conducted in a contained environment causing no direct threat to uninvolved parties. However, by exploring vulnerabilities and publishing them afterwards, pressure is applied to system providers for closing the respective security gap. Certainly, once rolled out in the market the C2X system represents also an attractive attack target for academia.

- **Traffic Rowdy**: C2X traffic efficiency applications such as GLOSA (see Section 2.2.2) are based on a fair treatment of all vehicles when performing the traffic flow control.

However, an adversary may actively try to obtain a *green wave*, by forging other vehicles on his lane (see Figure 4.3 in Section 4.1). Or instead, an adversary might claim to be an emergency vehicle in order to receive a prioritized traffic flow. Attackers of this category are assumed to have a deeper knowledge of the C2X system and are trying to influence respective applications according to their benefit. Actually, the primary motivation of a traffic rowdy is not to actively cause harm, but to gain an advantage over other participants. Such attackers are less likely to be found in other communication domains and may be compared best to the model of a *selfish attacker* in Mobile Ad Hoc Networks (MANETs) [50] (pages 77-79).

- **Script Kiddies**: According to *C. Eckert* [51] (page 21) and HPP [47] (page 53) the Script Kiddies denote a group of people, usually of younger age, which have enough free time, but do not necessarily have a deeper technical understanding. For conducting their attacks they use toolsets and exploits, already available on the market. Script Kiddies are rather driven by curiosity, play instinct and ambition than the intention to consciously harm other people. In most cases their awareness of doing something wrong is not very much developed. For the C2X communication domain this kind of digital vandalism is very likely to occur, too. Limited update possibilities of security software on vehicles allows attackers making use of the same exploit over and over again, until the security gap can be fixed. Below, the possible motivations behind Script Kiddies in C2X communication are discussed in more detail.

- **Amok**: For C2X communication the financial damage that may be caused is rather negligible, related to the potential risk of safety of lives. Due to its sensitivity towards safety, the C2X technology is particularly exposed to attackers whose intention is to cause as much harm as possible.

Regarding the severity and likelihood of the different attacker types in this work the Script Kiddies are considered as most critical for C2X communication. The study carried out in [47] (Chapter 6) yielded, that the following properties of a system generally may encourage this category of attackers:

1. Technical barriers for performing the attack: How much effort does an attacker have to spend?

2. Impact on the attacked system: How much attention can be attracted?

3. Likelihood of prosecution: How big is the risk of getting caught?

Obviously, answering these questions reveals that the C2X communication system may be considered as highly encouraging for Script Kiddies to perform their attacks:

First, an attack is realizable with only few efforts. After an introduction phase, C2X communication devices will be available either from junked vehicles, retrofit or portable C2X systems. Getting access to appropriate sender hardware is of no major issue then. Due to the harmonization of all cooperative C2X protocols, the respective attack software needs be programmed only once and can then be used to attack any other C2X station.

Second, the impact on the attacked system can be considered as significantly high. Depending on the kind of C2X application being affected, an attacker may redirect traffic flow by simulating traffic jams. Or, even worse, she/he might try to actively cause accidents by sending forged messages. In both cases, an attack certainly will find echo even beyond the borders of hacker communities.

And **third**, criminal prosecution can hardly be enforced. It should be recalled that C2X uses wireless broadcast communication for exchanging anonymized messages. Hence, with a communication range up to 600–700 meters, a possible attacker may be located several hundred meters away from the roadside, invisible to target vehicles and investigators. Detecting the attacker's location via direction-finding transmitters is a rather complex task, and considered as almost impossible if the attacker is even moving within inner-city scenarios.

Consequently, in the following parts of this thesis, as the assumed attacker model, a Script Kiddy is taken as reference.

3.1.2 Privacy Motivation

Over years, the personal car was considered as a private place, where no information was communicated directly to the outside world. Automated tracking or identification of vehicles was possible only via optical recognition using high resolution cameras and sophisticated image evaluation algorithms. Implementation costs as well as limited accessibility of installed cameras, prevented adversaries from a seamless and comprehensive tracking of vehicles so far.

The situation changed with the introduction of mobile telephony into cars. Most emergency or diagnostic services available with these systems require to include a geographical position and an identifier into the transmitted messages. Regarding the identification and localization of vehicles this facilitates tracking considerably. However, communication via telephony takes place only sporadically and is limited to the connection between the vehicle and the service provider, which reduces the degree of dispersion for sensitive data.

With the deployment of Car-to-X communication, tracking and tracing of vehicles finally becomes scalable and efficient. Once rolled out in the market, the C2X technology will be available and affordable to almost everyone. Compared to camera based systems, C2X receiver hardware is relatively cheap and object detection algorithms are easy realizable, using frequently sent CAMs. Whereas cameras usually have a relatively short detection range, C2X messages may be still received properly even hundreds of meters away from the sender. A high message sending frequency up to 10 Hz not only allows precise localization of vehicles. Furthermore, the detailed mobility information contained in these messages may be used to create a profile of the drivers driving behavior. In the following, possible threats on privacy are divided into location-based threats and threats based on an analysis of the driving behavior.

Before pointing out the different privacy threats, the connection between the vehicle and its driver is discussed briefly. In fact, there is a strong correlation between both, as many vehicles are used only by very few drivers. For instance, in Germany a total number of 51 Million vehicles were recorded in 2011 [52]. In comparison the number of people, which own a driving license is kept stable over the years at 53 Million [53]. Taking into account, that especially in larger cities, a major part of people use public transport and do not possess a vehicle at all, every vehicle registered may be assigned to a single person. Considering the previous analysis, a vehicle can no longer be regarded separated from the driver's identity. All, an adversary will have to do, is to establish a link between the person and the vehicle. From then on, any data emitted by the vehicle can be regarded as personal data. In Chapter 5.1, a more detailed discussion on linkability of traces and individuals is given.

Assuming an adversary may unambiguously determine the identity behind the driver of a vehicle, several privacy threats arise. In the following some examples are given, where being able to locate a persons position via C2X raises privacy concerns:

- **Surveillance**: For private investigators, following people without getting noticed becomes way easier by evaluating C2X messages from a long distance. Also an employer might use C2X messages to assess working times more precisely by monitoring arrival and departure times of his employees' vehicles.

- **Criminal Intentions**: Obtained location information may be used by criminals to profile a person's daily routines. Knowing when somebody usually leaves home for work and returns again might be useful information to burglars.

- **Targeted marketing**: Knowing the exact location of potential customers, could enable companies to adjust advertisements on the road side in a way that they reflect the needs and backgrounds of the drivers passing by. Depending upon everyone's own sensitivities, some people might regard targeted advertising as a helpful service, while others consider this as an intense way of manipulating their buying decision.

- **Blackmailing, Discrimination**: Location data may also reveal other, even more sensitive information. For instance, very frequent stays at a hospital might indicate medical problems. People with bad intentions could record this data and use it to blackmail or discriminate others.

Sharing single location information is not the only privacy issue within C2X. Moreover, C2X message can be used to analyze a persons driving behavior. By evaluating the path history of a vehicle including velocity and heading information, the following privacy violating use cases become possible in principle:

- **Traffic Violation Ticketing**: Mobility data sent within CAMs include sufficient information for comprehensive traffic surveillance by the police. For example, the included velocity may be used for speed tolling; equipped traffic lights may detect red light violation; relative data between two vehicles may be used to verify if safety margins are kept properly; and even an automated tolling for unauthorized parking becomes possible.

- **Adaptive Insurance Rates**: Assuming a comprehensive covering of RSUs, third parties such as insurance companies may be interested in getting access to the observed data. Based on frequently sent CAMs as well as additional context information obtained from DENMs, traffic situations may be assessed and the behavior of involved drivers may be analyzed. Over time the insurance company may then create a profile of its customers and charge them, depending on their risk propensity.

Privacy protection in C2X communication becomes crucial for achieving acceptance of this technology in society. Only if previously described scenarios can be impeded to a certain extent, customers will accept this novel communication system, which is absolutely necessary in order to achieve the required C2X penetration rate.

3.2 Security and Privacy Objectives

Security and privacy requirements have strong dependencies on each other. Any comprehensive C2X security architecture will have to answer the question on how to meet the apparently contradictory requirements between authenticities on the one hand and anonymity of vehicles on the other. In the following a compact overview over different security and privacy objectives is given. An excerpt of this discussion has been published by the author of this theses in [54].

3.2.1 Security Objectives

In the following, the main security objectives, already known from other areas of secure communication [51], are stated and mapped to the Car-to-X scenario.

Sender Authentication

The primary objective of security in Car-to-X communication is to ensure that only trust-worthy vehicles are included into the communication, and that all receivers are able to corroborate their validity, respectively.

Sender Authorization

Whereas authentication ensures, that the sender entity has been proven as a valid C2X unit by a trusted instance, e.g., the certification authority, a more fine grained delegation of rights is required, which reflects the different roles, a vehicle may take within the C2X network. For example, an emergency vehicle, which demands prioritized traffic flow has to be differentiable from other common vehicles. Hence, for C2X a general authentication is followed by a verification of the authorization of the sender.

Message Integrity

Because of its broadcast nature, the C2X message content is sent in plaintext over the wireless channel. Such a communication mode does not enable an a priori protection against message manipulation. Instead, techniques are required, which allow a posteriori detection of unauthorized manipulation as demanded in *C. Eckert* [51] (page 8). In this sense ensuring the messages integrity in C2X includes, that no vehicle, other than the originator can modify the content without being detected by receiving vehicles.

Message Freshness

An external adversary, without security credentials may still cause considerable damage by replaying previously observed warning messages. In order to reduce the likelihood of such attacks, an application dependant check for message freshness has to be applied. Message freshness is not mandatory for security reasons only. Event based messages like, e.g., *Traffic Jam Ahead Warnings* (see Section 2.2.1), loose their validity over time and therefore have to be filtered before processing.

Message Plausibility

The C2X message content has to be checked for consistency and plausibility. Depending on the message type (i.e., CAM or DENM), those checks are either performed by a central component or by each application individually. Verifying message plausibility represents "the last line of defense" and is applied for detecting very severe insider-attacker, which do not violate previously stated objectives.

Communication Availability

According to *C. Eckert* [51] (pages 10-11) a system ensures availability, if authenticated and authorized subjects cannot be affected by any other unauthorized entity. For the wireless Car-to-X technology, methods are required that enhance communication availability in order to keep communication operational, even in presence of strong disturbance. Disturbance may be caused, e.g., by an adversary, which is jamming the channel with invalid messages or noise, i.e., a *Denial-of-Service (DoS)* attack.

The definitions made above are to a great extend in line with the security requirements stated in the SEVECOM project [55] and sim^{TD}[9]. In contrast, the analysis performed by the authors in [56] is based on different assumptions regarding the importance for sender authentication. Instead of explicitly requiring a strong sender authentication, only a very general recommendation for ensuring message reliability is made.

3.2.2 Privacy Objectives

For safety purposes, vehicles constantly broadcast both, their current mobility data and static identifiers in form of CAM messages. These messages may be observed by an adversary and then be used to track the vehicle's trajectory, which poses a threat to the driver's privacy as outlined in Section 3.1.2. Compared to centralistic communication technologies like cellular networks (e.g., GSM/UMTS), the C2X data is considered as more privacy relevant due to its broadcast nature. Furthermore, the higher spatial and temporal resolution of the transmitted position data enables a more precise tracking of vehicles, than for cellular communication. Objectives from various stakeholders influence and constrain the privacy solution, as outlined in the following:

Message Confidentiality

CAMs and DENMs are broadcast messages and as such do not carry confidential contents. However, other ITS applications like, e.g., payment-oriented applications (see Section 2.2.3) usually require identification and therefore a high confidentiality of the exchanged messages. For safety messages in general, *Schaub et al.* [57] recommend to not include more information into broadcasted messages, than really needed by the receiving application.

Anonymity

In this work the term anonymity is applied as defined in *C. Eckert* [51] (page 12). Accordingly, in order to achieve *driver* anonymity, safety messages must not reveal a person's identity. Thus, any exchanged C2X message shall only include information on the respective vehicle. In contrast, *vehicle* anonymity is not intended for C2X, since this would be conflicting to requirements for non-repudiation and accountability as stated below.

Pseudonymity

According to [51] pseudonymity is regarded as a weaker form of anonymity and is considered as a compromise between requirements of anonymity on the one hand, and accountability on the other. A pseudonym is not directly linkable to the identity of the vehicle and can be resolved only by the respective trusted authority. However, in order to impede driver profiling, using a single pseudonym is not sufficient. Moreover, to ensure a long-term pseudonymity of vehicles, techniques to avoid tracking have to be defined.

Accountability

There is tension between privacy on the one hand and misbehavior detection and revocation on the other. For some proposed C2X public key infrastructures, misbehavior detection and revocation of credentials represents an integral part. However, revocation generally requires identification, thus discarding privacy of potentially misbehaving vehicles. Hence, a too high level of privacy complicates identification of individual vehicles and eventually prohibits revocation.

3.3 Security Protection

Up to now various projects have been dealing with security and privacy issues in cooperative vehicular networks. In the U.S. a first safety pilot [58] is being conducted, which builds up a security architecture based on the IEEE 1609.2 trial-standard [3]. In Germany early C2C projects like NoW [59],[60] already included security measures. The project *SEVECOM (Secure Vehicular Communication)* [61] further detailed concepts for key management and identified modules and interfaces necessary for integrating security into an overall C2X architecture in the vehicle. On an European level, the PreDrive C2X project has formed the basis for a harmonized security architecture among all stakeholders [62]. There, the security architecture does not only constitute additional concepts, but furthermore has been developed in appropriate detail for implementation and deployment purposes. The German field operational trial sim^{TD} deploys a security and privacy architecture by putting the results of previous research projects into practice [29], [9].

One major outcome obtained from all these projects is the insight that the requirements for data security in vehicular networks are very different from those in traditional computer networks. Hence, the broadcast communication pattern as well as the decentralized organization scheme excludes solutions based on symmetric cryptography (see *C. Eckert* [51] chapter 7.3.1) from the outset. In case the global symmetric key is getting revealed the entire system is affected and cannot be trusted anymore. A rekeying mechanism would have to update a new key for *all* vehicles. In a distributed vehicular network the nondisclosure of the secret key cannot be ensured and a synchronous and comprehensive key update is hardly realizable without costly recall campaigns.

Instead, for the Car-to-X communication technology, data integrity as well as sender authenticity are ensured by means of a PKI. Digital signatures are used to detect message manipulations, whereas the public keys used to create the signatures are certified by a trusted Certification Authority (CA). In the following the actual approach for securing C2X communication is outlined, as it is presently constituted, by standards and respective C2X projects. First, common measures for securing outgoing C2X messages are described. Then, a classification scheme for categorizing trustworthiness of incoming messages is proposed by the author of this thesis.

3.3.1 Cryptographic Message Signing

The IEEE 1609.2 trial-standard [3] is currently deployed in field operational tests such as sim^{TD} [26] or DriveC2X [4] and proposes a PKI based on *Elliptic Curve Cryptography (ECC)* for securing all exchanged C2X messages. The ETSI and C2C-CC have created a European

Figure 3.1: Secured message format (186 byte security overhead) [5]

Figure 3.2: Pseudonym Certificate (PC) for vehicles signed using ECDSA 224 (121 byte security overhead) [5]

profile of this standard, which additionally takes into account the secure multihop distribution of DENM messages. Since CAMs are created on facility layer, the definitions for secure message formats are adapted in order to support security operations also on lower layers.

IEEE 1609.2 foresees signatures based on *ECDSA (Elliptic Curve Digital Signature Algorithmus)* to ensure integrity of messages. The public keys are certified by a CA using the NIST P-224 curve [3]. In the context of privacy those certificates, together with other station identifiers within a message are referred to as *pseudonyms*. The simplified format of a *Pseudonym Certificate (PC)* according to the C2C-CC [5] is illustrated in Figure 3.2. Accordingly, the first 8 bytes denote, which Pseudonym Certification Authority (PCA) has issued the respective certificate. In order to save bandwidth, only the *signer ID* is attached, whereas the PCA certificate is assumed to be known by all vehicles. ITS stations with extended privileges, like, e.g., emergency vehicles, are indicated by respective attributes within the *Certificate Specific Data* field. In order to reduce the impact of compromised certificates, the C2C-CC proposes to assign reduced lifetimes to certificates and to establish update mechanisms, respectively. In Figure 3.1 the assembling of the final message is illustrated, as it consists of the message itself and the security overhead in terms of the signature and certificate.

For the purpose of preventing replay attacks, a timestamp and sequence number is included into every signature. Thus, messages, whose timestamp is either expired or dated to a future point in time, are discarded by the receiving vehicles. Note that due to the high mobility of vehicles, the expiry date of CAMs is assumed to be in the order of microseconds. In contrast, the temporal validity of a DENM highly depends upon the respective event type and consequently has to be set by the originator vehicle. The sequence number is included for impeding short-term replay attacks.

3.3.2 Cryptographic Message Verification

Signing outgoing messages is a prerequisite for authenticated communication in vehicular networks. For interoperability purposes any applied security parameters like, e.g., cryptographic algorithms or secure message formats have to be specified by respective standards uniquely among all participants. However, on receiver side the definition of an appropriate verification strategy lies within the responsibility of every C2X system provider individually. While for some safety critical applications, trustworthiness of messages is absolutely

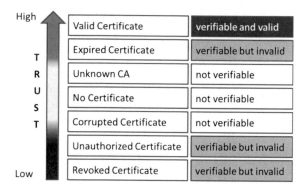

Figure 3.3: Trustworthiness rating of certificates

mandatory, less critical applications may work properly even without verifying the sender via cryptography. The presented concepts in this section aim at supporting C2X application designers in interpreting the results of the cryptographic verification correctly.

In the following, three different certificate clusters are proposed for distinguishing between *full*, *partial* and *non-valid* certificates. The basics of the following classification have been developed and presented by the author of this thesis in the context of the PreDrive C2X project [4]. In Figure 3.3 the rating according to the assessed trustworthiness is illustrated.

The first cluster includes all those certificates, which cannot be associated to any of the public known CAs. Having received a message with such a certificate, the receiver will not be able to authenticate the sender by means of cryptographic primitives. A non-verifiable certificate thereby may have different reasons:

(a) **No Certificate**: The C2X message format is generic, which includes also that messages might be send via the channel in an unsecured way, i.e., without attaching any cryptographic signature or certificate. Such messages are assigned to a rather low trust level, since no authenticity can be ensured.

(b) **Corrupted Certificate**: A certificate is considered as corrupted, if its signature of the public key cannot be verified using the specified CA-key. From the trust perspective, vehicles, which are constantly sending bogus certificates, may be considered even more suspicious as vehicles, which are not attaching a certificate at all.

(c) **Unknown CA**: The certificate might be valid but has been issued by a CA, which is not known to the receiver vehicle. This may be especially the case for vehicles coming from different regions (e.g., America or Asia) with different CAs. The PKI, as proposed in Section 3.5, is dynamic, in a way that additional CAs may be issued via the Root CA over time. In subsequent sections a protocol is outlined, by which a vehicle can learn newly authorized CAs. Until the authorization protocol has been completed, the certificate is rated with a medium (i.e., neutral) trust level.

In the second cluster, all those certificates are grouped, which can be processed by the receiver but possess only a limited validity. In the following, examples of such certificates are given:

(a) **Expired Certificate**: As described in the introduction of this section, certificates possess a limited temporal validity. If not updated regularly, certificates, in particular those, related to safety applications will expire. Especially during an early deployment phase, permanent backend connection to the CA cannot be guaranteed comprehensively. However, if issued by a commonly accepted CA, the certificate still maintains technically verifiable for the security module. And, furthermore if it is generally required to store private keys within secure hardware like proposed by the C2C-CC [6], even an expired certificate possesses some entropy of trustworthiness.

(b) **Unauthorized Certificate**: Nevertheless, the principle processability and freshness of a certificate does not necessarily include an unrestricted validity of a certificate in general. Also a vehicle, which is sending with a certificate, not authorized for that vehicle profile, receives a lower value of trustworthiness. A possible example for the latter case is a common vehicle, which is claiming to be an emergency vehicle, but is not. In this case it would be reasonable to expect an adversary, which is trying to receive prioritized traffic flow.

(c) **Revoked Certificate**: In Section 3.5, a proposal for a PKI is presented, which intends to avoid a direct revocation of invalid vehicle pseudonym certificates. Instead an implicit approach is chosen where misbehaving vehicles are refused to receive new pseudonyms during the update cycle. However, a certificate might be revoked locally on receiver side, if the related CA has been compromised. Certificates whose CA is revoked, are assigned to the lowest trust level.

The third cluster represents the common case of a valid and authorized certificate:

(a) **Valid Certificate**: A certificate associated to this cluster may be processed correctly and referenced to a trustworthy CA. Furthermore this certificate reflects the permissions required for sending the attached message.

Based on this analysis, a multistage warning system may be designed, by which, depending on the assigned trustworthiness and safety relevance of the message the driver is informed either via a basic remark, a warning or in — safety critical situations — an active braking. Note that for active braking it is highly recommended, that the certificate belongs to the third cluster, i.e., the cluster with the highest trustworthiness. However, within the PreDrive C2X security architecture no unified approach is aspired. Instead, it is left up to every C2X system provider individually, how to react properly to uncertain certificates.

3.4 Privacy Protection

For the scope of privacy in vehicular networks, the *C2C-CC Working Group Security (WG SEC)* generally distinguishes between

- privacy against the authorities (like, e.g., government, enrollment authority, etc.), and
- privacy against third parties (like, e.g., other ITS stations, service providers, etc.).

Privacy against the authorities has to be realized without violating the requirement for accountability as established in Section 3.2.2. Therefore for these cases the privacy protection is assumed to be based on a strong legal framework, which allows the processing of sensitive data only in specific cases.

| Signer-ID of LTCA | Cert-Specific Data | Public Key | Signature by LTCA |

8 Byte   18 Byte   35 Byte   64 Byte

Figure 3.4: Long Term Certificate (LTC) signed using ECDSA 256 (125 Byte Security Overhead)[5]

According to the author's opinion, privacy against third parties can be achieved best via a combination of both, legal and technical measures. In the Annex B of this thesis a survey over the legal background for processing and storing of personal data in different countries is given. Already existent privacy laws are presented and conclusions are drawn with respect to the area of Car-to-X communication. In the following the main focus is set on technical measures, which impede profiling of a vehicle's trajectory.

Although there are currently no dedicated standards yet available, which define measures to reduce linkability in C2X, a commonly accepted concept based on pseudonymization has already been established. Instead of assigning a single certificate to a vehicle, the CA issues several short-term certificates. Together with other station identifiers, such as network ID or MAC addresses, these short term certificates are denoted as *pseudonyms*. In order to reduce linkability, pseudonyms feature a limited lifetime and are therefore frequently changed within pre-defined intervals. For instance, in the sim^{TD} security architecture, every vehicle holds up to 24 pseudonyms, which are changed every 30 minutes.

In principle, shorter change intervals and pseudonym lifetimes are more advantageous for pseudonomyization. However, issuing new certificates requires a backend connectivity to the CA. Since during an early deployment phase it cannot be generally assumed that every vehicle is equipped with mobile telephony, alternative communication links have to be considered. Thereby, loading new pseudonyms in the garage during one of the vehicle's service intervals represents only one possible solution to this issue. To which extent certificates can be exchanged via C2X communication when passing a RSU has to be evaluated in future FOTs.

In Table 3.1 the different certificate types, as proposed by the C2C-CC Task Force PKI, are stated [5]. The *Long Term Certificate (LTC)* is issued via the *Long Term Certification Authority (LTCA)* and unambiguously identifies the vehicle station within the PKI. The lifetime of this certificate is in the order of the expected life-cycle of the vehicle itself. In case of misuse, or if the vehicle is getting de-registered the certificate is deactivated at the corresponding LTCA (see Table 3.1). In Section 3.5.2 a protocol is presented by which the vehicle can issue new pseudonyms using the LTC. Since the LTC represents the identity of the vehicle, additional attributes are included, which define the scope and permissions related to this vehicle. Such attributes may optionally include the *Vehicle Identification Number (VIN)*, software versions and configurations as well as security parameter, which define the trust level of the installed on-board security hardware (see [63] for the definition of trust levels). For reasons of privacy the LTC is never used for authenticating C2X messages and furthermore must not be communicated in plaintext to other entities. Mechanisms for revoking a LTC in the backend are described in subsequent sections. In Figure 3.4 the certificate assembling of a LTC is depicted using ECDSA 256 as defined in IEEE 1609.2.

	LONG TERM CERTIFICATE (LTC)	PSEUDONYM CERTIFICATES (PC)
Lifetime	Life-cycle of the vehicle	Minutes - Days
Authentication	Authenticates station towards the CA for PC refill, or revocation after de-registration	Authenticate stations in the C2X communication, e.g., CAM and DENM
Revocation	• At de-registration of the vehicle • In case of misuse → only in the backend	• No revocation necessary • Implicit revocation due to short lifetime → avoids transfer of long revocation lists to vehicles
Certificate Specific Data	Contains additional attributes for authorization, and identification	Contained data reduced to a minimum
Signer CA	Long Term Certification Authority (LTCA)	Pseudonym Certification Authority (PCA)

Table 3.1: Vehicle certificate types

In contrast, PCs are issued via the textitPseudonym Certification Authority (PCA) and possess a limited lifetime in the order of minutes up to several days. Because of their limited lifetime, ECDSA 224 instead of ECDSA 256 is applied as crypto algorithm, which reduces the certificate size. For similar reasons of reducing the channel load, the contained additional data inside a PC is reduced to a minimum. In principle, the pseudonymization strategy of a C2X station is defined by the following set of parameters:

1. **Pseudonym lifetime**: The pseudonym lifetime, in terms of start time and validity interval is set by the requested PCA in conjunction with the vehicle's LTCA (see Table 3.1).

2. **Pseudonym preloading interval**: The preloading interval depends upon how frequently a vehicle can contact the CA in case it is running out of certificates. Furthermore the total amount of issued certificates depends upon the capacity of secure memory available inside the vehicle to store the secret keys.

3. **Number of interleaving pseudonyms**: Current proposals for a PKI in the U.S. allow only one certificate to be valid at the same time period. While such an approach is beneficial to impede Sybil attacks in case a station has been compromised, it offers poor flexibility for more sophisticated pseudonymization strategies. Consequently, the C2C-CC proposes to increase the number of pseudonyms in order to be able to dynamically switch between pseudonyms. The concept of interleaving pseudonyms is a prerequisite for deploying sophisticated privacy protocols as proposed in Chapter 5.

4. **Pseudonym change strategy**: Only in a very basic implementation, pseudonyms are changed in an uncontrolled way. For a more advanced implementation it is strongly recommended to change pseudonyms while residing inside so called *Mix Zones*. In Chapter 5 and the Annex A, protocols for creating efficient Mix Zones are presented.

In case, the related private key of a certain certificate $Cert_i$ is getting revealed, the C2X system is considered as vulnerable until that certificate expires. And even more severe, if the entire set of private keys is compromised, the time window for authenticated attacks is increased to the pseudonym preloading interval. Therefore, the first two parameters, i.e., the pseudonym lifetime and preloading interval are one of the most sensitive parameter within the security architecture and consequently have to be chosen carefully. During an

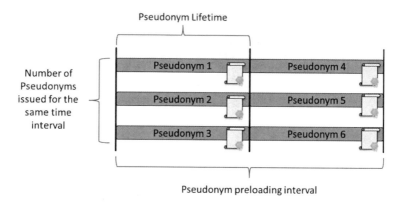

Figure 3.5: Overlapping validity of pseudonyms [5]

early deployment phase, where only sparse connection to backend facilities will be available, these parameters are expected to be dimensioned more generously.

Furthermore, ETSI recommends including nothing in broadcast messages from private vehicles that identifies the specific vehicle. Hence, any static identifier, like the MAC or IP address shall not be included. Also other, vehicle related information like, e.g., vehicle dimensions or vehicle color, may be used to unambiguously identify a vehicle among others and therefore threatens the pseudonymization concept. How to provide sufficiently high information granularity to safety applications, without creating a privacy threat is subject to current discussions between the C2C-CC and the ETSI.

3.5 Public Key Infrastructure

Designing a security architecture that provides low complexity and operational costs, while at the same time security and privacy constraints are not violated, is regarded as one of the remaining challenges to be solved before the roll-out of the C2X technology. It is the strong belief of the C2C-CC that besides communicational protocols also, to some extent, organizational security aspects should be subject to harmonization and standardization work.

3.5.1 PKI Architectural Overview

The PKI architecture as illustrated in Figure 3.6 has been designed by the C2C-CC [5], [6] and is currently being standardized by ETSI WG5. The proposed solution is composed of a hierarchical structure with a maximum of two levels of organization. At the top level a *Root Certification Authority (RCA)* takes over the task of certifying subordinated CAs. Following the subdivision of a PC and LTC, as outlined in the previous Section 3.4, two different CAs are assigned, i.e., a LTCA and a PCA. Since each certificate type possesses a different scope, also different policies have to be applied. Defining appropriate policies is subject to ongoing discussions between the C2C-CC, legislators and potential operators. A

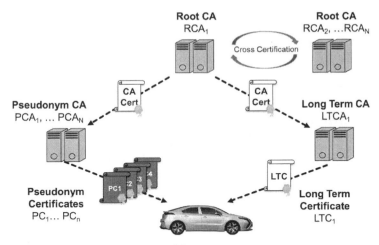

Figure 3.6: Hierarchical PKI architecture [5]

CA has to prove frequently that it is in compliance with the established policies in order to receive a valid CA certificate from the Root CA. Different Root CAs generate self-signed certificates and perform a cross-certification among each other.

During an early deployment phase, the different stakeholders inside the C2X network may take the following roles: Since the RCA serves as a central trust anchor inside the entire system, only a limited number of RCAs should be instantiated. Furthermore, such a sovereign task has to be carried out by governmental authorities. For example, for the states in Europe, one single root can be established, which cross-certifies itself with other RCAs in the U.S., China, etc., respectively. The LTCAs and PCAs are likely to be operated by separate, independent entities due to privacy reasons. LTCs are created during the manufacturing process of the C2X module or are finally introduced into the vehicle at the end of line. Hence, either automotive suppliers or manufacturers are considered as possible LTCA operators for vehicles. In contrast, RSUs, which are installed for supporting C2I/I2C applications, are operated by respective road authorities, which are also in charge of issuing respective LTCs.

It is considered as one key advantage of the advocated hierarchical PKI structure that any organization may operate a LTCA as long as it follows the policies of the RCA. The same is true for the operation of PCAs. A possible scenario is imaginable where an operator of gas stations offers an additional service for refilling a vehicle's pseudonym storage. Also the C2C-CC may found a legal entity by which it can operate a LTCA or PCA. The latter allows dividing financial costs as well as organizational complexity between several C2X system providers.

3.5.2 PKI Management Protocols

While in the previous section the architecture in terms of involved entities and relations between them has been described, in this section the individual protocols for managing the PKI are presented. In particular protocols and processes are of interest, by which a vehicle can request new pseudonyms in a secure and privacy-preserving way. Furthermore, a process for initializing C2X modules with LTCs is presented. Other processes to be defined, are related to certificate chain request, CA creation, as well as certificate revocation.

Long-Term Certificate Upload

The long-term certificate is regarded as the digital identity of a vehicle and therefore is supposed to be valid for the entire life-cycle. However, this value may vary even for vehicles of the same model. If the vehicle is kept in operation for longer time periods, as expected, the LTC will expire and consequently, will have to be renewed. A LTC replacement becomes also necessary, if the LTC has been (intentionally or not) corrupted or damaged. In principle, the LTC upload process may vary between different manufacturers and does not necessarily need to be standardized. However, since any LTC treatment is regarded as highly security critical, the C2C-CC aims at a harmonized approach among all system providers.

The process for LTC assignment is exemplarily depicted in the sequence diagram in Figure 3.7. For LTC upload, a mutual authentication scheme between both, the assigning authority and the C2X *Security Module (SM)* is anticipated. Assuming, that the *Security Module Provider (SMP)* and LTCA operator may be two separate entities (e.g., supplier and vehicle manufacturer), the initialization is performed as follows:

1. The SMP triggers the public/private key pair generation of the SM.
2. The SM generates an initialization public/private key pair: K_{inital}, k_{inital}.
3. The SM returns the initialization public key K_{inital}.

After the generation of the initial key pair, the C2X security module provider delivers the hardware module to the vehicle manufacturer for LTC assignment and the following process is executed:

4. The SMP sends the Security Module Information (SMI), which includes the public key K_{inital} and the corresponding Module-ID to the LTCA.
5. LTCA triggers public/private key pair generation for LTC of the SM.
6. The SM generates the LTC key pair: K_{LTC}, k_{LTC}.
7. The SM signs the public key K_{LTC} using k_{inital}.
8. The SM requests a signature for the public key K_{LTC} at the LTCA.
9. The LTCA verifies the signature of K_{LTC} using K_{inital}.
10. If valid, the LTCA signs K_{LTC}, which results into the LTC for that vehicle.
11. The LTC is returned back to the SMP.
12. The SMP verifies the LTC signature, using the pre-loaded key K_{LTCA} of LTCA.

Applying the presented process, allows instantaneous and secure LTC uploads. Hence, by signing the public key K_{LTC} with the private initial key k_{inital}, the security module authenticates itself towards the LTCA. In contrary, the authenticity of the assigning LTCA may be easily proven by verifying the signature of the obtained LTC. For LTC verification it is assumed, that the security module has been pre-loaded with the respective LTCA

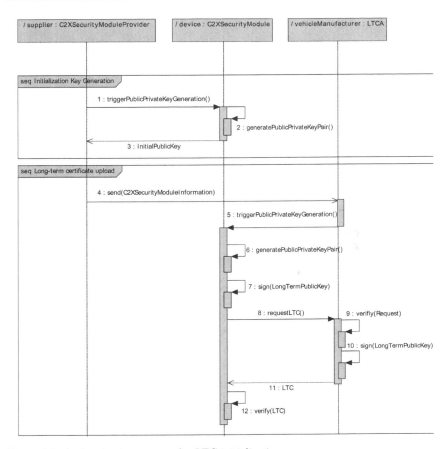

Figure 3.7: Authentication process for LTC initialization

certificate in advance by the SMP. Note that besides the public key K_{LTC} also related permissions are signed in order to yield the certificate format as depicted in Figure 3.4. A posteriori update of expired or corrupted LTCs is possible any time, by applying the same process.

Certificate Roaming

Due to legal requirements, it is conceivable that in different markets the usage of separate PCAs is enforced. In consequence, the C2C-CC advocates assigning a regional validity to certificates, denoted inside the Certificate Specific Data (see Figure 3.2 in Section 3.3). A vehicle permanently assesses the geographical context and chooses the certificate accordingly. In order to save bandwidth, region IDs are included into certificates, which are associated to polygon lines. If a vehicle leaves the geographical region, defined by that set of a certificates, it issues a new set, as soon as connection to the PCA becomes available.

Certificate Revocation

Within the C2X security community a major discussion focuses on the necessity for distributing *Certificate Revocation Lists (CRLs)* to vehicles. Whereas a common understanding has been established upon the distribution of revoked CAs and LTCs inside the backend, a comprehensive reachability of all vehicles in an ad-hoc network is considered as challenging. The distribution of CRLs is facing some challenges, as identified in the following:

- **CRL Size:** According to the assumption of the C2C-CC, a vehicle will be equipped with more than a thousand pseudonyms at once. If, for some reason, a vehicle is getting revoked, the entire set of pseudonyms will have to be declared as invalid. It is absolutely mandatory to keep the CRL lists reasonably small in order to save bandwidth over the C2X communication link.

- **Distribution Latency:** The overall latency for revoking a misbehaving vehicle from the C2X network is determined by the following sum:

$$T_{latency} = T_{detection} + T_{report} + T_{notify}. \tag{3.1}$$

  where $T_{detection}$ denotes the timeframe until vehicles (or RSUs) have gathered enough information to report a misbehavior. T_{report} denotes the timeframe (for vehicles) to get connected to the revocation authorityin order to deliver the report. And finally, T_{notify}, denotes the timeframe until every vehicle in the network is informed. Especially during an early deployment phase, as well as for less developed regions it is likely that RSUs will be sparsely placed, and thus, vehicles may not have connection to the revocation authority frequently.

- **Misbehavior Detection Reliability:** Detecting and reporting misbehavior represents a non-trivial task in vehicular networks. First, reliable detection algorithm are hardly available. And second, misbehavior reports introduce new attack trees (like, e.g., denigration).

In *Haas et al.* [64] the first challenge, regarding the size of CRLs is addressed. The presented approach is focused on an enhanced organization and storing of revoked certificates. Instead of listing each and every certificate identifier individually, a secrete key is added, which is used as seed during generation of the certificates. This secret key is known only to the CA and serves as revocation key to link related certificates, which reduces CRL sizes significantly. Having knowledge on this key, allows vehicles to generate the entire set of revoked certificates, independently of the CA. For efficiently storing and searching, the generated certificates are stored within a *Bloom Filter*.

In *Papadimitratos et al.* [65] a distribution system is presented, which relies on the usage of RSUs for dissemination of CRLs in a timely manner. In order to reduce CRL size, *Erasure Codes* or *Fountain Codes* are advocated, which reduce the required bandwidth considerably. Compared to Bloom Filters as applied in [64], [66] these encoding schemes are less prone to false positive errors.

The major argument against the deployment of CRLs is the fact that currently no reliable misbehavior detection algorithms are available. Although in [66] and [67] promising approaches are presented, none of them has been elaborated in detail enough to be seriously considered for deployment. Due to the absence of well-defined misbehavior detection algorithms and the assumption that RSUs will be available only sporadically, the C2C-CC has decided to abstain from a direct revocation of PCs via CRLs. Instead, the LTC itself is subject to revocation in case a vehicle gets de-registered. The registration and de-registration process may be carried out by two possible entities. Either a central registration authority takes the task of assessing the status of vehicles. Or, if not available, the end-of-lifetime management of a vehicle manufacturer is employed. Temporarily de-registered vehicles as well as vehicles, which are permanently withdrawn from service are excluded from communication by deactivating the LTC.

Authors in *Pietrowicz et al.* [68] come to similar conclusions than the C2C-CC. Actually, the strategy described by [68] is comparable to the one advocated by the C2C-CC, though both solutions differ in detail. Especially the processes for requesting new pseudonyms are based on different assumptions as outlined in the next section.

Pseudonym Certificate Request

The requesting of new pseudonyms is regarded as one of the most crucial protocols to be specified within the PKI. This is mainly because a major part of the security and privacy requirements as stated in Section 3.2 depend on a carefully designed request protocol. In particular, in this section the question is answered, how the requirements for accountability on the one hand, and unlinkability on the other can be met efficiently.

Algorithm 1 createPseudonymRequest()

In: Number of required Pseudonym Certificates N
Out: Certificate Request Req, Signature of Request Sig_{Req}

1: Req {Request Message Container}
2: **for all** $i \in N$ **do**
3:     $(K_i, k_i) \leftarrow$ generatePublicPrivateKeyPair()
4:     $Req \leftarrow Req + K_i$
5: **end for**
6: $Req \leftarrow Req +$ getRefPosition()
7: $Req \leftarrow Req +$ getPermissions()
8: $Req \leftarrow Req +$ getLTCAIdentifier()
9: $Time \leftarrow$ getUTCTime()
10: $VehicleID \leftarrow$ getVehicleID()
11: $VehicleID_{secured} \leftarrow$ Encrypt($Time, VehicleID; K_{LTCA}$)
12: $Req \leftarrow Req + VehicleID_{secured}$
13: $Sig_{Req} \leftarrow$ Sign($Req; k_{LTC}$)
14: **return** Req, Sig_{Req}

The process, described in Algorithm 1 is executed on a vehicle's C2X system for creating a pseudonym request Req, including the following components:

- the set of public keys,

- the vehicle's current position, which enables a certificate roaming according to Section 3.5.2,

- the vehicle's required permissions, which ensure the authorization objectives, stated in Section 3.2.1,

- the LTCA identifier for forwarding within the PKI backend,

- an authentication token $VehicleID_{secured}$, which includes the vehicle identifier (associated to the vehicle's LTC), encrypted with the public key K_{LTCA}. In order to impede correlation attacks, and to introduce a time-dependency, the current UTC (Coordinated Universal Time) timestamp is also included,

- a signature Sig_{Req}, created over the entire request, using k_{LTC}, which proves the requester's authenticity towards the LTCA.

In order to set up a pseudonym request, the vehicle may contact any of the known PCAs. If a strong privacy is required, the request, as composed by Algorithm 1, is transmitted via a secure channel in order to avoid any disclosure of the public key set (see step 1 in Figure 3.8). Depending on the module settings, any available communication link, such as, e.g., 802.11p communication at RSUs, cellular communication, or even On Board Diagnosis (OBD) at service garages may be considered for retrieving new pseudonyms.

PCs may have a regionally restricted authorization validity (see Section 3.5.2). Therefore, the request is forwarded to a second PCA in case the addressed PCA is not responsible for the specified region. An authorized PCA creates a forwarding package according to Algorithm 2, which includes the following components:

- the region, for which the PCs are going to be issued,

- the PCA identifier, used to identify the PCA towards the LTCA,

- the secured vehicle identifier $VehicleID_{secured}$,

- a hash value of the original request Req, which enables the LTCA to perform integrity checks, without revealing the public key set,

- the original request signature Sig_{Req},

- a signature $Sig_{Fwd_{LTCA}}$, created over the forwarded request Fwd_{LTCA}, using k_{PCA}, which proves the PCA authenticity towards the LTCA.

As depicted in Figure 3.8 the encapsulated vehicle request is then forwarded to the LTCA (see step 2 in Figure 3.8), which verifies the following criteria:

1. The message integrity of the forwarded request is given.

2. The forwarder PCA is not listed on the PCA revocation list (see step 3 in Figure 3.8).

3. The associated LTC is not listed on the LTC revocation list (see step 4 in Figure 3.8).

4. The requested PC permissions are covered by the given LTC.

Algorithm 2 forwardPseudonymRequest()

In: Incoming Request Req, Signature of Request Sig_{Req}
Out: forwarded Request Fwd_{LTCA} via PCA to LTCA, Signature of Request Sig_{Req}, Signature of forwarded Request $Sig_{Fwd_{LTCA}}$

1: **if** Req.getRefPosition() $\notin$ getRegion() **then**
2:    $PCA = \text{findPCA}(Req.\text{getRefPosition}())$
3:    **return** PCA.forwardPseudonymRequest()
4: **else**
5:    $Fwd_{LTCA} \leftarrow \text{getRegion}()$
6:    $Fwd_{LTCA} \leftarrow Fwd_{LTCA}+ \text{getPCAIdentifier}()$
7:    $Fwd_{LTCA} \leftarrow Fwd_{LTCA}+ Req.\text{getSecuredVehicleID}()$
8:    $Fwd_{LTCA} \leftarrow Fwd_{LTCA}+ \text{hash}(Req)$
9:    $Sig_{Fwd_{LTCA}} \leftarrow \text{Sign}(Fwd_{LTCA}, k_{PCA})$
10:    **return** $Fwd_{LTCA}, Sig_{Req}, Sig_{Fwd_{LTCA}}$
11: **end if**

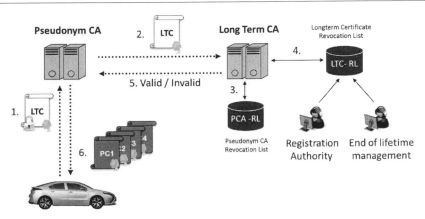

Figure 3.8: Pseudonym certificate request protocol

5. For the given region and preloading interval (see Figure 3.5 in Section 3.4) no pseudonyms have been issued, yet.

Only, if these criteria are met simultaneously, the made request is confirmed (see step 5 in Figure 3.8). Besides the verification result, the LTCA, as a central instance, also defines the next preloading interval for that vehicle. The PCA uses this preloading interval, to assign appropriate lifetimes to each pseudonym. Then, the PCA signature is applied and the entire set of pseudonyms is returned back to the vehicle (see step 6 in Figure 3.8).

Certificate Chain Request

The certificate represents a large part of the overall C2X message size (see Figure 3.1). In order to save bandwidth and to keep security overhead low, every vehicle attaches only the PC to every message. The receiver vehicles can then verify the validity of the PC by means of a set of preloaded PCA-Certificates. However, PCAs may change over time and consequently, the set of known PCAs has to be kept updatable and extendable. The C2C-CC recommends sending certificate chains (i.e., the authorization of the Pseudonym Certificate up to the Root CA) only, if requested by other vehicles. By evaluating the certificate chain once, further messages authorized with any certificate from that PCA can be verified, from then on.

3.5.3 PKI Implementation

In Section 2.1.1 the sim^{TD} architecture has been presented as a first near series implementation of the Car-to-X technology. Hence, regarding available communication channels and interfaces, the sim^{TD} architecture is considered as close to what will be deployed in the near future. As one of earliest field trials for C2X, sim^{TD} has also implemented a PKI, which provides vehicles and roadside stations of all involved project partners with valid security credentials. As a member of the sim^{TD} security group the author of this thesis was involved into the design of the overall sim^{TD} security architecture [29], [9], [11]. Experiences and partial results of sim^{TD} have been communicated back to IEEE and ETSI for improvements of respective standards.

In Figure 3.9 the security protection for each sim^{TD} communication channel is illustrated. Any unauthorized access via one of the available communication links may affect the security level of the entire ITS system. Consequently, sim^{TD} aims at covering each and every communication link with strong security measures. This includes in particular, the protection of communication links, other than 802.11p, i.e., IP-based communication, and communication between traffic authorities in the backend. In the following security measures for the different channels in sim^{TD} are summarized.

802.11p Safety and traffic efficiency messages exchanged within the 802.11p channel are signed, using asymmetric cryptography (see Section 3.3). Due to limited computational resources on the sim^{TD} target platform, it has been decided to use RSA algorithms instead of ECC. Respective timing measurements performed on the target platform yielded an approximately 28 times faster verification and 5 times faster signature processing when using RSA. However, applying RSA leads also to a significantly increased message size up to 25% compared to ECC [29], [9], [11]. In order to achieve an acceptable security level, 512 bit RSA keys had to be chosen, which increases signature and certificate size significantly. In general the usage of RSA for C2X represents an exceptional case applied for the sim^{TD} field trial only. For later deployment of C2X, hardware accelerator will be required to perform ECC algorithms in timely manner. In *Jaeger et al.* [69], [70], the author of this thesis has jointly developed a conceptual design for a C2X security hardware module. The design aims at integrating all cryptographic operations as well as key management into a single system-on-chip design. In the European project PRESERVE (Preparing Secure V2X Communication Systems) [71] a close-to-market security ASIC is being developed, which is meeting the performance requirements of future C2X scenarios.

802.11 b/g On the sim^{TD} test site commercial WiFi (802.11 b/g) access points can be accessed in a secure way using IEEE 802.11i with WPA2. In sim^{TD} all access points and vehicles are equipped with a pre-shared common key. The WPA2 protocol uses *AES 128 (Advanced Encryption Standard)* for encryption, which represents the quasi-standard for securing WiFi, today.

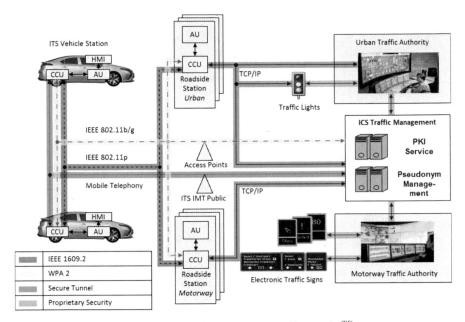

Figure 3.9: Comprehensive ITS channel protection according to sim^{TD}

Cellular Communication Connection establishment and maintenance of cellular communication is handled by a SIM card, installed in every vehicle. For IP-based access to additional services, a secure tunnel via *VPN (Virtual Private Network)* is established. In contrast, DENM messages, which are send via the cellular link are already authenticated using IEEE 1609.2 (see Section 3.3), and therefore do not require additional security measures for authentication.

Traffic Backend Communication Communication between road authorities and traffic facilities (i.e., traffic lights and sign bridges) is secured using proprietary security solutions. These backend systems benefit largely from the fact that they are physically isolated from any other network. Hence, an attacker has to get physical access first in order to perform attacks, which is considered as a rather complex task.

The sim^{TD} project realizes a minimalistic PKI, which already includes several concepts as foreseen for deployment by the C2C-CC. Hence, sim^{TD} also makes a division between certificates used to identify the vehicle in the backend and those used for authenticating safety and traffic efficiency messages. Every sim^{TD} vehicle and roadside unit obtains a secure token (i.e., a private 1024 bit RSA key), which is installed on every station manually and can then be used to request a basic identity certificate. This concept is comparable to the LTC upload protocol as described in Section 3.5.2, though the authentication process slightly differs (for more details please refer to [11]). In sim^{TD} a single CA incorporates functionalities of the LTCA and PCA at the same time. As part of the provided PKI services, the CA issues new pseudonyms, manages certification lists and resolves pseudonyms to respective basic identities for evaluation purposes during the field trial. The communication between vehicles and the CA is performed using the cellular communication link.

3.6 Conclusion

Security and privacy is considered as mandatory for successfully deploying the Car-to-X technology in the market. In order to motivate its necessity, in this part of the thesis the original motivation for different attackers has been discussed. The performed analysis has unveiled that a very likely attacker for the C2X systems will be the Script Kiddies located near the roadside and trying to inject forged messages. With respect to privacy, two categories of threats are presented, depending on whether an adversary is able to observe single geographic locations or is able to analyze the person's driving behavior, given a trace of messages.

Based on the general security objectives outlined in [51], respective security and privacy objectives are transferred to the Car-to-X domain. Current field operational trials and standardization works aim at a PKI solution for securing outgoing messages. Although a PKI only represents a first baseline for C2X security protection, most security and privacy objectives as stated in Section 3.2 are addressed in principle:

Accordingly, **Message Confidentiality** may be achieved by encrypting the message content using the cryptographic primitives as provided by IEEE 1609.2. **Sender Authentication** and **Authorization** can be ensured by issuing certificates to valid vehicles, including associated roles and permissions. By evaluating the digital signature attached to every message, any unauthorized bit manipulation can be detected on receiver side. Since a timestamp is also included into the signature generation, expired messages can be discarded. This property of the PKI solution fulfills the objectives for **Message Integrity** and **Message Freshness**.

However, cryptographic measures have their limitations, too. The objective for **Message Plausibility** is an upper layer topic and cannot be addressed via cryptography adequately. Therefore, in Chapter 4 of this thesis an efficient and robust approach for mobility data verification is presented. Apart from higher layer security, also low layer security issues such as **Communication Availability** cannot be realized via a PKI solution. In Chapter 6 the concept of Secure C2X Beamforming is introduced, which can remedy this problem.

Regarding, privacy the negotiated solution based on changing identifiers forms the cornerstone for realizing **Anonymity** and **Pseudonymity** in C2X. In Chapter 5 the effectiveness of this approach is discussed again with respect to a stronger adversary model. Considerable weaknesses are identified and consequently, enhancements based on Mix Zones are proposed.

The presented, hierarchical public key infrastructure realizes a split of powers between responsible certification authorities. Hence, long term CAs know which vehicle requested certificates, but do not know which certificates have been assigned. In contrast, pseudonym CAs know, which certificates have been assigned, but do not know which vehicle has actually requested them. If **Accountability** is required by law, a resolution of pseudonyms may be performed by integrating legal authorities. That way *Privacy-by-Design* is not only ensured in the C2C link, but also in the C2I link and within the communication between CAs. Its generic structure makes this PKI applicable for many communication domains even beyond C2X applications.

Facility Layer Security: Mobility Data Verification

This part of the thesis is dedicated to message content verification in vehicular ad-hoc networks. In particular the focus is set on an evaluation of the trustworthiness of transmitted mobility data in terms of position, speed and heading. Mobility data represents the main component of frequently sent Cooperative Awareness Messages (CAMs) and thus is highly relevant for most safety applications. However, this makes mobility data also an attractive attack target for most adversaries.

The developed mobility verification approach consists of three increments, which are constituted by an overall framework. The basic version of the framework has been presented first by *Stübing et al.* in [7] and has been honored with a an outstanding paper award. As a major component of this framework, a Kalman filter has been included as a means for detecting the continuum of motion as a verification criterion. The framework has been developed and fully implemented in the context of the sim^{TD} field operational trial [8], [9], [10], [11]. In *Jaeger et al.* [12] the framework has been further extended by additional measures for effectively handling vehicles in the near-communication range. In *Stübing et al.* [14], [15], [16] the security level of the framework is further increased by including traffic maneuver recognition algorithms based on Hidden Markov Models (HMMs) according to *Firl et al.* [13].

In the following, Section 4.1 outlines the underlying attacker model and thereby motivates the necessity for mobility data verification in C2X networks. Related work in the area of C2X message verification is summarized in Section 4.2. Section 4.3 is dedicated to the description of the mobility verification approach including respective refinements. Implementation details are given in Section 4.4 and experimental results are presented. Finally, in Section 4.5, the contributions of this part of the thesis are summarized and some remarks on future work are given.

4.1 Motivation

Securing inter-vehicular communication by means of cryptography as outlined in the previous Section 3.3 represents a necessary, though not fully sufficient countermeasure against forging of messages. Any adversary, who has gained access to secrete key material stored within the security module, will be able to send authenticated messages. Therefore, the

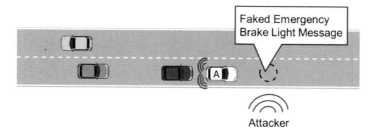

Figure 4.1: Attack on the Emergency Electronic Brake Light Warning (EEBL) application

C2C-CC strongly recommends to store security credentials within tamper proof hardware and to process it only in a secure environment [5]. Recently, much progress has been made for hardening cryptographic algorithms against threats like, e.g., side channel attacks (see *Stöttinger et al.* [72]).

Installing secure hardware within vehicles is mandatory for C2X, but furthermore needs to be complemented by additional measures for authenticating the information interchange between local sensors and the C2X communication module. For instance, C2X applications such as *Weather Hazard Warning* [73] or EEBL (see Table 2.1) trigger their action upon the information obtained from the vehicles local CAN bus. In *Koscher et al.* [49] vulnerabilities regarding missing authentication within todays automobile buses have been revealed. Due to imposed high busload, and verification delays when deploying security on the CAN bus, no quick solutions are conceivable. Flex Ray bus systems aim to remedy this problem, but will not be available for all vehicle types in the near future.

In this work a severe adversary is assumed, which has gained access to a vehicles internal network (CAN, LIN, etc.) and therefore is able to manipulate the information sent to the C2X module. Depending on the adversary's motivation, several attack scenarios are imaginable. For instance, in Figure 4.1 an attack on the EEBL application is illustrated. Thereby a roadside attacker is assumed, which is equipped with a common C2X module, including valid security credentials. By simulating a full brake to the C2X module, the respective warning message is created. If the adversary has also capabilities for manipulating the internal GPS interface, any reference position can be introduced. Since the final message will be signed using valid keys, those faked messages cannot be detected on the receiver side by means of cryptography. Hence, the driver will be alerted of a sudden full brake in front of him. As it is generally expected that drivers will instantly react upon C2X warnings, such a situation may lead to unexpectedly performed collision mitigation maneuvers.

A similar scenario is depicted in Figure 4.2. For the ICW application, vehicles are monitoring cross traffic when entering an intersection in order to detect possible upcoming accidents (see Table 2.1). In the illustrated scenario a static roadside attacker is sending faked CAMs, indicating a vehicle approaching the intersection with a very high speed. The application running on *vehicle A's* C2X unit detects a potential hazard and will erroneously notify the driver.

Mobility data verification is not only necessary for Car-to-Car use cases only, but can also prevent roadside facilities from processing faked data. For instance, in Figure 4.3 an attack

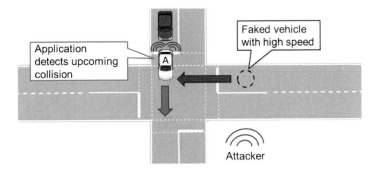

Figure 4.2: Attack on the Intersection Collision Warning (ICW) application

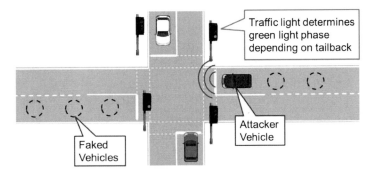

Figure 4.3: Attack on the Green Light Optimum Speed Advisory (GLOSA) application

is depicted, which intends to manipulate the GLOSA application (see Section 2.2). In the context of this traffic efficiency application, RSUs determine the tailback at every traffic light. Depending on the vehicle density on each lane, a prioritized flow control is performed. If an attacker may get access to the private keys of the certificate storage, she/he may take advantage of the GLOSA functionality by simulating virtual cars on her/his lane (i.e, performing a *Sybil* attack), in order to reduce the waiting time at the detriment of other road users.

Furthermore, falsified position claims have an effect also on the safety of multi-hop communication. Applications like, e.g., Traffic Jam Warning or Weather Hazard Warning are forwarding DENMs via several hops and therefore rely upon accurate position information. In *Leinmüller et al.* [74] the effects of falsified positions on the delivery ratio of multi hop messages have been examined. Simulations showed that especially greedy forwarding algorithms, which select always the node closest to the destination as next forwarder, are highly sensitive towards malicious nodes.

4.2 Related Work

This chapter provides an overview over existing attempts for verifying the mobility data, contained in frequently broadcasted CAM messages. The first part refers to verification approaches, which can either be applied to single parts of the mobility data (i.e., position, speed and heading) only, or to the claimed mobility data as whole. In the second part, verification frameworks are described, which aim at combining the output of different verification approaches into an overall trust value for the respective vehicle. Finally, each verification approach is evaluated in the last section.

4.2.1 Mobility Verification Approaches

As one of the early works on C2X security and privacy, *Hubaux et al.* [75] have identified the necessity for verifying a vehicle's position in Car-to-X networks. In order to impede falsified position claims *Hubaux et al.*, advocate two possible approaches. The first proposal obliges C2X system providers, to implement a tamper-proof GPS receiver into every C2X station. However, *Hubaux et al.* reveal that this approach is considered as rather ineffective, since protecting the GPS device against tampering does not prevent attackers from jamming or spoofing the GPS signal itself. The second approach is based on *multilateration* and requires at least three trustworthy RSUs to collaborate in order to verify a vehicle's position while driving through a certain region. While being inside the communication range of the RSUs, every vehicle executes a *challenge-response* protocol. Assuming that involved RSUs are capable of measuring the round trip time at nanosecond precision, a vehicle cannot claim to be closer to the RSU than it really is. By performing triangulation between three RSUs, the position can be fixed in two dimensions. Integrating an additional RSU furthermore allows a verification of the entire position vector, i.e., longitude, latitude and height.

Golle et al. [76] advocate a comparison of incoming data with a pre-defined model, taking into account the physical boundaries of vehicular scenarios (e.g., two vehicles cannot be located at the same position at the same time, vehicles rarely travel faster than 160 km/h, etc.). It is assumed that a vehicle can link a certain message to the physical source of that message, and furthermore is able to sense the distance to that source, using, e.g., camera technology. In order to extend the distinguishability beyond the direct observation range, a vehicle may also communicate observations to vehicles farther away. In case an adversary sends spoofed positions, inconsistencies in the taken observations may occur. Vehicles then generate possible explanations for these inconsistencies, taking into account, that the adversary may also be capable of generating additional spoofed vehicles, which communicate observations, supporting its own position claim. Among the set of different explanations, a vehicle chooses the one, which includes the fewest number of malicious vehicles and is consistent with the pre-defined model.

In order to motivate the necessity of position verification approaches *Leinmüller et al.* [67] analyzed the influence of falsified position data on geographic routing and observed a significant reduction of successfully delivered messages depending on the network size and the percentage of malicious nodes. As a countermeasure *Leinmüller et al.* propose a combination of both, autonomous as well as cooperative verification approaches. The classes of autonomous sensors according to [67] include basic checks, which are summarized in the following:

- **Acceptance Range Threshold (ART)**, verifies if the position denoted inside a message is located inside the receivers communication range.

- **Mobility Grade Threshold (MGT)**, verifies if the difference in positions obtained from two succeeding messages are reachable within the given time delta.

- **Maximum Density Threshold (MDT)**, verifies if the observed vehicle density exceeds a maximum threshold with respect to physical vehicle dimensions.

- **Map-based Verification**, verifies if received vehicle positions are located on the street.

- **Overhearing**, has been introduced first by *Marti et al.* [77] and verifies the claimed positions by monitoring the vehicles routing behavior.

The class of cooperative sensors inlcude the exchange of information with trustworthy neighbors in order to detect falsified positions. In *Leinmüller et al.* [67] two cooperative sensors are advocated:

- **Proactive Exchange of Neighborhood Tables**, detects inconsistencies in position claims by exchanging entire Neighborhood Tables between vehicles.

- **Reactive Position Requests**, allows vehicles to instantly query other vehicles for further information about a certain vehicle. By combining information from different sources, falsified positions may be detected.

In *Schmidt et al.* [78] the authors further go into detail with the module *Minimum Distance Moved (MDM)*. Assuming that attacks are likely to be launched by a stationary roadside attacker, the MDM module constantly assesses the trajectory of neighboring vehicles. Since the communication range of a stationary attacker is limited, any sender, which is still received by the host vehicle after a certain time cannot be a roadside attacker and consequently will be assigned to a higher trust value. Besides already known checks, further modules are introduced to detect suddenly appearing vehicles or irregularities within the CAM message frequency. In [79] and [80] the authors recall the main concepts of their approach and further extend their evaluation by means of more detailed simulations. Effectiveness has been shown especially for highway scenarios, where position falsification has a great impact on the number of successfully delivered messages.

While previous approaches are based on information obtained from received C2X messages only, *Yan et al.* [81] focus on techniques based on a cross verification via a vehicles onboard Radar sensor. Assuming that every vehicle taking part in the C2X network is also equipped with a multitude of Radars, covering 360° around the vehicle, a fusion between both information sources is performed, taking into account the respective inaccuracies for each technology. In order to overcome the spatial limitations of a Radar sensor, furthermore a cooperative exchange of observations among neighboring vehicles is proposed. For that purpose vehicles in communication range are grouped into geographical cells and one vehicle is selected, which functions as a cell router to forward information between adjacent cells.

4.2.2 Mobility Verification Frameworks

Schmidt et al. [82] take up the checks proposed by *Leinmüller et al.* [67] and include them into an overall evaluation scheme called *VEBAS (Vehicle Behavior Analysis and Evaluation Scheme)*. In VEBAS the different checks are grouped into checks, which are confirming and those, which are rejecting a given position claim, respectively. Outputs of different modules are averaged over time and assigned to an aging function to reflect the influence of past ratings on the current evaluation. In order to increase the reliability of evaluations, *Schmidt et al.* propose to share recommendations between vehicles in a cooperative way. For instance, in [83] the results of the aforementioned MDM test are proposed to be exchanged among neighbors in order to shorten the evaluation time and to cope with attackers, which are increasing their communication range above common thresholds.

A further attempt for combining outputs of different mobility verification modules in terms of an overall framework is presented by *M.Gerlach* [84]. There, the trustworthiness of mobility data is evaluated by means of a *Bayesian Network (BN)*. The BN models a hierarchy of three levels, representing the trustworthiness of the mobility data as a root node and the individual elements of the mobility data, i.e., position, speed and heading, as leafs. On the bottom level respective observers are located, which provide information to assess the trustworthiness for each element on the layer above. In *M.Gerlach* [84] the following different observers have been selected:

- The **Geographic Tolerance Observer** filters position claims by applying the ART check, suggested in [67].

- The **Received Signal Strength Observer** monitors the radio channel and intends to draw conclusions from the *Received Signal Strength Indicator (RSSI)* on the actual distance of the sender, considering the maximum transmission power defined for C2X stations. In *Gerlach et al.* [85], this approach has been further elaborated, which revealed that due to unpredictable influences of the channel, the RSSI is only of limited use for highly dynamic environments like vehicular networks.

- The **Certificate Observer** is related to the evaluation of the digital signature and the certificate attached to every C2X message. For assessing the trustworthiness the included attributes like, e.g., timestamp and signer CA are plausibilized.

- The **External Measurement Observer** includes observations taken by additional vehicle sensors, like, e.g., camera, to cross-verify this information with the received position claims.

- The **Map Matching Observer** is similar to the Map-based Verification approach suggested by *Leinmüller et al.* [67].

- The **Mobility Model Observer** verifies if two subsequent position claims are related to each other using the equation of motion.

Each of these observers translates the evaluated information into a certain probability, which is denoted inside the BN. Having the BN filled with respective probabilities from each observer, either the trustworthiness of a particular mobility datum or the trustworthiness as a whole can be assessed.

4.2.3 Assessment

Approaches using infrastructure-based position verification as suggested by *Hubaux et al.* [75] are promising in terms of their effectiveness and reliability. However, such approaches can be only applied locally, since they rely upon a comprehensive covering of roads with

RSUs. Outside the monitored region, the trustworthiness of sent positions cannot be ensured anymore. Hence, a smart attacker who is able to forge any position inside the sent C2X message may easily adapt to that scheme. While executing the attestation protocol suggested by [75], the attacker might try not getting revealed by sending correct position data. After having passed the local verification, she/he may easily continue sending forged positions. As a possible solution to that issue, the author of this thesis proposes to perform the triangulation continuously by including other trustworthy vehicles. Synchronization may be achieved, using the global UTC time. In order to make this approach applicable in practice, further sub protocols have to be specified for permanently exchanging attestation results among neighboring stations.

The approach suggested by *Goll et al.* [76] requires permanent exchange of observations among nodes. For highly mobile nodes in vehicular networks this may cause a considerable communication overhead.

Performing an information fusion of data coming from different in-car sensor, like applied by *Yan et al.* [81], will certainly enable a more sophisticated verification of C2X messages. However, the possibilities for applying Radar systems to comprehensively verify C2X data are rather limited, since only objects in line-of-sight can be verified. Hence, multi hop messages like DENMs are not verifiable with this approach and as such are exposed to possible attacks. Futhermore, in general, deploying a more reliable sensor (like, e.g., Radar) for the purpose of verifying data coming from a less reliable sensor (like e.g. C2X) is not considered as expedient.

VEBAS [82] represents a first attempt for creating a more holistic evaluation of trustworthiness in C2X networks by taking also into account the history of past ratings. However, VEBAS is missing a concise mobility model by which the current mobility data can be assessed with respect to the vehicle's entire trajectory. Hence, while a single message might pass the threshold checks successfully, it still may be rated as invalid in the context of all previously received messages. In the following sections, a framework is proposed, which evaluates mobility data with respect to the entire path history of a vehicle.

Applying Bayesian Networks as suggested by *M.Gerlach* [84] represents a feasible approach for modeling evidences and assessing trustworthiness of received mobility data. However to work effectively, suggested observers have to be elaborated in more detail. For instance, besides already mentioned shortcomings for applying RSSI in C2X, it can be further argued that the transmission power of the sender vehicle cannot be assumed as constant. Congestion control techniques may vary the transmission power in case of traffic jams. Also the concept of Secure C2X Beamforming, as introduced in Chapter 6, is based on an adaptive adjustment of the applied transmission power, dependant on the trustworthiness of surrounding vehicles.

4.3 Mobility Data Verification Framework

In the following a novel approach for mobility data verification by means of *Path Prediction*, *Sensor-based Verification* and *Maneuver Recognition* is presented. The core components are described in three separate sections. Each component is first motivated, and then described in detail. In the second part of each section the integration of the individual concepts in terms of an overall framework is stated.

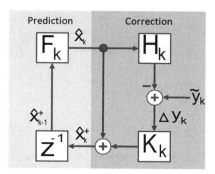

Figure 4.4: Kalman filter block diagram with prediction and correction phase

4.3.1 Path Prediction

In this section the basic concept and implementation of the first evaluation stage is presented, which consists of a Kalman filter for predicting and evaluating the mobility data of adjacent vehicles. Compared to other works, in this approach the entire path history of a vehicle is included into the verification process. Furthermore, the concept takes into account, that vehicles may suddenly change their identifiers due to privacy reasons. Especially the last issue has not been addressed by any of the proposed solutions so far.

Kalman Filter for Mobility Estimation

In the following a brief introduction into Kalman filter theory is given. Then, the performed adaptions for using the filter for the purpose of vehicle tracking are outlined.

Kalman Filter Theory The *Kalman Filter (KF)* method as denoted by the equations originally published by *R. Kalman* [86] represents a well-known and effective approach to multi-target tracking. It intends to minimize the mean squared estimation error of a system state, taking into account noise of the measurement data as well as uncertainties of the underlying system model. Compared to other minimum square methods, the Kalman filter has the clear advantage that it works recursively. Hence, this approach does not require to store and to process the entire set of previously received data for predicting the next estimate. Besides that, the KF is based on a time-discrete model and may consider dynamic noise for its calculations. The KF will generate an optimal prediction, if the measurement error is Gaussian distributed. Indeed, this is the case for position data delivered in C2X. Because of these properties, this method is particularly well-suited for the purpose of estimating future vehicle states based on C2X messages. For further reading, in *Blackman et al.* [87] a comprehensive survey over other possible application fields for KFs is given.

For every received measurement sample, received at time step k, the KF executes two recursive phases, i.e., *prediction* and *correction* (see Figure 4.4). The KF requires some a priori information on the system properties, in order to correctly predict the next state. This knowledge is modeled by the *state transition matrix* F_k. Hence, to predict the next *system state* $\hat{x}_k$ based on the *current state* $\hat{x}_{k-1}^+$, the following state space equation is applied:

$$\hat{x}_k = F_k \cdot \hat{x}_{k-1}^+. \tag{4.1}$$

Furthermore, an estimate on the inaccuracies related to the current prediction is determined during that phase. These inaccuracies are mainly due to unavoidable uncertainties within the applied system model. Accordingly, the *prediction error covariance* P_k is calculated recursively by accumulating the *previous prediction error* P_{k-1}^+ (taking into account the transition matrix F_k) to the *system noise* Q_k:

$$P_k = F_k \cdot P_{k-1}^+ \cdot F_k^T + Q_k. \tag{4.2}$$

For every time step k, the prediction phase is followed by an update phase, which consists of a correction of the predicted state by means of the *sampled data* $\tilde{y}_k$ observed from the system. For that purpose, the *distance* Δy_k between sampled data $\tilde{y}_k$ and predicted data $\hat{x}_k$ is determined, using transition matrix H_k, which reflects the correspondence between system state and measurement:

$$\Delta y_k = \tilde{y}_k - H_k \cdot \hat{x}_k. \tag{4.3}$$

A significant part within the KF is related to the calculation of the *Kalman gain* K_k:

$$K_k = P_k \cdot H_k^T \cdot (H_k \cdot P_k \cdot H_k^T + R_k)^{-1}. \tag{4.4}$$

The Kalman gain K_k represents a measure for weighting predicted and measured data, taking into account both, the system noise (accumulated in P_k) and the noise contained in the measurement itself (denoted as *measurement variance* R_k). Note that system and measurement noise are assumed to be statistically independent. Accordingly, the corrected system state $\hat{x}_k^+$ is calculated as:

$$x_k^+ = \hat{x}_k + K_k \cdot \Delta y_k. \tag{4.5}$$

As a final step, the prediction error covariance matrix P_k is updated by means of the Kalman gain:

$$P_k^+ = P_k - K_k \cdot H_k \cdot P_k. \tag{4.6}$$

Kalman Filter for Path Prediction The KF method is widely used in the automotive domain for applications like, e.g., navigation. There, techniques based on *dead reckoning* [88] are applied, which intend to overcome the reduced quality of GPS signals by taking into account the vehicles local data, such as, e.g., yaw rate and steering angle. This application is well comparable to our scenario, even though the state parameters are different.

For the purpose of vehicle tracking, the related matrices are defined as follows. The system state is denoted in terms of the vehicle's mobility data represented in Cartesian coordinates. Hence, a vehicle's position (p_x, p_y) and velocity (v_x, v_y) are components of a vector of the form:

$$\hat{x}_k = \begin{pmatrix} p_x \\ p_y \\ v_x \\ v_y \end{pmatrix}. \tag{4.7}$$

The accuracy of the system model is limited by the entropy included in the data of received C2X messages. Since in the present version of the CAM specification, only position, speed, and heading are transmitted, the system model is defined under the assumption of *constant velocity*. Consequently, the previous system state will be transferred to the next state according to the physical laws of motion by applying the following matrix:

$$
F_k = \begin{pmatrix} 1 & 0 & \Delta t_k & 0 \\ 0 & 1 & 0 & \Delta t_k \\ 0 & 0 & 1 & 0 \\ 0 & 0 & 0 & 1 \end{pmatrix}. \tag{4.8}
$$

For calculation of the prediction error covariance matrix P_k the error related to the system model described by the matrix F_k in Equation (4.8) has to be elaborated. This tuning process is generally referred as *system identification* and is performed offline with the help of several reference traces. In the context of the work done by *Stübing et al.* in [7] a slightly deviant behavior for different road scenarios, i.e., motorways, rural or city roads has been observed. Although not yet implemented in the current version of the framework, in general a dynamic switching of the applied system noise matrix Q_k is anticipatedd.

In the following, an estimator for the measurement variances R_k is derived. According to message specification of CAMs, the sender is obliged to attach a position confidence eclipse for the transmitted position (i.e. longitude and latitude). In [36] (page 13) a 95 % confidence interval (i.e., R95 accuracy measure) is defined for the horizontal plane. This means, that there exists a 95% probability that the true position falls into the region bounded by the defined intervals [89] (page 48). Within the CAM definition, the position confidence is expressed by an ellipse along major and minor axis with the corresponding orientation as illustrated in Figure 4.5. In principle, if considered as trustworthy, these transmitted confidence values are appropriate for the measurement variances in R_k. However, an attacker, which is capable of forging mobility data, may also easily forge the corresponding confidence values. Since the measurement variance has influence on the results of the verification process, an attacker with a less sophisticated mobility model might claim low confidence values in order to influence the Kalman gain on the receiver side according to her or his own interest.

Given the above discussion, in this thesis, it is anticipated to estimate the measurement variances in R_k locally at every receiver, instead. In general, defining an accurate confidence estimator for each mobility data at the receiver side is a non-trivial task and will be subject to future research work. In the following, a basic approach is advocated:

In C2X systems, the position accuracy is basically determined by GPS accuracy. This accuracy is affected by several parameters including the total number and geometry of satellites in reception range, clock inaccuracies between satellites as well as atmospheric effects due to reduced propagation speed in the troposphere and ionosphere. According to *Grewal et al.* [90], this set of errors is common among receivers, which are close to one another.

Besides these common errors, further errors are introduced at every receiver individually. This set of errors is due to noise caused by the environment and the GPS module, local clock inaccuracies, as well as multipath effects. With the exception of multipath effects, these sources of errors are rather negligible compared to the large influence introduced by the common errors. Multipath effects can be further reduced, e.g., by using proper GPS antennas, which mitigate the reflected signals. Furthermore, multipath effects are considered

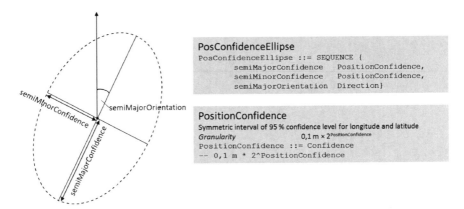

Figure 4.5: Position confidence ellipse for C2X position information

to be more an issue for urban city centers than for open highways, where this verification framework is primary intended for.

In a basic implementation of the advocated verification framework, as implemented in [7], [12], and [14], a static measurement variance R_k^{static} is assumed. The static values are determined by averaging the position error over several samples for different environments. Experiments conducted with this implementation already yielded notable results [12]. However, for the sim^{TD} architecture, a more sophisticated approach may be applied. In sim^{TD}, every vehicle is equipped with the same hardware and software architecture. Hence, for a given GPS quality, the same level of accuracy is achieved by all vehicles. If further assumed, that for vehicles within the same area, the GPS quality is comparable, the receiver vehicle may take his own, locally determined accuracy R_k^{local} as an accuracy estimator for the received data.

For the purpose of detecting adversaries, an estimator is generally aspired, which yields the best GPS quality achievable within a given area. The measurement matrix is therefore determined by the maximum of both values, i.e., the pre-calculated static variance and the actual variance, locally observed on the receiver vehicle:

$$R_k = max(R_k^{static}; R_k^{local}). \tag{4.9}$$

Note that this refined estimator is not part of the implementations as presented in [7], [12], and [14]. It has recently been included in the context of this thesis, only.

Framework Integration

In the following, the verification flow as depicted in Figure 4.6 is described. Accordingly, the evaluation is performed upon every received C2X message in a serial order. The mobility data as well as the sender ID are extracted and handed over to the mobility verification framework. After processing in this framework, each message will be classified either as *Approved, Neutral*, or *Erroneous*.

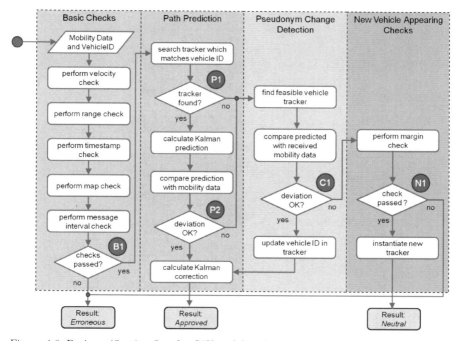

Figure 4.6: Basic verification flow for C2X mobility data

The possible results of the mobility verification framework are summarized in Table 4.1. Three validation classes are provided, which can easily be interpreted by applications on upper layers.

Validation Class	Description
Erroneous	The mobility data does not match the mobility model of the verification framework.
Neutral	The framework cannot make a reliable and meaningful statement.
Approved	Mobility data of the message was checked and accepted.

Table 4.1: Message validation classes

The first step of the verification consists of several threshold checks. Threshold verification prevents inconsistent data to corrupt the on-going mobility prediction. In particular, mobility data is filtered, which exceeds some physical or regulatory boundaries. For example, due to physics even in highway scenarios, vehicles may not drive with infinite speed. Furthermore, a message which indicates a position outside the host vehicles communication range is regarded as untrustworthy (refers to ART check according to [67]). A timestamp check is applied to filter messages, whose timestamp is either expired or dated to a future point in time. That way replay-attacks are impeded. Another threshold check monitors the repetition frequency of CAM messages. In order to prevent DoS attacks, CAM messages, which are sent with higher frequency as defined by standardization institutes (i.e., ETSI in Europe), are regarded as suspicious (refers to Maximum Beaconing Frequency according to [82]). The framework as presented in *Stübing et al.* [7], has been complemented by an additional map-based check for verifying, that the sender vehicle is located on the road.

For combining the different verification results into an overall trust value for that message, a weight factor may be applied to each verification check as proposed in [67]. For instance, the applied range check may be considered as more critical for evaluating the message trustworthiness as the map-based check and consequently may be assigned a higher weight. However, due to missing implementation proposals for the time-being, for the near-series implementation in sim^{TD} [7] a more straight-forward approach is applied. Since the aforementioned threshold checks can be considered as rather light-weighted and are furthermore designed with appropriated tolerances, each of them has to be passed seperately to continue verification. Hence, if one of these checks fails, the entire message will be marked as *Erroneous* (see B1 in Figure 4.6). In the following procedure, the message must undergo a more in-depth trajectory analysis.

The framework now evaluates the message with respect to previously sent messages from that vehicle, i.e., it is observed if all message lie on a continuous trace. For this reason a tracker based on KF predictions, like described in previous sections, is instantiated and maintained for every known vehicle within communication range. Assuming that the framework receives an already known vehicle ID, the assigned tracker is used to compare the received mobility data against the deployed mobility model (see P1 in Figure 4.6). Based on the given timestamp inside the message the expected mobility data is estimated by triggering the Kalman prediction phase. The difference Δy_k between predicted state $\hat{x}_k$ and received mobility data $\tilde{y}_k$ is determined. Considering a maximum tolerable difference (in Algorithm 3 and in the following course of this work, denoted as *Acceptance Threshold (AT)*), the trustworthiness of the message is assessed. Thus, it may be evaluated as *Erroneous* or *Approved* (see P2 in Figure 4.6). In case of an approved message, the Kalman correction phase is triggered, and the internal state is corrected using the newly received mobility data. In case no tracker was found (P1 in Figure 4.6), two possible reasons can be identified: Either an unknown vehicle is entering the host vehicle's communication range, or, instead, an already known vehicle has performed a pseudonym change.

For the latter case, the pseudonym change is made locally transparent. As described in Algorithm 3, the tracker list is iterated in order to find the candidate, which is most likely to fit the received mobility data. For the most feasible tracker the prediction phase of the Kalman filter is executed and the deviation is determined. If the vehicle movement fits the prediction of this tracker with respect to *AT*, then the message is evaluated as *Approved* and a pseudonym change is considered to be detected (see C1 in Figure 4.6). In order to identify the vehicle correctly for the next received message, the vehicle ID inside the corresponding tracker is updated.

For detecting a new vehicle entering the communication range, a rather light-weighted check is applied in this implementation variant. The check refers to the Sudden Appearance Check according to [82] and is based on the basic assumption, that vehicles generally first appear on the border of the communication range r_{max}. In Figure 4.7, the tolerance margin of this

---

Algorithm 3 resolvePseudonymChange()

In: Tracker List T, Incoming Mobility Data $\tilde{y}_k$, Vehicle Identifier $vehicleID$
Out: Boolean, *True* for pseudonym change detected, *False* for not detected

1:   $AT = 3m$ {Acceptance Threshold}
2:   $FeasibleTracker$ {temporary tracker variable}
3:   Δy_k^{tmp} {temporary deviation variable}
4:   **for all** $i \leftarrow 0, T.\text{size}()$ **do**
5:     **if** $i = 0$ **then**
6:       $FeasibleTracker \leftarrow T.get(0)$
7:       $\hat{x}_k \leftarrow F_k \times T.get(0).\hat{x}_{k-1}^+$
8:       $\Delta y_k^{tmp} \leftarrow \tilde{y}_k - H_k \times \hat{x}_k$
9:     **else**
10:      $\hat{x}_k \leftarrow F_k \times T.get(i).\hat{x}_{k-1}^+$
11:      $\Delta y_k \leftarrow \tilde{y}_k - H_k \times \hat{x}_k$
12:      **if** $\Delta y_k \leq \Delta y_k^{tmp}$ **then**
13:        $\Delta y_k^{tmp} \leftarrow \Delta y_k$
14:        $FeasibleTracker \leftarrow T.get(i)$
15:      **end if**
16:     **end if**
17:   **end for**
18:   **if** $y_k^{tmp} \leq AT$ **then**
19:     $FeasibleTracker.\text{setVehicleID}(vehicleID)$
20:     $P_k = F_k \times P_{k-1}^+ \times F_k + Q_k$
21:     **if** $R_k^{local} \geq R_k^{static}$ **then**
22:       $R_k = R_k^{local}$
23:     **else**
24:       $R_k = R_k^{static}$
25:     **end if**
26:     $FeasibleTracker.K_k = P_k \times H_k^T \times (H_k \times P_k \times H_k^T + R_k)^{-1}$
27:     $FeasibleTracker.x_k^+ = FeasibleTracker.\hat{x}_k + K_k \times \Delta y_k^{tmp}$
28:     $FeasibleTracker.P_k^+ = P_k - K_k \times H_k \times P_k$
29:     **return** true
30:   **else**
31:     **return** false
32:   **end if**

---

check is illustrated. Accordingly, only messages, which are indicating a vehicle that appears within the boundaries $r_{max} - d_{margin}$ and r_{max} will be marked as *Approved*. A more sophisticated approach for evaluating suddenly appearing vehicles is presented in Section 4.3.2. Since for unknown vehicles no sophisticated trajectory analysis can be performed, messages which have passed the Sudden Appearance Check will be marked as *Neutral*.

The described approach represents the foundation for C2X mobility verification framework and has to be extended by additional measures to increase its reliability. In the following sections further concepts are presented, which aim at reducing the false positive rate, i.e., the number of messages which are wrongly marked as *Erroneous*.

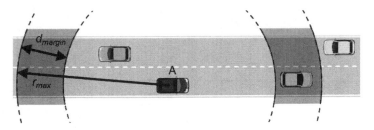

Figure 4.7: Acceptance margin range for verification of suddenly appearing vehicles

4.3.2 Sensor-based Verification

As one potential source of errors the Sudden Appearance Check, performed for unknown vehicles has been identified (see (N1) in Figure 4.6). The underlying assumption, for which unknown vehicles occur first at the border of the host vehicle's communication range may not hold for every possible C2X scenario. In the following some of the main challenges, the framework has to cope with, are stated:

1. Vehicles parked at the curb side may turn on the engine and start sending C2X messages. Especially in urban scenarios, such vehicles may suddenly appear close to the host vehicle.

As one possible solution to the first scenario, in this thesis, it is proposed to take into account a minimum velocity when applying the Sudden Appearance Check for a certain target vehicle. For instance, this check could be only applied to moving vehicles. Such an approach obviously weakens the mobility verification, but is considered as a necessary step to reduce the number of false positives.

2. Due to channel congestion, messages of the target vehicle might get lost. Depending on the number of lost messages, the first position received from that vehicle may be located within the near communication range, i.e., less than $r_{max} - d_{margin}$.

In order to cope with messages losses, there exist very few alternatives than to assign higher tolerances to the acceptance margin d_{margin}. It is subject to currently running field operational test like sim^{TD} to gain more insights into the C2X channel characteristics and the message loss rates depending on different traffic scenarios.

3. Further causes for suddenly appearing vehicles in the vicinity are shadowing effects. For instance, in Figure 4.8 a highway scenario is illustrated, where *vehicle B* is starting to overtake the truck in front of it. Due to shadowing, caused by the truck in the rear, the CAM messages sent by *vehicle B* are blocked and not received by the approaching *vehicle A*. In consequence, *vehicle A* will evaluate the first message received from *vehicle B* as *Erroneous*, since it cannot distinguish this scenario from any of the described attack scenarios in Section 4.1.

Regarding the impact on C2X functionality, this scenario is most critical, since suddenly appearing vehicles, which are located in the driving direction of the host vehicle represent

Figure 4.8: Vehicle shadowing due to large trucks at highway scenarios

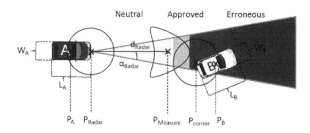

Figure 4.9: Radar and C2X message matching

a potential hazard. Obviously, a correct assessment of these messages has to be ensured in the interest of road safety. Verifying position claims based on a single message is limited, when applying message content verification, only. Therefore, the author of this thesis has examined the possibilits for including complementary checks via a vehicle's local sensors to overcome the described difficulties [12]. In the following section, the advocated countermeasure based on a local sensor verification is presented.

Radar Data and C2X Mobility Data Fusion

Within the introductory chapters of this thesis, the C2X communication technology has been introduced as the next logical step, in order to overcome the limited detection range of common automotive sensor systems, today. However, for the near field, local vehicle sensors like, e.g., Radar still possess a considerably higher accuracy than the data transmitted contained in C2X messages. Furthermore, different sensor systems, like, e.g., Camera, Radar, or Lidar may be combined to achieve even higher accuracies. However, besides the temporal and spatial alignment of different sensor sources, also the management and representation of the data is considered as an open challenge for sensor fusion and is still subject to ongoing research work [91].

In this thesis, for the purpose of verifying C2X position claims within the near field ($r_{max} - d_{margin}$) of a vehicle, a basic approach via a Radar sensor is applied. Available Radar systems, today, may detect obstacles with high accuracy of 0.25 m for the radial distance and 0.1° for angular measurements. The radar system available for the sim^{TD} architecture, provides a low cycle time (below 70 ms) at a high detection range (up to 200m) [92].

In the following, a brief description of the advocated approach for matching Radar data with C2X positions is given. Performed steps are described with respect to the example scenario as motivated by Figure 4.8:

1. The receiver *vehicle A* in Figure 4.9 determines the position of the Radar sensor P_{Radar} in geo-coordinates, considering its own position P_A and the physical dimensions (W_A,

L_A). Without the loss of generality, it is assumed that the transmitted GPS position denotes the center of the vehicle and the Radar sensor is mounted at the front. Since the center point is associated to a certain GPS error, this error translates also to the determined position of the radar mounting P_{Radar}. In Figure 4.9, related deviations are described in a simplified form as a circle around the given position for illustration purposes.

2. Considering the transmitted C2X position P_B, the heading and the vehicle dimensions in terms of width W_B and length L_B (attached to every CAM [36]), the geographical position of the four corners of *vehicle B* can be determined. The vehicle corner P_{Corner}, which possesses the minimum distance to P_{Radar} is taken as reference position for verification against the Radar measurement.

3. The deployed Radar sensor returns a measurement triple, consisting of the relative speed, distance d_{Radar} and angle α_{Radar} for a detected object. Considering the latter two parameter and the Radar position P_{Radar}, the position of the detected object $P_{Measure}$ is determined in absolute coordinates. The associated error related to this object position, results from a superposition of the GPS tolerances (translated from P_A) and the angle and distance tolerances, attributed to radar itself. In Figure 4.9 the superposed confidence area is depicted in a simplified manner, for illustration purposes.

4. Depending on the time delta between the radar measurement and the C2X message timestamp a temporal synchronization has to be performed, prior to conducting the final evaluation step.

5. In Figure 4.9, the coloring indicates the assessing scheme. Accordingly, the C2X message is considered to match the radar measurement, if the tolerance areas around $P_{Measure}$ and P_{Corner} do overlap. Objects, that fall into the *blue* shaded area may be due to other objects located in direct *Line of Side (LOS)* to the target *vehicle B*. For these cases no general statement can be made. In contrast, if the closest object detected by the Radar is located within the *red* shaded area, the position claim transmitted by *vehicle B*'s C2X message may be evaluated as erroneous.

Being aware that this sensor-based verification approach applies only to the vehicle driving infront of the host vehicle, it is strongly recommended to include additional sensors, in order to achieve 360° of verification coverage. However, for most safety relevant applications, like EEBL (see Section 2.2.1), a verification via the front Radar represents a feasible and easy realizable solution.

Framework Integration

For the prototypical implementation, a Radar sensor was used with a total detection range of 200 meters [92]. The Radar constantly measures the distance and angle of vehicles driving ahead. Matching Radar objects to positions indicated by C2X messages represents a non-trivial task when taking into account the different coordinate planes as well as error variances related to both systems. In the scope of this protoype implementation an approach is chosen where the relative distance of a measured object is transferred into absolute coordinates considering the host vehicle's position and a synchronization of the timeline.

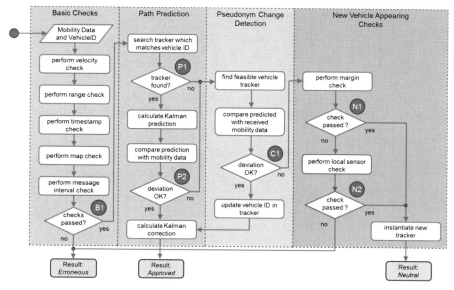

Figure 4.10: Extended verification flow including the local sensor check

In Figure 4.10 the extended verification framework is depicted. Accordingly, only in case the resulting Radar position can be matched to the C2X message's position (see N2 in Figure 4.10), the message is evaluated as *Approved*. In this comparison of positions, the vehicle's dimensions are considered, which are included as tagged value in every received CAM [36].

4.3.3 Maneuver Recognition

An essential part of the verification framework presented in previous sections consists of the path prediction and verification via the presented KF mobility model. While other threshold checks may be easily pre-empted by keeping sent mobility data within certain boundaries, the Path Prediction check requires an attacker to maintain a concise mobility model, taking into account additional context information of the respective traffic scenario. In this section this method is further refined, in order to make it even more effective and reliable, and by this, increase the overall security level of the C2X system.

These enhancements are driven by the insight, that the level of security provided by the verification framework is directly related to the predefined acceptance threshold AT between predicted and received mobility data (see decision point P2 and C1 in Figure 4.10). Within the previously described implementation state of the framework, the maximum tolerable value for AT is limited by the accuracy of the Kalman prediction model. Hence, the concepts described in this section aim at lowering AT by increasing the prediction accuracy of the Kalman based path prediction.

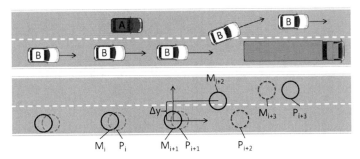

Figure 4.11: Lateral position offset due to overtaking maneuver. Black circles: real position, Green circles: correct prediction, Red circles: incorrect prediction

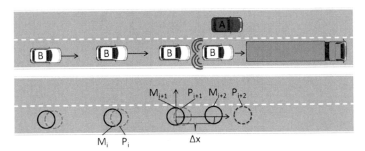

Figure 4.12: Longitudinal position offset due to hard braking maneuver. Black circles: real position, Green circles: correct prediction, Red circles: incorrect prediction

The Kalman Filter as described in Section 4.3.1, represents an effective estimator for predicting linear movements. In contrast, sudden changes in the trajectory may lead to discontinuities, which cannot be handled efficiently, using the deployed mobility model. With respect to the driving directions, such discontinuities may be reflected by a sudden position offset in lateral or longitudinal direction between two succeeding messages.

As an example, in Figure 4.11 a frequently occurring traffic situation is illustrated, where a *vehicle B* is accelerating in order to overtake a slowly driving truck to the front. Meanwhile on the left lane a second *vehicle A* is approaching with high speed, which causes *vehicle B* to perform a sharp lane change maneuver. In the graph below, the respective traffic situation from the viewpoint of *vehicle A's* internal Kalman tracker is presented. The transmitted positions of *vehicle B* are denoted by black circles. The dotted circles in green and red, illustrate the Kalman predictions for correct and incorrect predictions, respectively. Accordingly, due to the high lateral variation in *vehicle B's* trajectory and the steady state of the KF, the predicted and actual positions are diverging more than usual. In Figure 4.12 a similar traffic situation is illustrated. In this example, *vehicle A* is blocking the available free space on the left lane, which causes vehicle B, to perform a full brake. For this scenario, it is the longitudinal variance, which leads to a high deviation between predicted and received mobility data. Anticipating the experimental results from Section 4.4, it can be concluded

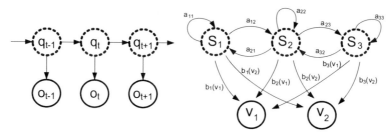

Figure 4.13: Structure of a HMM. Left: Markov Chain of hidden system states. Right:
HMM with 3 system states and 2 (discrete) observation symbols v_1 and v_2.

that the Kalman mobility model is appropriate for most traffic scenarios, but is actually
to inert in cases of highly dynamic traffic maneuvers like, e.g., suddenly overtaking or hard
braking vehicles. Therefore a strong need for complementary techniques can be identified
for efficiently detecting such maneuvers in order to subsequently calibrate the KF based
model. In the following, Hidden Markov Models as a means for detecting these kind of
traffic maneuvers are proposed.

Hidden Markov Model for Maneuver Recognition

In this section the concept and implementation of a second verification stage is presented. By
following the same structure as in previous sections, first the basic theory behind *Hidden
Markov Models (HMM)* and respective algorithms for effective calculation are reviewed.
Then, the appropriate deployment of HMMs for modeling and recognizing traffic scenarios
according to *Firl et al.* [13] is presented.

Hidden Markov Model Theory HMMs are stochastical models and can be considered as a
particular kind of dynamic Bayesian Network, which consists of one *Markov Chain* for the
sequence of hidden states and one for the sequence of observable emissions at each state.
As a basic property of HMMs, it is assumed that the system states of the model itself are
'hidden' and thus, are not directly visible to the observers. However, each state produces a
certain output with a given probability, which is visible to the observer, instead. Therefore,
if the system is traversing several states, a sequence of outputs are generated, which allow
to draw conclusions on the actual sequence of passed states.

The use of HMMs has grown in popularity over the last few decades. A major field of
applications for HMMs lies within speech recognition as presented by *L.R. Rabiner* [93].
M. Stanke [94] has applied HMMs for finding the most likely gene structure of a given input
DNA sequence, and *Marti et al.* [95] have established an HMM for recognizing words inside
handwritten text. In the area of cryptanalysis, HMM have been successfully applied by
Karlof et al. [96] for supporting side channel attacks against randomized keyed countermeasures. For this purpose, HMMs had to be extended to additionally handle inputs, which
model the influence of the secret key on the next system state. According to the notation
used by *L.R. Rabiner* [93] an HMM is determined by the following set of parameters (see
Figure 4.13):

1. N: the number of (hidden) system states in the model. The individual states are
   denoted as $S = (S_1, S_2, \ldots, S_N)$. The current system state at a specific point in time t

is denoted by q_t. The temporal sequence of system states $Q = (q_1, q_2, \ldots, q_T)$ represent a *Markov Chain*. A Markov Chain is a 'memoryless' random process, where the transition to the next state depends only on the current state, i.e., $P(q_t | q_{t-1}, \ldots, q_1) = P(q_t | q_{t-1})$.

2. M: the number of distinct observations. For HMMs, observations may be either countable, denoted by $V = (v_1, v_2, \ldots, v_M)$ or continous, denoted by $v_t \in \mathbb{R}$. The sequence of states Q emits a sequence of observations, denoted by $O = (o_1, o_2 \ldots, o_T)$ where $o_t \in \{v_1, v_2, \ldots, v_M\}$ and $P(o_t | q_t, \ldots, q_1, o_{t-1}, \ldots, o_1) = P(o_t | q_t)$ holds.

3. A: the state transition probability distribution matrix. The matrix A includes the conditional transition probability from each state i to every other state j of the system, denoted by

$$a_{i,j} := P(q_{t+1} = X_j | q_t = X_i) \quad 1 \leq i, j \leq N \quad \forall t \in 1, ..., T. \tag{4.10}$$

4. B: the observation model including the respective probabilities for observing a certain symbol when the system remains in state j. In the discrete case, B represents a matrix, denoted by

$$b_{j,k} := b_j(v_k) = P(o_t = v_k | q_t = X_j) \quad 1 \leq k \leq M \quad \forall t \in 1, ..., T. \tag{4.11}$$

In case the observed symbol is considered as a continous value, the corresponding observation probability distribution is also continous, denoted by

$$b_j(o) := P(o | X_j). \tag{4.12}$$

Note that, in order to describe the probability function $b_j(o)$, for the presented application a parameterization based on *Mixture of Gaussian (MoG)* is chosen. MoGs are generally used for approximating a certain probability distribution by superpositioning of several normal distributions.

5. π: the initial state distribution vector, includes the probability of each state for being that state, which has emitted the first observation o_1, i.e.,

$$\pi_i := P(q_1 = X_i). \tag{4.13}$$

Since the number of states N as well as the number of observations M are implicitly determined by the size of the matrices A and B, a HMM is fully specified by the following triple:

$$\lambda = (A, B, \pi). \tag{4.14}$$

For a respective application, an external observer is assumed to have knowledge about the HMM parameter λ. Depending on the complexity of the observed system several HMMs $\lambda_1, \lambda_2, ..., \lambda_K$ may be defined for modeling the different aspects of the system behavior.

Given a certain observation sequence $O = (o_1, o_2 \ldots, o_T)$ basically three different problems are of particular interest for most applications. According to [93] these are denoted as the *Evaluation*, *Decoding*, and *Learning* problem, respectively:

1. **Evaluation**: The purpose of the evaluation is to determine, how well a certain HMM λ can be associated to the given observation sequence O. Hence, the probability $P(O|\lambda)$ has to be determined.

2. **Decoding**: The decoding problem consists of finding those states within a given HMM, which are most likely belonging to the observed sequence O.

3. **Learning**: For most applications the accuracy of the chosen model parameters λ is essential. Therefore the model parameters $\lambda = (A, B, \pi)$ have to be determined in a way that for an emitted observation sequence, the probability $P(O|\lambda)$ reaches its maximum.

For the purpose of maneuver recognition in C2X communication, solving the **Evaluation** problem by determining $P(O|\lambda)$ is of major interest. A straighforward approach to identify how well a certain HMM matches the given observations O, is to calculate the probability of all possible state sequences Q which might have led to the respective observations $O = (o_1, o_2 \ldots, o_T)$:

$$P(O|\lambda_k) = \sum_{all\,Q} P(O, Q|\lambda_k). \tag{4.15}$$

Since there exist N^T possible state sequences, this calculation is computationally infeasible. Instead, in practice a more efficient procedure is applied. *L.R. Rabiner* [93] advocates a *forward algorithm* for solving the interference task efficiently with only linear efforts. For timestep t and state S_i, the probability of the partial observation sequence $o_1, o_2, \ldots, o_t$ which ends in state X_i is denoted by

$$\alpha_t(i) := P(o_1, \ldots, o_t, q_t = X_i|\lambda). \tag{4.16}$$

Due to the Markov property of HMMs, the forward variable $\alpha_t(i)$ and the unknown probability $P(O|\lambda)$ can be determined iteratively:

1. Initialization:
$$\alpha_1(i) = \pi_i b_i(o_1), \quad 1 \leq i \leq N \tag{4.17}$$

2. Induction:
$$\alpha_{t+1}(j) = \left[\sum_{i=1}^{N} \alpha_t(i) a_{ij} \right] b_j(o_{t+1}), \quad 1 \leq t \leq T-1 \quad 1 \leq j \leq N \tag{4.18}$$

3. Termination:
$$P(O|\lambda) = \sum_{i=1}^{N} \alpha_T(i). \tag{4.19}$$

The **Decoding** problem is concerned with finding the best state sequence for a given observation sequence and can be efficiently solved using *Viterbi* algorithm [93].

For each defined HMM, the model parameters A, B, π have to be determined in advance. During the **Learning** phase, the HMM is trained by introducing several input sequences, which can be directly associated to a given HMM. An observer then uses the emitted observation symbols to optimize the following equation:

$$\hat{\lambda} = \underset{\lambda}{\arg\max}\, P(\vec{o}_{train}|\lambda). \tag{4.20}$$

Solving this task is not possible using analytical approaches. Therefore, [93] advocates using an iterative approximation procedure namely the *Baum-Welch* algorithm, which solves the optimization problem locally. Note that the results are highly depending on the initial parameters, which have to be chosen wisely.

Hidden Markov Model for Maneuver Recognition Using HMMs for maneuver recognition in traffic scenarios has been advocated first by *Firl et al.* [13]. Accordingly, different HMMs $\lambda_{foll}, \lambda_{over}, \lambda_{flank}$ are defined for detecting *following-*, *overtaking-* and *flanking*-maneuvers on rural roads and motorways. Each HMM is modeled by 5 hidden states, which reflect the relation between two vehicles at a specific point in time during the maneuver. Neither the actual state, nor the transition between the states can be directly assessed. Instead, an external observer is assumed to measure the relative distance and speed between two relevant vehicles. During the Learning phase this data is directly obtained via a simulator, which has been used to train the model parameters A, B and π. For real world evaluations, test vehicles have been used which were equipped with a mono Camera and long range Radar. A sensor fusion has been performed between both sensors in order to accurately determine the relative dynamics to the vehicle driving ahead as well as road conditions.

In *Stübing et al.* [14] this approach has been transferred to the Car-to-X communication domain. For the purpose of traffic maneuver recognition, solving the Decoding problem is of less importance, since finding the correct HMM λ_i is of higher interest than to identify the exact states within the respective HMM. Hence, if the different HMMs are defined accurately enough, solving the Evaluation problem already gives sufficient information to calibrate the KF within the mobility framework.

In order to transform the obtained probability $P(O|\lambda)$ in Equation (4.19) into the required probability $P(\lambda|O)$, Bayes' theorem is applied. Thereby, the a priori probability $P(\lambda)$ may be used to include additional information into the evaluation. For instance, knowing that the observed vehicles are currently driving on a highway might increase the likelihood for performing overtaking maneuvers, compared to other road types (for more information see [13]).

Comparing the data obtained from Radar/Camera with the data included in C2X messages, like e.g. the CAM, basically two major differences can be identified. First, the generation frequency of CAMs is by a factor of 2 lower than the sampling interval of the Radar (see [36]). And second, the received position information may be noisy, due to GPS errors. Hence, the HMM algorithm has to get along with less data and a reduced accuracy. However, as shown in *Stübing et al.* [14], it turned out that the detection algorithm by *Firl et al.* [13] is surprisingly robust towards a reduced data set and accuracy. A more detailed analysis will follow in Section 4.4.

As outlined in the introduction of this section, the purpose of integrating HMMs into the mobility framework is to detect and if applicable, plausibilize suddenly appearing lateral and longitudinal position offsets. Lateral offsets are mainly due to lane change maneuvers, while a longitudinal buckling of a vehicle's trajectory may be caused by braking maneuvers.

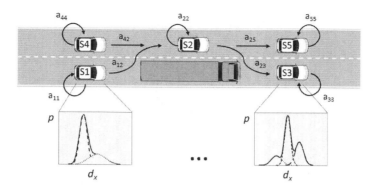

Figure 4.14: Different stages of an overtaking maneuver, corresponding to the (hidden) states of the HMM, with one exemplary observation distribution (MoG) for distance d_x

In the following, respective HMMs are described for modeling overtaking, following and hard braking maneuvers.

In Figure 4.14 the hidden states of the HMM for an overtaking maneuver are illustrated. In this example, the entire vehicle trajectory is observed by *vehicle A*, which is running the maneuver recognition algorithm. For using emitted C2X messages as input to this algorithm, absolute position coordinates have to be transformed into relative distances between the vehicle and the truck. The observation vector is therefore defined as follows:

$$o_t = \begin{pmatrix} d_x \\ d_y \\ v_{rel} \end{pmatrix}. \tag{4.21}$$

Obviously, the observation symbols are continuous, which leads also to continuous observation probabilities. The respective *probability density functions (pdf)* are parameterized using a MoG model. Note that for illustration purposes in Figure 4.14 the pdf for only exemplary observation symbol is depicted. A similar HMM is defined for modeling a following behavior of a vehicle. There, the hidden states lie on a continuous trace behind the vehicle driving ahead. Both HMMs, i.e. λ_{over} and λ_{foll} are used to predict an upcoming lane change. For doing so, the following ratio is evaluated as:

$$r_1 = \frac{P(\lambda_{over}|\vec{o})}{P(\lambda_{foll}|\vec{o})} \tag{4.22}$$

Accordingly, high values of r_1, indicate an imminent lane change.

The second types of maneuvers which are crucial to be detected are spontaneous brakings. For the KF application in this work, it is of particular interest to identify scenarios, where a vehicle is starting to accelerate in order to overtake the vehicle driving ahead. Due to insufficient free space to the left, the overtaking maneuver cannot be completed. Therefore the vehicle has to perform a hard braking in order to impede an accident (see Figure 4.12).

Detecting hard braking maneuvers is not possible by using relational data between two vehicles, only. Complementary issues need to be considered, such as the positioning of other surrounding vehicles or the given road geometry. Therefore, in *Stübing et al.* [14], [15],[16] an additional parameter $f \in [0, 1]$ is included into the observation vector which models the probability for having sufficient free space available. This leads into an extended observation vector, defined as follows:

$$o_t = \begin{pmatrix} d_x \\ d_y \\ v_{rel} \\ f \end{pmatrix} \tag{4.23}$$

Within the joint work in *Firl et al.* [16] a possible way for modeling the available free space by means of so called *occupancy grids* is presented. An occupancy grid is thereby composed of small geographical cells segmenting the area around the two vehicles. For each cell the probability of being occupied is determined. Whether adjacent lanes are occupied by other vehicles or not, can be determined by polling the C2X Neighborhood Table for the latest vehicles entries. Besides other vehicles, a road narrowing or construction zones may also impede a vehicle to perform an already initiated overtaking maneuver. This kind of information may be obtained from additional sources like, e.g., DENM messages, digital maps or on-board cameras.

For this work, of particular interest are traffic situations, where the drivers intention for overtaking, described by the probability $P(\lambda_{over})$, considerably diverges from the feasibilty of conducting that maneuver considering free space, denoted by $P(\lambda_{over,fs})$. Hence, the ratio of both probabilities may be used as indicator to predict braking maneuvers:

$$r_2 = \frac{P(\lambda_{over}|\vec{o})}{P(\lambda_{over,fs}|\vec{o})} \tag{4.24}$$

Similarly as for the lane change maneuver, a high value of r_2 gives indication that the driver is about to perform a full braking shortly.

Framework Integration

The enhanced framework as depicted in Figure 4.15 includes a two-stage verification process for evaluating a vehicle's trajectory. Accordingly, the first part of the evaluation is related to the comparison between received and predicted mobility data by means of a given mobility model as already described in Section 4.3.1. However, due to unavoidable inconsistencies of the deployed system model, the underlying Kalman prediction contains precision errors. In order to achieve a higher reliability for the overall system, a second stage of verification is introduced based on maneuver recognition via Hidden Markov Models. The maneuver recognition component is thereby deployed at two points of the evaluation flow.

Similar as in the basic scheme presented in previous sections, for known vehicle IDs (P1), the assigned vehicle tracker is selected and based on the given timestamp the Kalman prediction phase is triggered. According to Equation (4.3) in Section 4.3.1 the difference Δy_k between predicted state $\hat{x}_k$ and received mobility data $\tilde{y}_k$ is determined. Considering a maximum AT, the trustworthiness of the message is assessed. Note that the predefined acceptance threshold AT is established based on common GPS errors, which are typically in the range of $3 - 5$ meters. In [7] evaluations have been carried out, which yielded acceptable performance margins for most traffic situations. However, due to inherent system inaccuracies, the greatest deviations have been observed in high dynamic scenarios.

For the refined framework anticipated in this section, it is proposed to reduce AT to a maximum of 1 meter and to apply maneuver recognition algorithms for handling exceptional traffic scenarios, instead. Consequently, a message which exceeds the refined AT value, will not be directly marked as *Erroneous*, but is further evaluated by means of a second verification stage (see P2 in Figure 4.15).

The maneuver recognition component permanently assesses traffic situations of vehicles in the communication range and directly provides an estimate to the framework. The current implementation, as described in Section 4.3.3, is capable of predicting two dynamic manoeuvres, i.e., a suddenly overtaking or hard braking vehicles. In case the evaluated message is originated from a vehicle, which is currently performing such a maneuver, previously conducted experiments yielded that the applied KF reacts too slow on sudden changes of the vehicles trajectory and consequently has to be recalibrated. As already identified in Section 4.3.1, the Kalman gain represents the determining factor for weighting the predicted state against the measured data. Accordingly, in such highly dynamic maneuvers (M1 in Figure 4.15), the evaluation framework is adjusting the gain in a way that the system state is corrected more towards the measurement than the prediction. Hence, a higher trustworthiness is assigned to the measured data.

The Kalman Gain is adjusted at time step t, but has to be applied for correcting the system state x_k^+, one iteration step before, i.e., at time step *t-1*. For doing so, the previous prediction and correction phase are reversed and recalculated again. Considering an adapted Kalman Gain, the recalculation leads to an enhanced corrected state. Applying the prediction again, will lead to an enhanced corrected state, which is expected to be closer to the next mobility data received at time step t. The deviation is calculated again and if the threshold is passed by now (M2 in Figure 4.15), the message will be marked as *Approved* and the respective correction is performed. In contrast, if the deviation still exceeds the predefined threshold, the message will definitely be evaluated as *Erroneous*.

In case a *vehicle ID* is unknown, the tracker list is iterated, to evaluate whether any of the known vehicles has performed a pseudonym change (P1 in Figure 4.15). Since for dissolving pseudonym changes, the same technique based on path prediction is applied, this evaluation branch is equally prone to errors in case of dynamic maneuvers. That means, in principle a situation is conceivable, where a vehicle is switching from an old to a new pseudonym just before performing a lane change or hard barking. Such situations have to be detected and evaluated correctly via the described two-stage verification process. If a pseudonym change cannot be confirmed, using path prediction or maneuver recognition, the verification framework proceeds as described in previous sections (M3 and M4 in Figure 4.15).

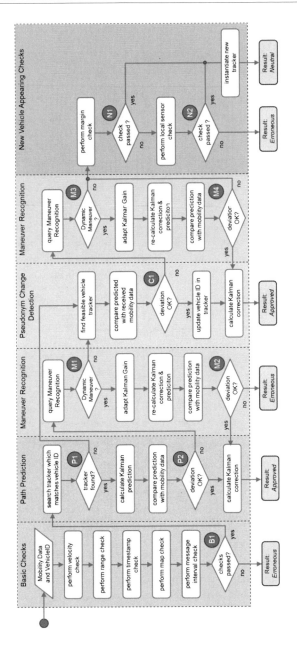

Figure 4.15: Verification evaluation flow including the maneuver recognition verification
          stage

4.4 Evaluation Results

This section provides a description of the prototypical implementation and carried out experiments. The obtained results are presented and commented.

4.4.1 Implementation

The mobility data verification framework, as outlined in previous sections has been fully implemented as Java/OSGi bundle, and integrated as a central system component on facility layer within the sim^{TD} vehicle architecture. Regarding the three different increments, presented in respective Sections 4.3.1, 4.3.2, and 4.3.3, the first stage is part of the official field trial. It has been implemented and integrated by the first three authors stated in [7]. The latter two stages are also fully functional, though they are implemented only on a smaller test fleet of three vehicles. The Radar system has been integrated and calibrated in a reduced version by means of students work presented in [97] and [98]. Considering the maneuver recognition stage, the first two authors in [14], [15], and [16] have jointly developed and integrated respective functionalities for the verification framework.

In Figure 4.16 the architectural integration of the mobility verification framework is depicted. As outlined in Section 2.1, sim^{TD} vehicles are equipped with two separate units. The CCU is based on a 400 MHz PowerPC with Linux running on top of it. It communicates via Ethernet to the AU, which consists of a Dual Core 2.7 GHz processor with Windows Embedded as operating system. While in respective project documents [35] and [8] a detailed description of the sim^{TD} system architecture can be found, the presentation in Figure 4.16 is restricted to components relevant for mobility verification, for brevity. Thereby the coloring indicates to which communication layer of the ITS reference model (see Figure 1.1) the components refer to.

Accordingly, incoming C2X messages are parsed by lower communication layers and are handed over to the network layer for cryptographic verification. Within the sim^{TD} architecture, security is implemented as a service, meaning that the network layer explicitly has to call a function and delegate the attached signature and certificate to the *Security Daemon* [99] for verification. The returned result is binary, i.e., either the message can be authenticated or not. In sim^{TD} invalid messages are not directly discarded but are marked for further evaluation on higher layers.

The second security evaluation consists of the advocated mobility verification framework, located on facility layer. Each verification stage (i.e., basic checks, Kalman filter, maneuver recognition etc.) is realized as a separate Java package, which facilitates testing and allows flexible switching between different configurations.

The sim^{TD} development environment offers various build-in test routines and debugging interfaces, which have been extensively used during the following evaluation. Especially the possibility for recording complete traces of received C2X messages together with own CAN data, using a *Trace Recorder*, was considered as very helpful for performing later offline evaluations.

4.4.2 Common Traffic Scenarios

The mobility verification framework is evaluated for technical feasibility by means of several trial runs, performed during the sim^{TD} preparation phase. Since the mobility verification

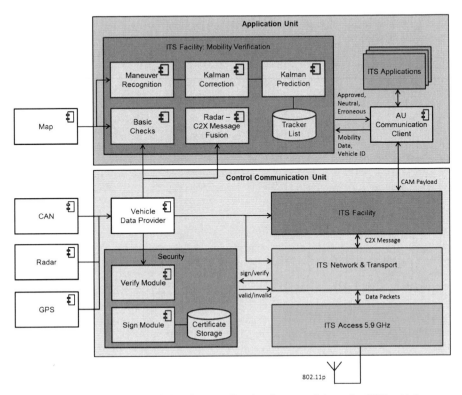

Figure 4.16: Integration of mobility data verification framework into the C2X vehicle architecture

is instantiated on the time critical path between network and application layer (see Figure 1.1), any introduced latency has to be kept as low as possible due to safety reasons. For the presented implementation and target platform, an average latency of about 2.7 ms is measured. Thereby, about 1ms can be attributed to performed threshold checks, as well as administrative tasks, like, e.g., function calls and search operations. The remaining 1.7 ms originate from the execution of the Kalman prediction and correction phase. This low latency is basically due to the light-weighted operations associated to that approach, and is considered as a clear advantage over conventional measures based on cryptography.

Regarding a validation of the effectiveness of the overall verification framework, two figures of merit are of general interest:

- *False Positive Rate-Path Prediction (FPR-P)*: The relative number of messages which are evaluated as *Erroneous*, though they are correct. That means, how many trustworthy messages are discarded by the framework?

- *False Negative Rate-Path Prediction (FNR-P)*: The relative number of messages which are evaluated as *Approved*, though they are *Erroneous*. That means, how many faked messages pass the framework without being noticed?

In practice, the FNR-P can hardly be derived from experiments, since it heavily depends upon the underlying attacker model. For instance, a basic attacker which is sending waypoints including discontinuities will be filtered out by this approach. In contrast, a very sophisticated attacker, which applies a mobility model, perfectly matching the C2X scenario is not detectable at all. Obviously, the point from where on, *False Negatives* will occur can be derived deterministically from the predefined *AT* value implemented by the mobility verification framework. Hence, in the scope of this work the focus is set on an evaluation of the FPR-P, i.e., the number of erroneously discarded messages. Especially in highly dynamic traffic maneuvers correct message shall not be discarded by the verification framework due to safety.

The first experiments are related to a general evaluation of the path prediction verification stage in common traffic scenarios, i.e., scenarios without very dynamic changes in the vehicles trajectory. Sim^{TD} equipped vehicles have been used to evaluate the prediction accuracy of the KF, which is considered as the determining factor for a correct assessment of received messages. Several test drives have been carried out with different road types and velocities, varying from 30-50 km/h in city scenarios up to 100-140 km/h on highway scenarios.

With respect to the different road types and scenarios, a deviating performance can be observed (see Figure 4.17). While for highway scenarios the prediction component proves an acceptable accuracy, city scenarios are more prone to errors. Besides the environmental differences in urban and highway scenario, also the message sending frequency has an impact on the prediction accuracy, as depicted in Figure 4.18. Obviously, the Kalman vehicle tracker performs best, with shorter message intervals. Note that the verification framework shows good performance, when being applied at the variable CAM frequency as specified by ETSI [36].

It can be concluded, that the path prediction component shows acceptable performance in more than 95% of all cases. However, the remaining cases, for which the deviation considerablty exceeds the 1.5 meter margin must not be neglected, since in these cases, valid and potentially safety-relevant C2X messages may be discarded by the framework. Analyzing the recorded traces in detail yielded, that the higher deviations in urban environments basically originate from the decreased GPS quality available in street canyons. However, in highway scenarios, the deviations are mainly due to dynamic driving. Consequently there exists further room for improving the FPR-P by means of the advocated maneuver recognition component.

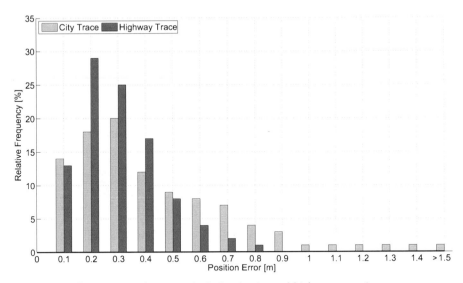

Figure 4.17: Comparison of average deviation in city and highway scenarios

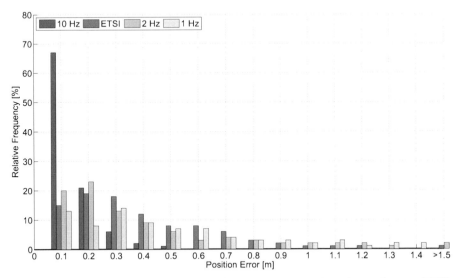

Figure 4.18: Exemplary city-highway route for path prediction algorithm evaluation (ETSI CAM frequency)

4.4.3 Dynamic Traffic Scenarios

One way of reducing the FNR-P in highly dynamic scenarios represents the maneuver recognition component based on HMMs as described in Section 4.3.3. In order to evaluate the effectiveness of this approach, overtaking and hard braking maneuvers have been reconstructed using 3 sim^{TD} equipped vehicles, considering a message sending interval as specified by ETSI [36]. Thereby, two vehicles are used to create the respective traffic situation on one lane, while the third vehicle is intended to model available free space on the second lane (see Figure 4.11 and Figure 4.12). In total, a sequence of approximately 30 overtaking and 20 braking maneuvers have been taken on rural roads.

The first assessment is dedicated to a general performance evaluation of both components (i.e., path prediction and maneuver recognition), when being applied in such highly dynamic scenarios. Since the C2X message channel is considered to be lossy, the sensitivity of any C2X application towards message loss is of particular importance. In order to determine the accuracy with respect to message loss, the given traces are averaged. Additionally, for each trace and percentage of the message loss rate, about 1000 different variants were created. This high diversity of different traces becomes necessary in order to yield the true averaged behavior, since the accuracy of the path prediction component depends exactly upon which messages are getting lost.

In Figure 4.19a the results for the average deviation between predicted and received mobility data is given depending on the message loss. The results when applying the component in dynamic maneuvers generally confirm the tendency already regarded in common driving situations (see Section 4.4.2), i.e., the accuracy of the path prediction declines with a reduced temporal and spatial resolution of the received messages. In the context of this work, of particular interest are those messages, for which the resulting deviation exceeds the predefined AT value. For these traces, such peaks will result into false positive hits and as a consequence, will introduce safety flaws into the system. The relative occurrence of peaks, as depicted in Figure 4.19b, is increasing linearly with the number of lost messages.

For reasons of comparability the proposed maneuver recognition has been evaluated under the same system assumptions, using exactly the same traces. The figures of merit of the maneuver recognition are defined as follows:

- *False Positive Rate - Maneuver Recognition (FPR-M)*: The relative number of messages, which are associated to a dynamic maneuver, though the vehicle is actually in a steady mobility state.

- *False Negative Rate - Maneuver Recognition (FNR-M)*: The relative number of peaks, that occur during a dynamic maneuver, though no braking or lane change maneuver is detected.

The evaluation results for the first error type are represented in terms of a *ROC (Receiver Operating Characteristic)* curve depicted in Figure 4.20a. Thereby, the ratio r_1 as denoted in Equation (4.22) represents the determining parameter for weighting the false-positive rate against the true-positive rate with regard to the respective application requirements.

Compared to the path prediction stage, the maneuver recognition is less sensitive towards possible message losses and proves a high accuracy above 90% even when losing up to 30% of all messages (see Figure 4.20b). This corresponds to a low *False Negative Rate (FNR-M)*

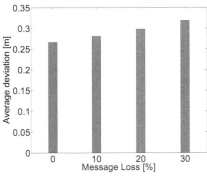
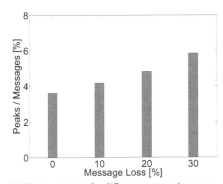

(a) Average Kalman deviation for different mes-   (b) Peaks per trace for different message loss rates
sage loss rates

Figure 4.19: Performance evaluation of the Kalman filter by comparison of predicted with
received mobility data.

and makes the maneuver recognition component particularly useful for compensating the
shortcomings of the path prediction stage.

In the following sections the working principle of the mobility verification framework is
illustrated by means of exemplary sequences for overtaking and braking maneuvers.

Lane Change Maneuver Evaluation

The graph at the top of Figure 4.21 shows the isolated behavior of the KF, when being
applied at a sharp lane change maneuver. The x-axis (primary axis) denotes the CAM
messages of the observed vehicle, as they are sequentially received by the host vehicle. On
the y-axis (secondary axis) the deviation between predicted and received mobility data is
plotted. The obtained results confirm the previously made hypothesis, that the deviation
Δy_k reaches its maximum during the last stage of the lane change maneuver (messages 37
− 52). For the given example, peaks with amplitudes up to 3 meters have been measured. In
order to cover even higher peaks that could principally occur, the AT value initially had
to be defined with large tolerance between $3 - 5$ meters.

Based on the same data set the maneuver recognition component is evaluating the traffic
situation in parallel. As it can be concluded from the middle part of Figure 4.21, the course
of the evaluated probabilities reflects very well the actual state of the vehicle during the lane
change maneuver. In fact, already when the first peak above 1 meter occurs (at message 37),
the likelihood for a following maneuver drops significantly. At the same time the likelihood
for overtaking maintains at a constant level, which gives a clear indication of a pending lane
change.

At the bottom of Figure 4.21 the characteristics of the overall verification framework, as
described in Section 4.3.3, are visualized. For reasons of comparability, the evaluation
has been carried out offline using the recorded real world traces. Taking into account the
dynamic traffic situation of the observed vehicle, the occurred peaks become plausible to
the observer vehicle. Therefore, the Kalman gain is adapted (at message 37) such that

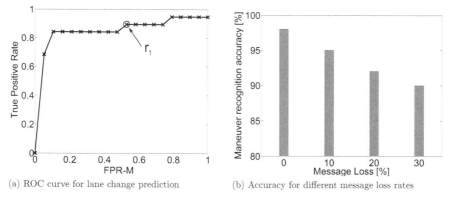

(a) ROC curve for lane change prediction   (b) Accuracy for different message loss rates

Figure 4.20: Performance evaluation of the maneuver recognition component

all subsequent peaks are decreased. In consequence, due to the enhanced reliability of the verification framework, the applied AT value can be refined to 1 meter. Note again, that in general a reduction of this threshold comes along with an enhancement of the security level of the overall C2X system.

Braking Maneuver Evaluation

The results for the hard braking maneuver are depicted in Figure 4.22. The setup for this experiment is similar to the one before, apart from the fact that this time, the overtaking maneuver cannot be conducted successfully, due to a third vehicle occupying free space on the left lane. In order to avoid crashing into the vehicle driving ahead, the observed vehicle is performing a sudden full brake, leading to a peak in the graph of the deviation Δy_k (message 70, top of Figure 4.22). The framework instantly queries the maneuver recognition component, which returns back the likelihoods for each traffic maneuver at the given instant of time. As illustrated in the middle of Figure 4.22, the driver's intention for overtaking (overtaking, no free space consideration) clearly diverges from the feasibility of actually conducting that maneuver (overtaking, free space consideration) due to insufficient free space. The dynamics of the traffic situation is correctly assessed by the proposed maneuver recognition and, thus, the path prediction model can be calibrated accurately. Adapting the Kalman gain, as outlined in Section 4.3.3, leads to a deviation $\Delta y_{k,new}$, which does not exceed the predefined AT value. In consequence, no messages are wrongly marked as erroneous anymore.

4.5 Conclusion

The correctness and trustworthiness of exchanged mobility data represents a cornerstone of future C2X communication systems. Up to now, standardization activities have mainly focused on cryptographic solutions for providing data security and integrity, disregarding that these measures are quite ineffective towards insider attacks. That means, any attacker who gains access to the secret key material will be able to bypass the security without being noticed.

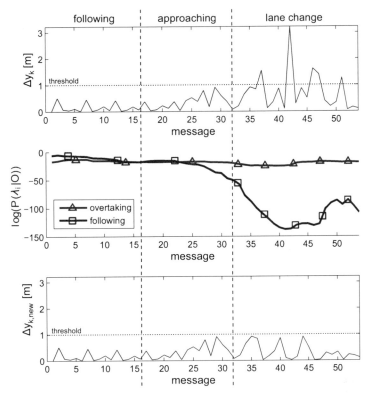

Figure 4.21: Lane change maneuver - Top: conventional Kalman deviation Δy_k - Middle: log-likelihood of maneuver recognition - Bottom: Maneuver-aware Kalman deviation $\Delta y_{k,new}$ with adapted Kalman gain

As a remedy to this problem, novel concepts for mobility data verification have been proposed in this part of the thesis. The presented approach foresees a behavior analysis in order to filter suspicious messages. The presented mobility data verification thereby puts previously research works into practice and besides that, introduces novel strategies for sophisticated verification of a vehicle's overall trajectory. The developed framework is characterized by its near series alignment in terms of provided level of detail and thorough architectural integration. It consists of three major increments, which aim at increasing the security level by lowering the component's false positive rate.

The advocated mobility concept is generally driven by the idea to collect as much information as possible in order to build up a model of the outside traffic world and to measure any incoming message against that model for plausibility. If the model reflects the traffic scenario accurately enough, even small deviations caused by an attacker will be made detectable. However, towards such a concise model, further information sources may be included in the future. For instance, in order to assess the traffic situation correctly in case

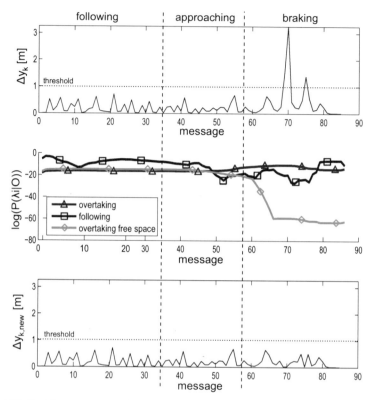

Figure 4.22: Braking maneuver - Top: conventional Kalman deviation Δy_k - Middle: log-likelihood of maneuver recognition - Bottom: Maneuver-aware Kalman deviation $\Delta y_{k,new}$ with adapted Kalman gain

of severe accidents, event based messages such as DENMs may be considered. Furthermore, a vehicle's on board sensors like camera or radar allow detection and consideration of other traffic participants, which are not equipped with the C2X technology. Map data may be used to include the respective road type and geometry, which principally has an influence on the likelihood for performing certain maneuvers.

Besides a comprehensive data capturing via a multitude of different sensors, an efficient data management and access is of equally high importance. One possible way for consolidating the different data sources represent the *Local Dynamic Map (LDM)* as anticipated first by the SAFESPOT project [91]. The LDM organizes all traffic related information into a hierarchy of different levels, connected via a digital map. Originally intended as a compact data representation for ITS applications, in the future, the LDM database may be further adapted for the purpose of enhanced plausibility checking.

Network Layer Security: Group Privacy Protocols

In this part of the thesis, a novel approach for obfuscating pseudonym changes based on dynamic cryptographic Mix Zones is presented. While geographical cells are used to establish a secret group key among all members, the group is maintained even when travelling along the road. Using the group key, a vehicle is able to send authenticated messages, though its anonymity is preserved. An essential property of the proposed protocol relates to its decentralized group key establishment. In this thesis two different approaches for establishing a decentralized group key in C2X networks are introduced.

First, an efficient group establishment protocol called *C2CGE.1* (Car2Car Group Establishment) is presented. By means of this protocol the group key is assembled based on multiple key fragments obtained from all group members. The basic concepts behind this protocol have been introduced by the author of this thesis in *Stübing et al.* [17] and will be recalled within this chapter. In addition, further implementation details are given and the protocol is analyzed for its benefits, when comparing to other state-of-the art approaches.

As an alternative to C2CGE.1, a second group establishment protocol, called *C2CGE.2* is proposed, which is based on an n-party Diffie Hellman scheme according to *Steer et al.* [100]. For the first time, in *Stübing et al.* [18], this approach has been applied to the requirements of vehicular networks. In the following, the basic adaptations are recalled and furthermore are complemented by respective sub-protocols for group maintenance.

A comprehensive evaluation has been carried out, which is divided into two major parts: First, the concepts for group establishment are verified for formal correctness by means of model checking methods. Then, the temporal behavior of the protocol is analyzed, using a dedicated C2X network and traffic simulator. Besides the protocol specifications in this thesis a detailed model of a global passive adversary is provided, which can be used by researchers working in the field as reference implementation. The achieved privacy enhancements are analyzed with respect to that defined adversary model.

The overall chapter is structured as follows: Section 5.1 sets the stage for the following protocol development by showing that traceability is an essential parameter for preserving the drivers's privacy. In Section 5.2 several known approaches for establishing Mix Zones for C2X communication are summarized and discussed. Based on this analysis, fundamental requirements for C2X group protocols are derived in Section 5.3. In Section 5.4 the underlying system model and protocol parameters are introduced. Then, in Section 5.5, the specification for the proposed group establishment protocol C2CGE.1 protocol is given. In Section 5.6 it is described, how an n-party Diffie Hellman scheme can be applied to the C2X scenario by means of the proposed C2CGE.1 protocol. Required sub-protocols for managing the groups are further specified in Section 5.7. Section 5.8 is dedicated to the protocol comparison, verification and evaluation. The simulation setup is described, a detailed attacker model is given and the advocated privacy protocol is evaluated for its effectiveness. Finally, in Section 5.9 this part of the thesis is concluded and some remarks on future work are given.

5.1 Motivation

The motivation for strong privacy protocols is following a step-by-step approach: First, a privacy metric, which is appropriate for comprehensive evaluation of the driver's privacy in Car-to-X is presented. According to that metric, traceability is identified as the determining factor for enhancing privacy. In consequence, the focus is set on traceability, and respective metrics are discussed. By applying traceability metrics to pseudonymization strategies like deployed within currently running FOTs, it can be concluded that those approaches provide only a basic level of privacy protection. Consequently further investigations on enhanced technologies have to be carried out, which motivates the development of the group privacy protocol presented in this part of the thesis.

5.1.1 Privacy Measure based on Driver Entropy

In the context of the PRECIOSA project [101], *Ma et al.* [102] have developed a trip-based location privacy metric for ITS applications. The advocated metric does not only reflect the capabilities of an adversary for tracking vehicles, but also takes into account how strong a certain driver can be associated to the respective origin or destination of the trip. The uncertainty in the information is quantified into entropy. In the following, the concepts of the privacy metric according to *Ma et al.* is summarized, and by means of an example calculation, the impact of sophisticated privacy protocols is analyzed.

For the adversary model behind the privacy metric, it is assumed that she/he can observe a vehicle driving from an *origin o* to a *destination d* with a certain probability $p(o, d)$. Depending on the accuracy of the tracking algorithm, several origins and destinations may come into consideration, in principle. Tracking a vehicle does not necessarily imply a privacy threat as long as the adversary cannot link the trip to the respective driver. Assuming several possible origins and destinations for a multitude of different vehicles, the adversary's knowledge is described by

- the probability $p(i_s, o_j)$ for linking the driver i_s to one of the possible origins o_j of the trip, and

- the probability $p(d_k, i_s)$ for linking one of the possible destinations d_k to the driver i_s.

The authors in [102] model the three linkage probabilities $p(i_s, o_j)$, $p(d_k, i_s)$, $p(o_j, d_k)$ as a weighted directed graph. The graph represents the information, an adversary has on the system, including the vehicle movements and their relations to the drivers in a given area and period in time. Thereby, the driver, the origin, and the destination of a trip are represented by nodes, whereas the associated probabilities are denoted on the edges between the nodes.

Another effective way of modeling linkability by means of a directed graph is presented by *Fischer et al.* [103]. Applying that model to the C2X domain, the nodes inside the graph might represent the vehicle owner, the respective vehicles, the certificates and the sent C2X messages. Similar to *Ma et al.* [102], weighted edges indicate the belief of an attacker, how strong two nodes of interest are related to each other. In fact, both models of [103] and [102] possess related characteristics and can be partly transferred into each other. Note that in subsequent sections, the notation according to *Ma et al.* [102] is applied as reference.

In order to combine all linkage probabilities into a single value, the authors in [102] advocate to determine the entropy of the given information. Information entropy according to *C. Shannon* is a means for quantitatively measuring the information content and uncertainty over a given probability distribution [104]. Originally used in communications to estimate the information content produced by a discrete information source, in [102] entropy is applied to quantify the driver's privacy level. Note that therfore, in the following, the terms *entropy* and *privacy level* are used synonymously. Accordingly, the driver's entropy (privacy level) is calculated by the following formulas according to [102]:

$$H(i_s) = -\left(\sum_{a=1}^{m}\sum_{b=1}^{m} \hat{p}_{ab} \log \hat{p}_{ab} + \hat{p}^c \log \hat{p}^c\right) \qquad (5.1)$$

$$\hat{p}_{ab} = \frac{p(i_s, o_j) \cdot p(o_j, d_k) \cdot p(d_k, i_s)}{\sum_{j=1}^{m}\sum_{k=1}^{m} p(i_s, o_j) \cdot p(o_j, d_k) \cdot p(d_k, i_s) + \hat{p}^c} \qquad (5.2)$$

$$\hat{p}^c = 1 - \sum_{j=1}^{m} p(i_s, o_j) \qquad (5.3)$$

The normalized probability $\hat{p}_{ab}$ denotes the likelihood of a certain individual for making a trip from origin o_j to the destination d_k, whereas $\hat{p}^c$ is the complementary probability for not making any trips at all. The number m represents the total number of possible trips. Privacy enhancing technologies generally attempt to reach a uniform distribution in order to maximize the entropy.

From the analysis of the metric above, it can be conclude, that there are two possible ways for increasing drivers privacy: First, any ITS application, service-oriented or safety-related, has to ensure that neither at the origin nor at the destination of a trip, personalized data is transmitted to un-authorized entities. And second, ITS stations have to impede that adversaries can link single traces to an overall trip. The first requirement has to be met by every application separately. Within the PRECIOSA project, several guidelines for developing privacy-preserving applications for ITS have been developed [105]. Since location privacy for individuals is not scope of this work, in the following, it is assumed that respective privacy preserving techniques are foreseen by every application individually and their effectiveness can be measured in terms of linkage probabilities. Hence, in this work the focus is set on strategies for reducing the probability for successfully assembling single traces to an entire trip.

In the following, the privacy level is calculated exemplary for two scenarios, as illustrated in Figure 5.1. Given are two individuals (i.e., drivers in this case), which are starting from different origin locations o_1 and o_2 and are driving to the destinations d_1 or d_2. While the probability for linking identities to one of these locations is kept the same for both scenar-

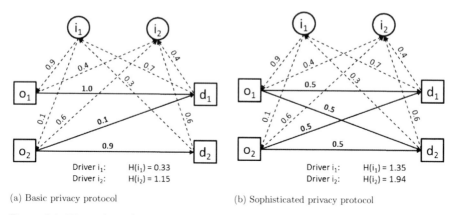

(a) Basic privacy protocol   (b) Sophisticated privacy protocol

Figure 5.1: Directed graph examples for entropy calculation

ios, the trip probabilities are assumed to be different. For both scenarios the entropy is determined and compared.

For the first example scenario, illustrated in Figure 5.1a, it is assumed that the adversary is able to completely track a vehicle, starting from the origin o_1 and driving to the destination d_1. This might be the case, if the adversary monitors the entire trip and the vehicle's C2X system is not providing any privacy protection at all, e.g., no change of pseudonyms while driving. The driver starting from origin o_2 is driving a vehicle that sporadically changes pseudonyms, which slightly obfuscates the true destination locations d_1 and d_2. However, due to the poor anonymity provided by both C2X systems, an adversary may easily match the origin to the respective destination of the trip. The dotted lines indicate complementary information, the adversary has on the driver itself. For instance, driver i_1 has used a service application at the origin, where she/he identified her/himself to the ITS system, e.g., via a credit card. If the adversary has access to such information, she/he can assign the driver to that origin with a high certainty as indicated. Furthermore, knowing that i_1 visits destinations d_2 less frequently than d_1, gives the adversary further details to increase the linkability.

For the second scenario, depicted in Figure 5.1b, the same location linkabilities for the individuals are assumed. However, this time, the individuals are using vehicles which change pseudonyms according to sophisticated privacy protocols, i.e., privacy protocols which obfuscate performed pseudonym changes in a way, that an adversary cannot follow any of the trips. This leads to a uniform probability distribution and in consequence, to a significantly higher entropy value for each driver.

From the previous analysis it can be concluded, that, to some extent, techniques for impeding traceability can outweigh a poor location privacy of an individual. Hence, in the remainder of this thesis, a more in depth investigation on metrics for measuring traceability is performed.

5.1.2 Privacy Measure based on Traceability

The success for tracking a vehicle, driving from an origin o to a destination d, is dependent upon several system parameters:

- **Message Interval**: The more frequently a vehicle distributes messages within a certain area, the more information an adversary will obtain to reassemble the track. The message frequency for sending CAMs is safety relevant and is specified by standardization [36]. It can be argued that any privacy enhancing technique must not change system parameters, related to road safety or traffic efficiency. Therefore, in this thesis the message density is considered as a fixed parameter, which must not be reduced by means of respective privacy solutions.

- **Communication Access**: This parameter is comparable to the previous one, as it defines the information basis an adversary may rely on, to perform the tracking. Since reducing the message frequency is not an option, in the context of this work, the focus is set on a reduction of the adversary's access to the exchanged messages, instead. In Chapter 6 approaches for effectively limiting the communication access by means of Secure C2X Beamforming are proposed. However, this chapter is dedicated to enhancements of the pseudonymization technique and therefore, a global passive adversary is assumed. Such an adversary has unlimited access to all broadcasted messages within the network.

- **Tracking Algorithm**: In *Gruteser et al.* [106] multi-target tracking algorithms have been applied, to successfully track pedestrians for an extended period of time. In *Wiedersheim et al.* [107] attacks have been carried out, where the attacker obtains mobility data in terms of position, speed, and heading in order to resolve pseudonym changes of the vehicle. In the following, an attacker is assumed, which is equipped with state-of-the art tracking algorithms, similar to those deployed by *Wiedersheim et al.* [107] or *Stübing et al.* [7], respectively. A detailed attacker model will be defined in subsequent sections.

- **Privacy Protocol**: The privacy protocol defines the respective countermeasure, a vehicle applies for not getting tracked by the adversaries tracking algorithm. Privacy protocols may vary from a simple pseudonym change, up to enhanced obfuscation techniques based on Mix Zones.

In conclusion, the *Message Density*, *Communication Access* as well as the adversary's *Tracking Algorithm* are supposed to be already given system parameters, which cannot be influenced. Under these assumptions, the presented privacy protocol in this part of the thesis, is aimed towards a reduction of the traceability by adversaries. Consequently, any enhancements gained by pseudonymization are measured by means of a reduced traceability. In the following, a brief survey over possible traceability metrics is given:

Gruteser et al. [106] have applied multi-hypothesis tracking system, to track pedestrians, based on frequently sampled geographical locations. Upon every received sample, a Kalman filter based tracking algorithm is used to calculate the assignment probabilities for each of the possible targets. A Kalman filter represents an adequate means for predicting movements, as already identified in Chapter 4.4. However, in the context of C2X communication, the model has to be adapted and further extended to the vehicular domain.

Sampigethaya et al. [108], [109] use the maximum tracking time of a vehicle to measure the achieved anonymity level depending on the vehicle density. Anonymity measurements have been carried out under the assumption of a global adversary. Tracking is performed by predicting the next location of a vehicle based on the previously received measurements. Whereas generally the *tracking time* is considered as an appropriate metric, a more accurate prediction model is desirable. The tracking method by *Sampigethaya et al.* neither takes into account the measurement errors, due to GPS inaccuracies nor system errors due to inaccuracies of the prediction model itself. In Section 5.8 an attacker model is presented and a metric, which takes *Gruteser et al.* [106] and *Sampigethaya et al.* [108], [109] as a foundation.

5.1.3 Privacy Level of Simple Pseudonym Changes

Applying traceability as a metric for the effectiveness of pseudonomyization, currently deployed strategies according to sim^{TD} [29], [9], [11] and the C2C-CC [5], [6] (see Section 3.4) provide only a rather modest privacy protection against attacks of a global adversary. Using temporal and spatial relations between two succeeding locations of a node, the old and new pseudonym can still be linked to the respective vehicle. Inspired by the measurements taken by *Gruteser et al.* [106], *Wiedersheim et al.* [107] have elaborated a dedicated Kalman-based tracking algorithm, to resolve pseudonym changes in vehicular networks. Assuming a powerful adversary, which has access to all sent messages of the target vehicle, it can be shown that a maximum sampling rate of 1Hz is already sufficient to resolve most of the pseudonym changes. *Wiedersheim et al.* [107] analyzed, that in most cases tracking errors occurred only at traffic scenarios where vehicle traces are crossing each other, e.g., at intersections.

The authors in [107] observed a reduced traceability for increasing vehicle densities. Same effects apply for reducing the intervals of pseudonym changes, i.e., the more often a vehicle changes its pseudonym, the more likely an adversary's tracking algorithm produces matching errors. In order to investigate the impact of noisy position information on tracking results, a GPS error in the range of 0-5 meters is added to the sampled positions. Simulation yielded that already a position error of 1-2 meters significantly reduces the mean tracking duration by more than 50%. However, the authors in [107] admit, that modeling the error as noise up to 5 meter into a randomly chosen direction does not a reflect a realistic GPS behavior. Instead, GPS error is much more constant in time and does only vary in case of changed surroundings due to shadowing effects. In [107] it is assumed that for real-world traces position errors will play a minor role for prediction accuracy.

In the scope of the work done by *Stübing et al.* [7], studies on how to effectively resolve pseudonym changes in vehicular networks have been carried out, too. Whereas the authors in [107] base their measurements upon simulations, the tracking algorithm applied in [7], has been calibrated and evaluated by means of real-world traces obtained from the sim^{TD} field trial. It has been observed that even in the presence of noisy position information the developed tracker was able to resolve most of the pseudonym changes, which confirms the assumptions made by *Wiedersheim et al.* [107].

From the previous discussions it can be concluded, that simple pseudonym changes are not sufficient for a comprehensive privacy protection against correlation attacks. And consequently, there exists a strong demand for further investigations into techniques, which restrict a tracking of vehicles. In the following section, the most recent approaches in this area are summarized and discussed.

5.2 Related Work

In this section several works, which intend to increase unlinkability by means of pseudonymization are presented. The concept of Mix Zones is introduced and available approaches are categorized into two classes: *Situational Mix Zones* and *Cryptographic Mix Zones*. For each approach the key components are stated and discussed.

5.2.1 Mix Zones

Early works on Mix Zones have focused on technologies for locating and tracking individuals in the area of pervasive computing. Based on prior works done by *Chaum et al.* [110], *Beresford et al.* [111] have introduced the term *Mix Zone*, for defining a connected spatial area, where a user is not reachable by a central service provider. Thus, their identities are *mixed*. If users change to a new pseudonym within such a Mix Zone, external observers cannot link ingressing users to those leaving the Mix Zone. The degree of location privacy is determined by the *anonymity set*, which is defined by *Beresford et al.* as the group of users visiting the Mix Zone during the same time period. Users might refuse communicating location updates until the Mix Zone reaches a minimum level of anonymity, i.e., a sufficient amount of users are present inside the region. *Beresford et al.* also point out, that the anonymity set is only a poor indicator for privacy, if the maximum size of the mix zone exceeds the distance a user covers in one period. In such a case an adversary may use temporal and spatial correlation to resolve the pseudonym change.

The concept of Mix Zones has been first applied to vehicular networks by *Buttyan et al.* [112]. Accordingly, a Mix Zone is defined as a geographical zone where vehicles are not observable by possible adversaries and thus can change their pseudonym without being tracked. If the provided level of privacy is high enough, vehicles which are traversing such a Mix Zone cannot be distinguished from each other. In Figure 5.2 the fundamental principle of a Mix Zone located on an intersection is illustrated.

While *Buttyan et al.* have restricted their definition of a Mix Zone to spatial regions, *M. Gerlach* [113] uses the term Mix Zone in a wider sense and introduces the term *Mix Context*, which takes into account any relevant information for performing a pseudonym change. In the context of this thesis, the term Mix Zone is used to describe a situation that obfuscates a pseudonym change in a way, that linking of the old and new pseudonym to the respective vehicle is impeded. In literature several proposals for creating Mix Zones in vehicular networks can be found. In the following, these approaches are categorized into two classes: *Situational Mix Zones* and *Cryptographic Mix Zones*. To the best of the author's knowledge this can be considered as the first attempt in general, for a categorization of the different Mix Zone concepts in vehicular networks. In Figure 5.3 the proposed taxonomy is illustrated and state-of-the-art protocols are categorized, respectively.

5.2.2 Situational Mix Zones

Even at a maximum beacon frequency of 10 Hz, a transmitted C2X message represents only a snapshot of the vehicle's trajectory. Although approximating the trajectory based on discrete mobility samples is of no major issue for most scenarios (see Section 5.1.3), there still remains an uncertainty in situations where multiple vehicles possess similar trajectories. In the following, approaches are presented, that intend to increase this uncertainty

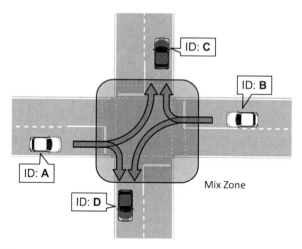

Figure 5.2: Working principle of a Mix Zone

either by using *Silent Periods* or *context-aware* Mix Zones. Since those approaches change pseudonyms only, if the traffic situation diminishes an adversary's tracking results, they are denoted as *Situational Mix Zones*.

Silent Periods

In order to reduce the success of correlation attacks, *Huang et al.* [114] introduce the concept of Silent Periods. A Silent Period is defined as the period that passes by from the point in time the old pseudonym is used last, until a node is allowed to start communicating again with the new pseudonym. It is divided into a constant period and a variable random period, in order to disrupt the spatial and temporal order between two successively observed messages. The authors introduce a *Maximum Tracking Round (MTR)* to measure, how many pseudonym changes a node has to perform until an adversary's average tracking success is considerably reduced. By means of simulations it could be shown, that a pseudonym change is most effective if several nodes are performing their pseudonym change simultaneously at the same location. Simulation results with varying silent periods indicate that longer silent periods also lead to a reduced MTR value.

The authors in [114] are assuming a point-to-point cellular communication scenario where nodes access services from central service provider using short-range radio such as Bluetooth or Wireless LAN. As exchanged network beacons generally do not contain position information, an adversary has to rely on signal metrics as *Angle of Arrival (AOA), Received Signal Strength (RSS)* or *Time of Arrival (TOA)* for estimating the locations of mobile nodes.

CARAVAN/AMOEBA In contrary, in C2X networks an adversary does not have to perform estimations on a node's position, because it is already included inside every transmitted message. Furthermore, the higher mobility of vehicular nodes plays a significant role for the tracking success. Therefore, the concept of Silent Periods has to be adapted to fit the requirements of C2X scenarios, which has been done first within the *CARAVAN/AMOEBA*

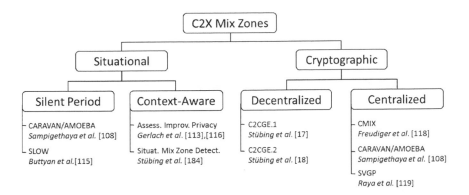

Figure 5.3: C2X Mix Zone taxonomy

concept by *Sampigethaya et al.* [108], [109]. When entering a network, a vehicle changes its pseudonym and remains silent for a randomly chosen time period. If neighboring vehicles update their pseudonym at the same time, the probability for tracking is possibly reduced. However, the maximum silent period is strongly limited by the maximum message interval, needed to maintain a certain safety level [36].

SLOW *Buttyan et al.* [115] pick up the idea of establishing dynamical Mix Zones by means of Silent Periods and introduce a Situational Mix Zone called *SLOW (Silence at Low speeds)*. The main objective of this approach is to reduce traceability without the need for vehicle synchronization or additional infrastructure support. As the name suggests, the SLOW concept enforces a Silent Period for slowly driving vehicles. Given a threshold of approximately 30 km/h, vehicles stop broadcasting messages if their velocity drops below that value. During each Silent Period a vehicle changes its pseudonym.

Buttyan et al. have simulated SLOW for urban intersections, with varying threshold velocities and vehicle densities. For single intersections, SLOW does not have the desired effect of reduced traceability, i.e., the attacker achieves a reasonable tracing success almost independently of the chosen threshold velocity and vehicle density. Only, if the target vehicle remains silent, while crossing multiple intersections in a row, obfuscation becomes sufficiently high enough to reduce attackers tracking capabilities.

Context Aware Pseudonym Change

Instead of applying Silent Periods *Gerlach et al.* [113],[116] propose every vehicle to continuously assess the traffic context in order to identify the best opportunity to change a pseudonym. In order to keep assessment complexity low, a simple approach based on the vehicle density is applied. If a vehicle detects a minimum number of vehicles in their vicinity, a pseudonym change is initiated. For regions with a low vehicle density a randomized pseudonymization interval is proposed. Simulations indicate, that although with this approach fewer vehicles could be tracked, the majority of vehicles remain traceable. It can be analyzed that this approach exactly represents the definition for an anonymity set according to *Beresford et al.* [111], but transferred to vehicular networks.

Assessment

Obviously, the concept of Silent Periods is most effective when coinciding with unpredictable changes in the vehicle's trajectory. Furthermore at least one additional vehicle is required in the proximity of the host vehicle, which possesses a similar trajectory and changes its pseudonym at the same poin in time, in order to create a possible obfuscation to adversaries. In *Sampigethaya et al.* [108], [109], apart from proposing Silent Periods for vehicular networks no investigations have been carried out to further specify and evaluate this concept. It can be argued that without inter-vehicular synchronization of pseudonym changes, Situational Mix Zones are not very likely to occur often enough, to provide a sufficient privacy level. In particular, if vehicles change pseudonyms with low frequency like deployed in sim^{TD} [29], [9], the likelihood of two vehicles changing pseudonyms in appropriate situations is further reduced.

An upper bound for the maximum silent period is given by the safety message interval, which may be reduced to 100 ms [36] in case of changing trajectories. While a reduced message interval is advantageous for road safety, it is rather disadvantageous for pseudonym changes. Although the general approach of introducing Silent Periods is very promising, additional investigations have to be carried out to synchronize the pseudonym change among several vehicles, in order to increase the effectiveness of this method. In the Annex A of this thesis an adequate approach is presented, respectively.

In comparison, the SLOW protocol advocated by *Buttyan et al.*[115], realizes a synchronization implicitly by enforcing Silent Periods for all vehicles, driving below a certain threshold speed. However, SLOW should be also evaluated under the effects of heterogenic traffic scenarios, with several lanes and different vehicle speeds. Some highway scenarios are imaginable, where a *vehicle A* is driving slowly on a lane, which is congested, and suddenly is changing to adjacent lanes, where another *vehicle B* is approaching with high velocity. Because *vehicle A* stays inside the Silent Period, it may not benefit from the C2X functionality. Furthermore, the authors in [115] are focusing on road safety only and are neglecting the relevance of beacon messages for enhancing traffic efficiency. Promising use cases, such as GLOSA (see Section 2.2.2) rely upon a precise traffic assessment to trigger their actions. Without frequently received beacon messages, a roadside station cannot determine the tailback at every traffic light and as consequence, prioritized flow control becomes impossible. While being effective for privacy in inner-city scenarios, it would be also interesting to see how the protocol performs on highway scenarios, where for an adversary, the trajectory is better predictable than at intersections.

The situation-awareness protocol proposed by *Gerlach et al.* [113],[116] represents a very attractive attempt to enhance privacy because of its low complexity. However, as simulations have shown, the vehicle density is an insufficient measure for detecting Mix Zones. Since the reliability for detecting such zones is crucial for the effectiveness of pseudonym changes, further work on finding additional context parameters has to be done.

A major advantage of Situational Mix Zones lies within their reduced communication overhead and low computational complexity. Despite those benefits, these kinds of Mix Zones have the undesirable effect of scaling best with a reduced data quality inside the sent messages. However, due to safety reasons, C2X application designers are interested in the highest accuracy achievable. The more precise a vehicle can assess the whereabouts of neighboring vehicles, the more effectively active safety systems inside a vehicle can be cal-

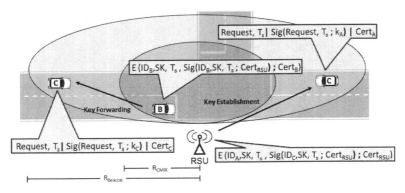

Figure 5.4: CMIX protocol according to *Freudiger et al.* [118]

ibrated. The contradictory requirements between high privacy requirements on the one hand and reliability on the other is not only an issue within vehicular networks, but can be also found in other areas, like, e.g., credit card systems or electronic voting [117]. All those systems do require a trade-off and so does the novel communication area of vehicular networks.

5.2.3 Cryptographic Mix Zones

Cryptographic Mix Zones represent a possible attempt to create anonymizing regions, while preserving the fundamental functionality of safety messages. In the next sections, the following protocols are discussed: *CMIX* [118], which creates Mix Zones around RSUs; *CARAVAN/AMOEBA* [108], [109], which establishes dynamic groups for accessing service applications; and third, *SVGP* [119], which defines aggregation techniques for groups.

CMIX

Freudiger et al. [118] propose to switch to symmetric cryptography every time a vehicle enters the communication range of a trusted RSU. The CMIX protocol is used to distribute a symmetric key from the RSU to every authenticated vehicle. As the CMIX protocol is based upon the same system assumptions, as already presented in Chapter 3, a vehicle can be authenticated by means of the certificate, attached to every periodically sent broadcast message. Once the vehicle has obtained the corresponding symmetric key, it stores it inside a *Tamper-Resistant Module (TRM)* allowing access to its contents only through its secure interface. While being inside the communication range of the RSU, the vehicle utilizes this symmetric key for encrypting all outgoing messages. That way broadcasted mobility data becomes only visible to vehicles, which posses the same key and, thus, are authenticated receivers. Changing pseudonyms while using symmetric cryptography turns the area around the RSU into a cryptographic Mix Zone.

Within the CMIX protocol three sub protocols are defined for *key establishment*, *key forwarding* and *key update*, respectively. For key establishment a vehicle creates a request, together with a timestamp and signs it with the currently used certificate. Upon reception of the request, the RSU verifies the sender's integrity, encrypts the symmetric key SK with the vehicles public key, and sends everything as a unicast message back to the vehicle. In Figure 5.4 the maximum communication range of the RSU is denoted as R_{Beacon} whereas the Mix Zone is described by the distance R_{CMIX}. The key establishment phase is supposed to be completed within the distance R_{Beacon}. When entering R_{CMIX} the vehicle starts sending encrypted messages only and meanwhile changes its pseudonym.

Due to shadowing effects, vehicles might not always receive messages sent by a RSU and therefore cannot switch to the symmetric cryptography. *Freudiger et al.* propose that neighboring vehicles take over the functionality of a RSU and forward the symmetric key via respective key forwarding protocols. For key updating, every RSU is expected to be connected to the CA to get access to new key material.

The CMIX protocol is aimed for creating Mix Zones at intersections. The success ratio for tracking a vehicle, that crosses such a Mix Zones depends on the delay characteristic of the intersection as well as the trajectory of the passing vehicle. Several attacks have been simulated to evaluate the effectiveness of CMIX against correlation attacks. Accordingly, the CMIX protocol scales best with increasing vehicle densities. The combination of several Mix-Zones into Mix Networks furthermore reduces traceability.

Dahl et al. [120] have identified a possible issue: within the CMIX protocol key requests are sent in plaintext together with the currently used pseudonym. If Mix Zones do overlap, vehicles may start sending new requests while still driving inside the old Mix Zone, which reveals the vehicles identity. It can be argued that a simple solution to that problem might be to encrypt requests with the RSUs public key. However, according to the opinion of the author of this thesis, this problem may be considered rather as an implementation and optimization issue, than a conceptual vulnerability of the CMIX protocol.

CARAVAN/AMOEBA

Besides proposing Silent Periods for enhancing privacy protection of CAM messages, the CARAVAN/AMOEBA [108], [109] protocol also foresees cryptographic Mix Zones when accessing *Location Based Services (LBS)* via infrastructure facilities. For that purpose, CARAVAN/AMOEBA includes a concept, by which vehicles form a group in order to mitigate the profiling of target vehicles. *Sampigethaya et al.* [108], [109], have defined four sub protocols, which are named as *group formation, group join, group leave* and *group operation*. In Figure 5.5 – Figure 5.7 the concepts for each sub protocol are illustrated. Note that for reasons of clarity the exchanged messages are denoted in terms of the notation introduced in Section 5.5.

Accordingly, the *group formation* protocol is initiated by a single vehicle, if no further group can be found within communication range. In order to become a group leader, that vehicle sends a signed request to the CA via the RSU as illustrated in Figure 5.5. The CA verifies the appended certificate and generates a group leader ID *GID*. The CA then signs the group leader ID, encrypts the entire response with the public key of *vehicle A* and sends it back to the vehicle.

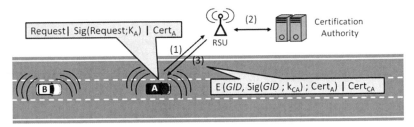

Figure 5.5: AMOEBA Group Formation [108], [109]

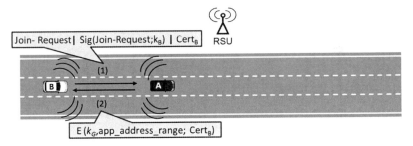

Figure 5.6: AMOEBA Group Join [108], [109]

Once the group leader has been determined, neighboring vehicles may join the group, using the *group join* protocol. As depicted in Figure 5.6, *vehicle B* makes a join request by sending a signed unicast message to the group leader. The group leader in turn checks whether the location of *vehicle B* falls under his responsibility and verifies the certificate accordingly. If the request is valid, then the group leader replies with a message including the group key k_G and the LBS application range of the group, encrypted with the public key of *vehicle B*.

The *group leave* protocol is executed without prior synchronization. Once a vehicle has left the communication range of the group leader, it either switches to another group, or initiates a new group in case no other group can be found.

A major application of the AMOEBA protocol lies within the anonymous access of LBS, like illustrated in Figure 5.7. Within the AMOEBA protocol the group leader serves as proxy for anonymous access. Accordingly, the *group leader A* forwards the service request via RSU from *vehicle B* to the CA (step 1-3), which validates the service request and sends an approval together with a session key back to the RSU (step 4). The communication between *vehicle B* and *group leader A* is always encrypted with the group key, whereas the service request itself is signed using the *vehicle B's* public key and furthermore is encrypted with the public key of the CA. The returned session key is encrypted with *vehicle B's* public key and the public key of the service provider, respectively. By doing so, none of involved stakeholders except the CA knows both parts of the critical information: Either the vehicles location is known, or the requested service, but never both. Every further message exchanged between *vehicle B* and the service provider is encrypted with the session key. A location server handles the geographically forwarding of messages.

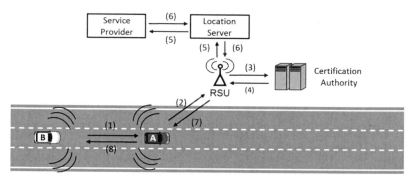

Figure 5.7: AMOEBA anonymous access for Location Based Services (LBS) [108], [109]

SVGP

Raya et al. [119] propose techniques for securely aggregating information in vehicular networks for the purpose of increasing channel efficiency, data correctness and non-repudiation. Although the proposed solutions are not primary aimed towards enhancements of privacy in first place, the concepts could be used for this purpose. The presented *Secure VANET Group Protocol (SVGP)* includes three independent proposals for secure and efficient aggregation: *Combined Signatures, Overlapping Groups,* and *Dynamic Group Key Creation.* The Combined Signature scheme intends to increase the channel usage by combining several signatures into a single message, rather than forwarding every message individually. Combining signatures of intermediate hops increases the reliability of the sent messages and avoids resending duplicated information. For the Overlapping Group scheme, *Raya et al.* propose to fragment roads into small overlapping cells. Every vehicle inside such a cell belongs to the same group whose group leader is determined as the vehicle closest to the cell center. The group leader creates a symmetric group key, encrypts it with the respective public keys of the group members and distributes it inside the cell. Instead of signing messages by means of their own private key, group members are adding an anonymous *HMAC (Hash-based Message Authentication Code)* to every sent message. As cells overlap, the vehicles located on the intersection of two cells receive the group key of both groups. These vehicles serve as relay station to forward message between the groups. The third concept called Dynamic Group Key Creation foresees the creation of groups by vehicles sharing the same velocity and driving direction. Neither the group formation processes nor the mechanisms for determining the group leader are further explained. When passing by a RSU with backend connection to the CA, the group leader instantly requests an asymmetric group key pair. The key pair is encrypted with the symmetric group key and sent to each group member.

Assessment

The proposed CMIX protocol according to *Freudiger et al.* [118] represents an effective solution for privacy protection against eavesdropping of pseudonym changes at intersections. Hence, from an adversaries perspective the CMIX protocol is very similar to the SLOW protocol [115], presented in previous sections. In both cases the adversary does not receive any C2X messages for determining the trajectory of the vehicles located inside the Mix Zone. This is also reflected by the simulation results of both works. Both protocols are creating Mix Zones at intersection scenarios and the provided privacy scales best with increased vehicle densities. Furthermore CMIX as well as SLOW foresee to concatenate several Mix Zones at intersections to an overall Mix Network in order to further increase the unlinkability. However, from a road safety perspective, the CMIX protocol is clearly preferable. Compared to the SLOW protocol, CMIX keeps the Car-to-X functionalities fully operational as vehicles continue to send messages while staying inside the Mix Zone.

Although *Freudiger et al.* [118] have not further detailed effects on the channel load, generally encrypted messages are expected to require less bandwidth than signed messages including the used certificate. Furthermore the computational overhead is reduced when using symmetric cryptography. Despite aforementioned advantages, the CMIX protocol also experiences some difficulties. For CMIX, to operate effectively it has to be ensured that a vehicle encounters an RSU equipped intersection, every time it intends to change its pseudonym. The author of this thesis agrees on the estimation of *K. Plößl* [121] (pp. 195 – 196) and *R. Resendes* [122], that a comprehensive covering of all intersections with trustworthy RSUs is not realistic due to high financial costs. Especially during an early deployment phase, RSUs with backend connectivity are very likely to be installed only on some selected intersections with very high traffic volume. Furthermore the CMIX protocol as well as its counterpart, the SLOW protocol are intended to create Mix Zones only at intersections. Motorways or rural roads are not covered by any of the proposed solutions. Since those road-types with an overall total length above 70.000 km [123] make up the vast majority of roads within Europe, respective privacy techniques are strongly required. The privacy protocol advocated in this thesis addresses this issue.

In contrast to CMIX [118], the Mix Zones created by AMOEBA [108], [109] are moving in time and space and the group keys are not distributed by a RSU, but are issued from a vehicular group leader. Although the main scope of AMOEBA are rather service oriented C2I applications, it would be interesting to see if those concepts may also be used for creating Mix Zones for safety applications. A first review of the AMOEBA protocol has been done by *K. Plößl* [121] (pp. 202 – 205). He basically analyzed that AMOEBA very well ensures the C2I security and privacy objectives in terms of integrity, confidentiality and accountability. However, *K. Plößl* has several concerns that especially during the group formation process a comprehensive covering of infrastructure facilities becomes necessary in order to ensure permanent backend connectivity.

Sampigethaya et al. [108] developed their protocols for C2I application in isolation of requirements of C2X safety applications. The proposed Silent Period for safety messages is not very much related to the group concept. Anonymous C2I communication via a group leader does not lead to the desired effect of increased unlinkability, if meanwhile the vehicle is revealing its identity by sending CAMs and pseudonyms via one of the safety channels. To stop sending CAMs while accessing LBS applications is a not feasible solution for reasons of road safety.

Compared to AMOEBA, the scope of the SVGP protocol according to *Raya et al.* [119] is more aimed towards C2X safety applications. Nevertheless the protocols are not specified far enough to be seriously considered for further deployment. As already elaborated by the authors in [119], none of combined signatures schemes yields significant enhancements compared to the common solution. The presented signature combination schemes either lead to an increased message size or, in case of onion-signatures, to a reduced reliability. Without further refinements the author of this thesis has concerns putting the Overlapping Group concept into practice. Determining the group leader based on a vehicles distance to the cell center is not an effective solution, due to the high mobility of vehicles especially in motorway scenarios. Within the order of milliseconds the geometric arrangement can change, which inherently leads to a change of the group leader role. Every change of the group leader triggers a new group formation process. Given a distance of only several hundreds of meters between two adjacent cell centers, it may nonetheless be questioned whether the group lifetime is high enough, such that the proposed aggregation technique would bring any benefit. Although the idea of creating dynamic groups is quite promising, essential questions regarding synchronization and operational feasibility are left unanswered.

5.3 Privacy Protocol Objectives

From the previous review of related work it can be concluded, that none of the proposed solutions fully applies to all Car-to-X scenarios. In the following, major requirements are derived, which any group privacy protocol has to fulfill in order to be in line with the safety, security and privacy demands. Then, in subsequent sections a novel privacy protocol is proposed, which is meeting those criteria.

- **Privacy Enhancements**
  Obviously, the main objective of any privacy protocols lies within the enhancement of the driver's anonymity. According to the analysis performed in Section 5.1.1, a strong dependency between driver's anonymity and the vehicle's traceability has been identified. Consequently, for the development of group privacy protocols, in the context of this thesis, a metric is intoduced, which quantifies how effectively a certain approach can obfuscate a pseudonym change with respect to time. More details on the proposed metric for measuring the achieved privacy level will be given in Section 5.8.

- **Decentralization**
  Relying upon the trustworthiness of RSUs to establish cryptographic Mix Zones is considered as problematic in many ways. A centralistic instance, which is in charge of all protocol parameters (e.g., symmetric key), weakens the privacy protection. For instance, in case of the CMIX protocol [118], no privacy towards the RSU operator can be ensured. And second, the centralistic approach requires a comprehensive covering of all roads with RSUs, which is hardly achievable, especially for rural roads. Furthermore, concentrating the key generation within a single station violates the peer nature of the group, because trust is getting centralized and key agreement is being replaced by a mere key distribution. A centralistic instance always represents a single-point of failure and is in general an attractive attack target for any adversary. Therefore, for cryptographic Mix Zones, a decentralized way of creating and maintaining the group is preferable instead.

- **Robustness**
  Car-to-X messages are generally sent via broadcast through a wireless channel, which gives no guarantee that messages are received correctly by all recipients in communication range. Due to shadowing effects messages might get lost, a situation which has to be taken into account for any protocol design. In consequence, any privacy

protocol is required to be able to cope with message losses and the high mobility of communication nodes.

- **Flexibility**
  C2X networks are highly dynamic, i.e., vehicles may enter and leave the network spontaneously and unannounced. Consequently, besides the initial group establishment, further mechanisms to manage the group have to be defined. Among others, these mechanisms have to include protocols for vehicles to join and disjoin the group.

- **Efficiency**
  Since the bandwidth of the C2X communication channel is limited and primarily dedicated for exchanging safety related information any privacy protocol is required to keep the communication overhead as low as possible. Similar requirements apply for the computational overhead on involved stations.

- **Safety-Preserving**
  The main purpose of Car-to-X Communication is to enhance both road safety and traffic efficiency. Hence, establishing a privacy solution at the expense of safety has to be avoided. Although certain implications cannot be fully circumvented, a trade-off has to be found in a way that safety use cases can still work properly to serve their purpose.

- **Accountability**
  This requirment refers to the general privacy objective already stated in Section 3.2.2. One can argue further that designing a privacy solution that provides privacy against authorities is risky, since legislation might always overrule the design and require a change of the entire architecture. Lawful interception might become a major issue in case of severe traffic accidents, where C2X messages might become legally binding.

The privacy protocol presented in this chapter aims at fulfilling all previously stated requirements. In the following section the underlying system model and prerequisites for carrying out the proposed privacy protocol are described.

5.4 System Requirements

Both privacy protocols presented in this work are built on top of the common C2X architecture as described in Chapter 3. Data security is ensured by means of a PKI, which foresees pseudonym-certificates and signatures to verify the trustworthiness of all sent messages. Additionally, for the purpose of this privacy protocol, every vehicle is provided with a symmetric key. This symmetric key is only known by the vehicle and the CA and is involved to implement the requirement for accountability during the group phase. The advocated novel key fragment protocol is executed in a cooperative manner, which demands every participant to be aware of all additional protocol parameters. In particular, those protocol parameters are related to the spatial and temporal synchronization during the group formation process.

5.4.1 Spatial Synchronization

Especially for the group setup, a measure for defining all initial group members has to be given. For the purpose of creating cryptographic Mix Zones, a geographical measure seems to be the natural choice. In order to meet the requirement of decentralization, an

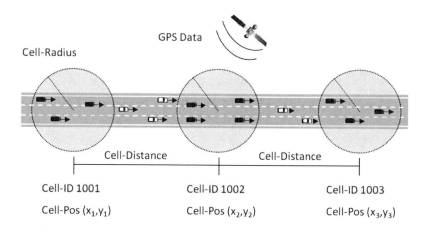

Figure 5.8: Cell concept and protocol parameters

approach comparable to the cell concept by *Raya et al.* [119] is applied. Accordingly, a group is defined by all vehicles located in a cell. In contrary in this work cells are defined to be non-overlapping and a separation between neighboring cells is introduced (see *Cell-Distance* in Figure 5.8). Every cell holds a unique identifier (*Cell-ID*) and geographical position (*Cell-Pos*), which are both known parameters to all vehicles. The *Cell-Radius* is defined as a constant and therefore does not have to be attributed to every cell separately. Two possibilities exist to ensure synchronization of cell parameters among vehicles: Either every vehicle preloads all cell parameters into an internal database during manufacturing or, instead, all cells within a current region are polled on demand via some backend facility. In general selecting the appropriate solution is implementation-specific and is not essential for interoperability of the protocol as long as it can be guaranteed that vehicles are always aware of the next cells in their proximity. In the context of this work it is assumed, that cell parameters are available from a database inside every vehicle.

Selecting the right dimensions and locations of cells is essential for the effectiveness of the proposed privacy protocols. On the one hand, the cell radius should be as large as possible in order to ensure a maximum number of group members. On the other hand, the maximum dimension of a cell is limited by the vehicle's communication range of approximately 600 meters, assuming open space at highway scenarios [124]. This threshold comes from the necessity that all vehicles within one cell have to be able to communicate per one-hop communication with each other to successfully create a common group key. As a trade-off, the cell radius is defined as approximately half the communication range (Cell-Radius = $300m$) to meet both requirements. In order to avoid interference between cells, a minimum separation of 1200 meters is defined such that there is no cross-talk between groups of neighboring cells.

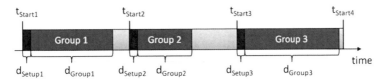

Figure 5.9: Cyclic group formation process with fixed starting times and variable group lifetimes

5.4.2 Temporal Synchronization

Forming a group and dissolving it again is a cyclic process, which has to be synchronized among all participating vehicles using the UTC time. In Figure 5.9 the different group phases are exemplarily shown for a single cell. Upon commonly agreed *starting times* t_{Start} the group formation process is triggered and executed until the group key has been established (d_{Setup}). During the *group lifetime* d_{Group}, the size of the group varies, since vehicles are constantly joining or disjoining the group. After the group has reached a sufficient level of anonymity, it is dissolved again. Finding the exact point in time, where an obfuscation has become high enough such that tracking of group members is impeded, represents a non-trivial task. It depends upon the actual traffic density as well as on the adversary's tracking capabilities. In Section 5.8 an attacker model is defined and appropriate group lifetimes are elaborated with respect to different traffic densities.

5.5 Group Establishment Protocol I: C2CGE.1

In this section, C2CGE.1, a protocol for Car2Car group establishment by means of encrypted key fragments is presented. The protocol anticipates four successive phases, which are repeated at every starting time t_{start}. Parts of the following protocol description have already been published by the author of this thesis in *Stübing et al.* [17].

5.5.1 Initial Group Definition

During the initial group definition of C2CGE.1, vehicles are frequently broadcasting CAMs, which are used by surrounding vehicles to determine, which neighbors are located in the cells. In Figure 5.10 a basic scenario is illustrated, where at the starting time t_{Start}, *vehicle A, B, and C* are located within a cell, whereas *vehicle X, Y, and Z* are located outside the cell. In Table 5.1 the related notations are summarized.

Given the cell center and radius, every vehicle can determine whether it is located inside a cell or not. The cell concept serves as a kind of geographical *stamp* to mark initial group members at starting time. In the following procedure, the marked *vehicle A, B, and C* do not necessarily have to remain in the cell to successfully complete the initialization process.

NOTATION	DESCRIPTION
t_{Start}	starting time for group establishment (periodic)
d_{Setup}	setup interval to establish the group key
d_{Group}	group lifetime
k_i	asymmetric private key of vehicle i
$Cert_i$	certified public key of vehicle i (pseudonym)
$Sig(data; k_i)$	signed data, using k_i, (ECC 224)
$KeyFrag_i$	16 bit random number of vehicle i
$E(data; Cert_i)$	encrypted data using $Cert_i$
k_i^{CA}	symmetric CA key of vehicle i
k_{group}	symmetric group key
$HMAC(data; k_i)$	HMAC of data using k_i

Table 5.1: Notations Overview

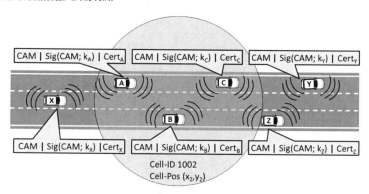

Figure 5.10: Scenario at the starting time t_{Start} of the group

5.5.2 Key Fragment Distribution

As a result of the previous phase, *vehicle A, B*, and *C* have been selected to create a group and are instantly starting to distribute key fragments. In the context of the C2CGE.1 protocol the term *key fragment* ($KeyFrag_i$) is defined as a confidential 16-bit random number, which is created individually by every *vehicle i*. In order to assemble the common group key, each fragment has to be communicated among all group members via a secure channel. Hence, all key fragments are encrypted by means of asymmetric cryptography before sending.

For instance, in the accompanying example in Figure 5.11, *vehicle A* requires the key fragments from *vehicle B* and *C* and in turn sends its encrypted key fragment to them, respectively. From previously received CAMs, *vehicle A* may extract *vehicle B*'s and *C*'s certificate and use the included public key to send the encrypted key fragment. Only the receiver vehicle holds the related private key, and thus will be able to decrypt the message. In order to meet previously stated requirements for low message overhead, it is recommended

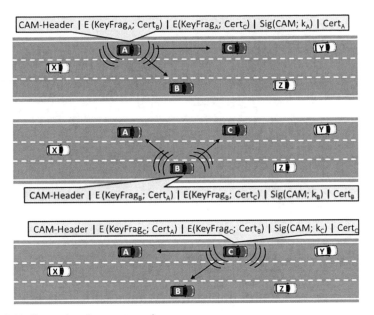

Figure 5.11: Secure key fragments exchange

to include the encrypted key fragments into the payload of the next regularly sent CAM broadcast.

In Figure 5.11 the packet structure as sent by *vehicle A* is illustrated. It consists of the CAM header, including *vehicle A*'s mobility data, as well as the

- *Vehicle A*'s key fragment $KeyFrag_A$, encrypted using *vehicle B*'s certificate $Cert_B$,
- *Vehicle A*'s key fragment $KeyFrag_A$, encrypted using *vehicle C*'s certificate $Cert_C$,
- Signature over the entire message, created using *vehicles A*'s asymmetric private key k_A, and
- *Vehicle A*'s certificate $Cert_A$.

Vehicle B and *C* distribute their key fragments similarly.

5.5.3 Group Key Generation

After completing the previous phase, all vehicles are aware of the same set of key fragments. These key fragments are then aggregated to a common *group key* k_{group}. By including the *Cell-ID* and *starting time* t_{start}, the resulting group key now features both a spatial and a temporal dependency. This way the likelihood of a group key correlation is reduced for the cases, where the same vehicles are initiating a new group at some other point in time. Furthermore, for later identification of the group, an identifier is chosen, which is also based on the *Cell-ID* and the t_{start}. The group key generation function is further detailed in Section 5.5.5.

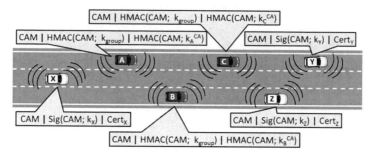

Figure 5.12: Anonymous message exchange within the group

5.5.4 Anonymous Message Exchange

After key establishment, vehicles continue signing messages using the symmetric group key k_{group}. In doing so, both objectives are met at the same time, i.e., a reliable authentication of messages, while the anonymity of the sender is maintained. Having a common group key, furthermore, enables the usage of symmetric authentication techniques during the group phase, which require lower channel bandwidth than the respective asymmetric techniques. In this thesis the usage of the Keyed-Hash Message Authentication Code (HMAC-256) is advocated, which is approved by the NIST to provide message authentication. Accordingly, every sender creates an unique hash value from the message content, which cannot be reproduced without having knowledge ons the symmetric group key.

Besides creating a HMAC for integrity checks within the group, every vehicle additionally employs a second HMAC computed with the symmetric CA key k_i^{CA}. By means of this second HMAC, the CA can confirm, if a given message has been sent from a certain vehicle. Any bit manipulation of the message or the attached HMAC performed by an adversary will be detected by the CA. Furthermore, in order to be able to use the second HMAC for accountability purposes, it is required that the HMAC creation is performed within a tamper proof module inside every vehicle. In Figure 5.12 the exchanged messages right after the group establishment phase are depicted. *Vehicles A, B, and C* are broadcasting CAMs, which are authenticated using symmetric cryptography, whereas *vehicles X, Y, and Z* rely upon asymmetric cryptography.

In order to overcome interoperability problems at the border of a group, join operations have to be defined, which allow transferring the group key to non-members as well. Related methods are detailed in the following section.

5.5.5 Implementation

While the previous chapter gave a more general description of the proposed key establishment protocol, in this section the implementation is further detailed by means of pseudocode descriptions. In particular, the question is addressed, how the protocol copes with message losses and the high mobility of the network. In Algorithm 4 and Algorithm 5, the protocol synchronization approach is outlined, which is triggered at every starting time t_{Start}.

In the reference implementation, given in Algorithm 4, the next starting time t_{start} is determined by evaluating the current UTC time, as a multiple of the globally predefined *Protocol*

Algorithm 4 determineInitialMemberSet()

In: Starting Time t_{Start}, Closest Cell Region C, Neighborhood Table N_{Table}
Out: Initial Member Set M

1: $SI = 3000ms$ {Protocol Start Interval}
2: **if** getUTCTime() mod $SI = 0$ **then**
3: t_{Start} = getUTCTime()
4: **if** getPosition()$\in C$ **then**
5:    **for all** $n \in N_{Table}$ **do**
6:      $NeighborPosPredict$ = doPrediction(n.getPosition(), t_{Start});
7:      **if** $NeighborPosPredict \in C$ **then**
8:        M.add(n)
9:      **end if**
10:   **end for**
11:   **return** M
12: **end if**
13: **end if**

Start Interval (see line 1 in Algorithm 4, with example initialization). The host vehicle instantly queries the internal cell database to obtain the location of the cell closest to its own position. If at starting time the host vehicle is located inside the cell, it forms a group with its neighbors. For that purpose each vehicle calculates the *MemberSet*, which is defined as a list including all vehicles from which the host vehicle assumes that they are taking part in the group establishment process. The *MemberSet* is determined by iterating the Neighborhood Table, which includes the received last positions of all surrounding vehicles. Because of deviating timestamps, the entries do not necessarily reflect the precise scenario at starting time. In order to bring all entries down to a common time basis, linear approximation is used to find the location of all vehicles at starting time and the *MemberSet* variable is defined accordingly. However, inconsistent member sets between group participants cannot be fully circumvented as there always remains space for some errors due to the high mobility of the network. If not treated carefully, those different member sets will result into an inconsistent calculation of the group key among the group members. In order to solve this issue, a basic voting scheme for defining the group members is followed. Accordingly, every group member communicates its own *view on the group* to all surrounding neighbors. By adding a vehicle's own Member Set to every outgoing message, a common awareness between all group members can be established. The given approach ensures that every member determines the greatest common subset among all Member Sets, as described by Algorithm 5.

Due to message loss and shadowing effects key fragments might get lost. In order to cope with such effects, assigned group members further attach a *VehicleReady* flag to every outgoing message. This flag signalizes to other group members, that the respective vehicle has received all required key fragements with respect to his own Member Set and is about to enter the group mode, once the group setup time d_{setup} is reached. The detailed message format is given exemplarily for *vehicle A* in Figure 5.13. The concept of the *VehicleReady* flag is introduced not only to enable reliable key fragment exchange. It furthermore ensures, that before entering the group modus, each vehicle may again verify whether a minimum number of vehicles (MIN_GROUP_SIZE) has received all required key fragments.

In all cases, the key establishment phase will terminate after d_{setup} and each vehicle will decide to switch into the group mode, or not. This temporal synchronization is introduced, to avoid that one group member is sending already group signatures, while others are still sending messages with their own certificate. During the group establishment phase d_{setup}, vehicles constantly broadcast encrypted key fragments including an updated version of its Member Set and internal reception status, as indicated in Algorithm 5.

Algorithm 5 receiveGroupEstablishmentMsg()

In: Received Message $ReceiveMsg$, Group Setup Interval d_{setup}
Out: Sent Message $SentMsg$
1: G {Monitor for Group Status}
2: R {Request Set}
3: M {Initial Member Set}
4: **if** getUTCTime() $\leq t_{start} + d_{setup}$ **then**
5:    **if** getVehicleID() $\notin$ $ReceiveMsg$.getMemberSet() **then**
6:       leaveGroup()
7:    **else**
8:       **for all** $i <$ MAX_GROUP_SIZE **do**
9:          M.get(i) = M.get(i) $\wedge$ $ReceiveMsg$.getMemberSet().get(i)
10:      **end for**
11:   **end if**
12:   R.get($ReceiveMsg$.getSenderID()) = 0;
13:   **if** R.get(j) = 0 $\forall$ $j <$ MAX_GROUP_SIZE **then**
14:      $VehicleReady$ = true
15:   **else**
16:      $VehicleReady$ = false
17:   **end if**
18:   G.get(getVehicleID())= $VehicleReady$
19:   G.get($ReceiveMsg$.getSenderID())= $ReceiveMsg$.getVehicleReadyFlag()
20:   $SentMsg$.add(M)
21:   $SentMsg$.add($VehicleReady$)
22:   send($SentMsg$)
23: **else**
24:   **if** G.getOnes() $\geq$ MIN_GROUP_SIZE **then**
25:      startGroup()
26:   **else**
27:      leaveGroup()
28:   **end if**
29: **end if**

In Figure 5.14 the connectivity of the key generator function is depicted. According to the respective vehicle ID all key fragments are listed in ascending order. Sorting the fragments in a defined order is important in order to yield the same group key for all members. The key fragments are then concatenated with the respective Cell-ID and the starting time. In this thesis, it is proposed to apply *Secure Hash Algorithm SHA-256* to map an input string with variable length to a fixed unique 256-bit value. As the resulting value is a common secret among all group members, it may be used as the group key k_{group}.

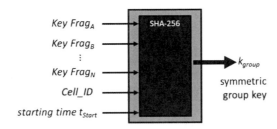

Figure 5.13: Detailed message format for group establishment

Figure 5.14: Group key generator function

5.6 Group Establishment Protocol II: C2CGE.2

Based on the same system assumptions as outlined in Section 5.4, this section presents a further approach for establishing a common group key among all group members. This approach is called C2CGE.2 and is based on the *Diffie-Hellman (DH)* scheme, which has been extended to meet the requirements for flexibility of highly mobile nodes in a n-party scenario of C2X communication.

The DH protocol, as introduced by *Diffie et al.* [125], is generally used to establish a common secret of two parties via an insecure channel. For Car-to-X networks, the DH approach is particularly well-suited, since the establishment process does not require an encryption of messages. Hence, protocol parameters can be exchanged in plaintext via broadcast, which reduces complexity. In order to apply the basic DH protocol for n-party scenarios like, e.g., C2X networks, subordinate protocols have to be defined, which coordinate the key establishment between all group members. In [126], [127], and [128] n-party DH protocols are proposed based on binary trees for creating and managing groups in ad-hoc networks. However, such hierarchical approaches are considered as rather inefficient and inflexible for the fast changing topology of C2X networks.

In *Ingemarsson et al.* [129] group participants are arranged in a logical ring structure (e.g., $M_1 \rightarrow M_2 \rightarrow M_3 \rightarrow \ldots \rightarrow M_n \rightarrow M_1$). Following a round-based approach, a node M_i always receives the DH result from the preceding node M_{i-1}, raises that value to the power of its own secret number, and forwards the result to the succeeding node M_{i+1}. For n participants, $n - 1$ rounds are required until the final group key can be computed. Since the ring structure has to be maintained during the establishment process, a total number of $n * (n - 1)$ unicast messages have to be exchanged within the network. Besides this high communication overhead, the scheme does not provide any additional reliability in case of a failure of single nodes. Hence, a malfunctioning of any participant will prevent all other nodes from calculating the final group key.

Burmester/Demstedt [130] have advocated a generalized Diffie-Hellman protocol taking into account the broadcast capabilities of involved nodes. Similar to *Ingemarsson et al.* [129], nodes are arranged in a logical ring. First, every node M_i calculates $K_i = g^{k_i} mod\ p$ (considering a *prime p* and *primitive root g*) and broadcasts the DH result to its predecessor M_{i-1} and successor M_{i+1}. After this step, every node determines and broadcasts the ratio $X_i = (K_{i+1}/K_{i-1})^{k_i} mod\ p$ to all nodes. Then, every node determines the final group key according to [130]:

$$k_{group} = (K_{i-1})^{nk_i} \cdot X_i^{n-1} \cdot X_{i+1}^{n-2} \cdots X_{i-2} mod\ p. \qquad\qquad (5.4)$$

Steiner et al. [131] advocate two different n-party DH schemes, namely GDH.2 and GDH.3. The GDH.3 scheme follows a centralized approach in letting a single node gather all intermediate values and calculate the final key fragments. For comparison in this thesis, GDH.2 is selected, since it fits best to the requirement for decentralization stated in Section 5.3. GDH.2 consists of an upflow and downflow stage. During the upflow stage contributions from all members are collected. The highest indexed group member then broadcasts the last round of intermediate values during the downflow stage. Compared to [130], the number of exchanged messages is reduced significantly. However, this approach still implies too many rounds until the final key can be calculated. Thus, due to high mobility of C2X nodes, a minimum number of sequentially sent unicast messages is aspired. Instead, group protocols shall make more use of the broadcast capabilities of C2X networks for key establishment. A more detailed comparison of the previous protocols and the protocols proposed in this thesis is subject to Section 5.8.

One of the most promising n-party DH approaches has been proposed by *Steer et al.* [100]. This approach comes along with only two rounds of broadcast. In the context of this work, this protocol is taken as a basis for group establishment C2CGE.2 and is further adapted to the requirements of vehicular networks.

According to *J. Alves-Foss* [132], existing solutions for n-party Diffie-Hellman can be categorized into two classes: The first class of solutions is based on key distribution via some trusted group controller. In contrast, the second class assembles the final key based on contributions obtained from all participants. When considering this categorization, the privacy protocol, presented in this thesis, represents a hybrid of both, i.e., the initialization process is entirely contributory, whereas for the group extension the shared key is distributed.

5.6.1 Initial Group Definition

Defining the initial set of group members for C2CGE.2 is done in a similar way as described for the key fragment protocol C2CGE.1 in Section 5.5. By polling the Neighborhood Table, every vehicle determines the respective group members at starting time. In Figure 5.15 a scenario is depicted, where *vehicles A, B, C,* and *D* are supposed to create a group. Like in the 2-party DH scheme all members agree a priori on the same *prime number p* and *primitive root (g mod p)*, which are assumed to be public. As detailed in further sections, the prime p is selected on a geographical basis, whereas the corresponding primitive root g features a temporal dependency.

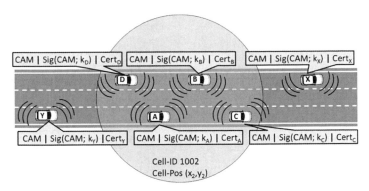

Figure 5.15: Initial group definition

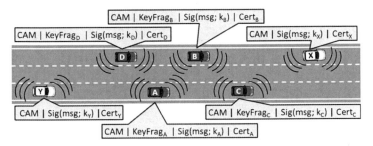

Figure 5.16: Key fragment distribution

5.6.2 Key Fragment Distribution

Each vehicle inside a cell selects a secret random number first and then determines the DH result. These results are used later on to assemble an overall group key and are therefore denoted as key fragments $KeyFrag_i$, following a similar terminology as already introduced for the previous key establishment protocol C2CGE.1 in Section 5.5.

$$KeyFrag_{\{A,B,C,D\}} = g^{\{a,b,c,d\}} mod\ p \tag{5.5}$$

Since DH applies a one-way function to determine Key Fragments, it is computationally infeasible to obtain the secret private number given the public parameters only, i.e., $KeyFrag_i$, prime p, and primitive root g. In order to ensure authenticity and to impede man-in-the-middle attacks [51] (page 432), key fragments are signed using the private key k_i (see Figure 5.16).

5.6.3 Group Key Calculation

The outlined group formation process in C2CGE.2 works iteratively. Hence, starting from a *Root Group* the 2-party DH scheme is repeated repetitively until the final common group key has been created. For this iterative process, a chronological order has to be defined by which key fragments are processed. For this reason, every vehicle takes a 'snapshot' of the geographical vehicle distribution within a cell at starting time t_{Start} (see Figure 5.15). Based on this snapshot, the two vehicles located closest to the cell center are supposed to create the Root Group. Due to their location in the center of the group, those vehicles are being received equally well by all group members and therefore are assigned a keyrole for distributing parameters.

In the scenario depicted in Figure 5.15 *vehicle A* and *B* create the Root Group. Since key fragments have been exchanged during the previous phase, no further communication between these two vehicles is necessary to calculate the common group key:

$$\begin{aligned} GroupKey_{AB} &= (KeyFrag_A)^b \ mod \ p \\ &= (KeyFrag_B)^a \ mod \ p \\ &= g^{ab} \ mod \ p. \end{aligned} \qquad (5.6)$$

After completing this step these vehicles share the common secret $GroupKey_{AB}$, which, for an outsider, is undistinguishable from a true random variable. Hence, this value can be used to calculate the next group key fragment by means of the DH equation:

$$KeyFrag_{AB} = g^{GroupKey_{AB}} \ mod \ p. \qquad (5.7)$$

For subsequent steps always the key fragment of the vehicle with the smallest distance to the cell center (as defined by the snapshot) is processed in every time step. In order to integrate the next *vehicle C* in Figure 5.16 into the group, the members of the Root Group are broadcasting the key fragment $KeyFrag_{AB}$ via the next sent CAM. The common group key between *vehicle A*, *B*, and *C* is now established accordingly:

$$\begin{aligned} GroupKey_{ABC} &= (KeyFrag_{AB})^c \ mod \ p \\ &= (KeyFrag_C)^{GroupKey_{AB}} \ mod \ p \\ &= g^{c \cdot GroupKey_{AB}} \ mod \ p. \end{aligned} \qquad (5.8)$$

Following this scheme, the final group key is calculated as:

$$GroupKey_{ABCD} = g^{d \cdot GroupKey_{ABC}} \ mod \ p. \qquad (5.9)$$

5.6.4 Anonymous Message Exchange

After group establishment, all initial group members are aware of the same group key and continue sending messages as depicted in Figure 5.17. Since every group member is signing messages using k_{group}, an adversary needs to use error-prone temporal and spatial relations to correctly assign messages to vehicles. For accountability purposes, every group member furthermore creates a second HMAC using the symmetric key k_i^{CA}. In order to overcome interoperability issues at the border of a group, related join operations are defined in Section 5.7 to include further vehicles. So, once the final group key has been established via the presented contributory scheme, the proposed protocol is switching to a centralized scheme for the purpose of distributing the group key to *vehicle X* and *Y*, respectively.

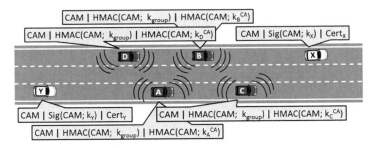

Figure 5.17: Anonymous message exchange within the group

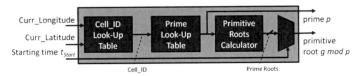

Figure 5.18: Calculation of Diffie-Hellman protocol parameters according to C2CGE.2

5.6.5 Implementation

While in the previous section, the basic working principle behind the C2CGE.2 protocol was described, in this section, more implementation details related to the synchronization of the protocol parameters are given.

Diffie-Hellman Parameter Synchronization

In order to reduce the channel bandwidth and to keep the overall latency low, no setup protocol for negotiating initial parameters is anticipated. Instead, the parameter selection is performed in a decentralized manner via the scheme illustrated in Figure 5.18. Based on its current position, a vehicle queries the related *Cell-ID*, which is directly associated to a large prime number p.

Given the prime p, the corresponding primitive roots are found using *Fermat's little theorem*. Accordingly, as a first step, *Eulers's totient function* is determined for prime p [133] (ch. 3.22, pp. 55 – 56):

$$\varphi(p) = p - 1. \tag{5.10}$$

Then, for $\varphi(p)$ a prime factorization is performed. A number $g \in \{1, 2, \ldots, p-1\}$ is considered a *primitive root mod p*, if for every obtained *prime factor p_i* the following equation holds:

$$g^{\varphi(p)/p_i} \neq 1. \tag{5.11}$$

Note that determining prime roots analytically for C2X is feasible only if a factorization of $\varphi(p)$ is achievable on automotive processors and, furthermore, efficient algorithms for modular exponentiation (e.g., exponentiation by squaring) are deployed. As an alternative implementation an offline prime roots calculation is anticipated. The pre-determined prime roots are stored inside a look-up table, which is queried at every t_{Start} of a group. The starting time is also used to select the primitive root among all possible candidates.

In principle, it is also possible to define public parameters prime p as well as prime root g globally the same for all vehicles, which would further reduce the computation overhead. However, the temporal and spatial dependency of these group parameters is considered as a desired property to ensure that only assigned vehicles are creating the respective group.

Group Parameter Distribution

According to the calculation scheme presented in previous sections, the final group key is established by executing the DH scheme sequentially. Hence, for *vehicle D* in Figure 5.19 to be able to determine the group key, all intermediate key fragments are required for its calculation. In contrast, members of the Root Group, i.e., *vehicles A and B*, may determine the final group key as well as all intermediate key fragments directly. In order to reduce the overall delay, vehicles A and B, are proposed to broadcast the entire set of key fragments. In doing so, any group member, who receives the broadcast, can instantly determine the final group key without having to wait for other vehicles, thus reducing the overall delay significantly. The mathematical background of such an approach has been also described by *Steer et al.* [100].

Regarding the overall security of this approach no vulnerabilities are constituted, since all distributed DH parameters are public by definition. If the 2-party key establishment is considered as intractable, the same is true for the proposed n-party scheme. Once a vehicle has determined the final key, it starts broadcasting the set of key fragments as illustrated in Figure 5.19. Broadcasting simultaneously the set of key fragments is an asset in two ways: First, the likelihood for other vehicles to receive key fragments in a timely manner is increased. Second, redundancy allows cross-checking between multiple sets of received key fragments in order to identify possible inconsistencies. For reliable key fragment exchange, C2CGE.2 applies a similar scheme of *MemberSet* variables and *VehicleReady* flags as already outlined for C2CGE.1 in Section 5.5.5 .

5.7 Group Management

Each of the previously described protocols C2CGE.1 and C2CGE.2 may be applied to establish a group and determine a group key among all group members. While C2CGE.1 requires only low communication overhead, the alternative C2CGE.2 comes along without the need for encryption. Depending on the respective preferences one or the other may be chosen for deployment. A more detailed comparison will follow in Section 5.8.2. This section is dedicated to group management. In particular, it is explained in more detail, how new vehicles can be integrated into the group and how interference between adjacent groups can be handled. The following sub protocols are independent of the group establishment process and therefore may be applied to C2CGE.1 and C2CGE.2 similarly.

5.7.1 Group Join

Immediately after the group establishment process has completed, vehicles in the vicinity have to join the group for reasons of interoperability. Like before, authentication towards the group is implicitly realized by evaluating the certificate and signature of received CAMs.

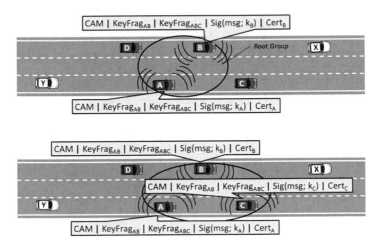

Figure 5.19: Successive group key calculation

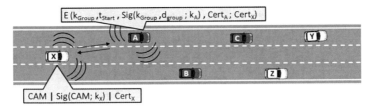

Figure 5.20: Group join protocol

Non-members, like, e.g., *vehicle X* in Figure 5.20, can migrate to the group by requesting the group key. In response, the closest group member (i.e., *vehicle A*) is encapsulating the group key k_{group} and the group lifetime d_{group} into a message. The group lifetime depends upon the vehicle density at the starting time t_{Start} of the group and is determined by means of simulations (see Section 5.8.5). Signing the message with the forwarder's pseudonym is necessary to ensure authenticity. The entire reply-message is encrypted using the certificate of *vehicle X* for keeping the group key as well as the sender identity confidential to the adversary. Note that the reply-message of *vehicle A* does not include any mobility data (i.e., position, speed, and heading). Hence, if *vehicle A* uses a new unused pseudonym for signing, *vehicle X* still can verify the overall authenticity, but cannot reveal the sender's identity using spatial-temporal information. In this way privacy of group members is preserved, even when answering to group join requests.

5.7.2 Group Interference

The previously presented join protocol allows extending the group far beyond its initial group size. Groups are expanding into all directions simultaneously and, at some point in time they will possibly interfere with adjacent groups. Group interference might also be caused by single vehicles, which are traveling faster than other group members and are therefore reaching some other group ahead. In principle, four different strategies for handling interfering groups are possible:

- Dissolving both groups
- Merging both groups
- Assigning multiple group memberships
- Leaving of single vehicles

In the following, each of these possible solutions is discussed with respect to its computational complexity, message overhead and privacy impact. In Table 5.2 the findings are summarized.

The first approach is not considered as a feasible solution. The costs in terms of exchanged messages are high, because every group member has to be notified about the cancellation. The impact on privacy is seen critical as the gained anonymity of a group scales best with long lifetimes of the group. Dissolving the entire group too early will reduce the effectiveness of the privacy protocol.

A merging of both groups is less problematic concerning privacy but would require even more messages for group re-synchronization, since a new group key has to be negotiated among all group members.

A third approach consists in assigning two group memberships to those vehicles, which are located at the borderline of both groups. This can be realized via the privacy preserving join operation. The problem is that mutual authentication between two vehicles, which are members of different groups is hardly realizable, i.e., the group key k_{group} can only be used for authentication within the same group.

The fourth approach represents a trade-off between privacy and complexity. If vehicles of different groups meet, those vehicles which are located inside the interference area, instantly will leave their group. They continue sending messages with their regular pseudonym and are requesting the unknown group key of the adjacent group. Having received the respective group keys allows those intermediate vehicles to verify messages sent by both groups. However, instead of using a group key, those vehicles use their own pseudonym to authenticate messages. For those vehicles no anonymity is provided by the group anymore. This trade-off is considered as most appropriate, since it includes the lowest complexity at an acceptable privacy level for the remaining group. In Figure 5.21 the resulting scenario is illustrated, where *vehicle A* and *B* serve as a sort of buffer to separate both groups.

POSSIBLE STRATEGIES	COMPLEXITY	MESSAGE OVERHEAD	PRIVACY PROTECTION
Dissolving both groups	Medium	High	Low
Merging both groups	High	High	High
Assigning multiple group memberships	High	Medium	High
Leaving of single vehicles	Low	Low	Medium

Table 5.2: Group interference handling assessment

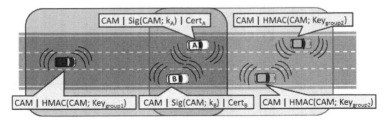

Figure 5.21: Group interference

5.7.3 Group Disjoin

If a vehicle has to disjoin a group, it switches over to one of its own pseudonyms for signing subsequent messages. A notification to other group members is not required. In general, there might be two reasons for a vehicle to disjoin the group: Either the group lifetime d_{Group} has exceeded and the group is dissolving, or the vehicle has left the communication range of the other group members. This may especially be the case when the vehicle is taking an exit of the highway, or is traveling much faster than its mate group members.

5.8 Evaluation Results

The following evaluation and has been carried out to analyze the privacy protocol with respect to its technical feasibility, temporal behavior, and anonymity achievements. Thereby, different types of evaluations are applied to analyze the different protocol properties:

First, the protocol specification is verified for formal correctness. The expected high mobility of nodes and unreliability of the communication channel in C2X networks requires a high robustness and flexibility of any applied cooperative protocol. For the proposed C2X privacy protocols, this mainly affects the synchronization of vehicles during the group establishment phase. Though, the communicational overhead for synchronization is kept to a minimum, the environment includes several unpredictable processes, like, e.g., the mobility of group members or the message loss of the channel, which significantly increases the possible state space of the system. Thus, due to the complexity of the C2X environment mathematical proofs of correctness become difficult, or even impossible. A promising alternative to mathematical proofs represent mathematical verification approaches based on model checking. Formal verification helps to reveal design flaws that lead to a violation of the protocol requirements for any possible sequence of events that can occur.

In the second part of the evaluation, it is analyzed whether the proposed protocol has been specified accurately enough to ensure a reliable group establishment and maintenance when being simulated by means of a more advanced simulation environment. These simulations have been carried out in the context of the Master's thesis done by *M.Pfalzgraf* [134] and *M. Ceven* [135], which both have been instructed and supervised by the author of this thesis. State-of-the-art simulators are used to study the protocol behavior under realistic traffic scenarios and vehicle movements. By observing the behavior of the groups over time, protocol characteristics are obtained like, e.g., the duration for group establishment or the point in time until group interferences appear. Based on these values the protocol parameters, such as appropriate cell distances or the minimum group lifetime, are defined for a specific road segment. Then, a global passive adversary is modeled and tracking capabilities are evaluated when deploying the protocol at varying vehicle densities. It should be noted here, that protocol parameters like cell distances and group lifetime heavily depend upon the actual road geometry. In the following evaluation sections those parameters are shaped to be appropriate for an exemplary case study. Similar simulations will have to be carried out for every other road section, on which the privacy protocol is going to be deployed.

This evaluation part is structured as follows: In Section 5.8.1 the protocol is verified for formal correctness. The correctness claims are stated, and based on these, an appropriate system model is derived and the verification results are presented. The group establishment protocols, advocated in this thesis, are compared to other state-of-the-art approaches in Section 5.8.3. In the core of this evaluation, the privacy protocol is evaluated with respect to its gained privacy enhancements. Therefore, in Section 5.8.4 the simulation setup is presented. Then, in Section 5.8.5 the temporal protocol behavior in terms of group establishment and management is analyzed. And finally, for privacy evaluation, a detailed reference attacker is modeled and appropriate group lifetimes are derived for different traffic densities.

5.8.1 Protocol Verification

As a well-known automated tool for model checking, in this thesis SPIN [136] is applied to verify correctness properties of the C2X privacy protocol. Using SPIN, in this thesis, the following verification flow is applied:

1. In a first step, the to be verified properties like, e.g., deadlock freedom or liveness are stated. Starting with an informally notation, later on, the correctness properties are specified using *Linear Temporal Logic (LTL)*, once the system has been modeled in detail.

2. Considering the previously stated properties the underlying system and protocol is modeled in a way that all relevant aspects are covered. PROMELA (a Process Meta Language) is a C-like verification language and allows modeling of concurrent asynchronous processes, which may communicate via buffered or unbuffered message channels.

3. For a quick debugging of the system during the modeling phase, SPIN offers the possibility to simulate the model over one random sequence of events. This random simulation is further complemented by an interactive mode, which enables a step-by-step execution of the model.

4. For a full verification of the protocol with respect to a given property, SPIN may produce a verifier, which performs a simulation of the entire state space. For larger systems, in order to reduce memory consumption, the verification can be performed in *supertrace* mode, applying bit state space techniques [137]. The supertrace mode uses hashing without collision detection, which implies that in case a collision occurs, the search path is terminated prematurely. However, an excellent coverage of the state space is still retained with this technique. The specified LTL formulas (see step 1) are translated by SPIN into a PROMELA never-claims. A never-claim consists of an endless loop, which is terminated only, if the given correctness property is violated.

Correctness properties

For the advocated C2X privacy protocol two general correctness properties are specified. The first one is related to the absence of deadlocks, while the second ensures that inside every vehicle the protocol status proceeds over time:

Deadlock Freedom: By no means, the protocol flow executed on a vehicle gets stuck in an invalid end state, from where it cannot recover.

Liveness Freedom: By no means, the protocol flow executed on a vehicle reaches a state where it shows an infinite behavior, and no progress is made anymore.

While these two properties are generally mandatory for any cooperative protocol, the next two properties are especially defined to verify the feasibility of the advocated protocol for creating a common group key among the participating group members:

Satisfiability 1: By means of the protocol, it is possible to create a group, which includes a *minimum* number of 2 group members.

Satisfiability 2: By means of the protocol, it is possible to create a group, which includes *all* initial members of the group.

Considering the stated correctness properties, in the following, the system model is derived, which later on will be subject to verification.

System Model

For any model checking attempt, an abstraction of the underlying system is a mandatory process. On the one hand, simplifications and certain assumptions have to be made in order to keep the computational complexity low. On the other hand, the model still has to be detailed enough to cover all aspects of the system, relevant for verification of the correctness properties stated in the previous section. The schematic of the overall system model, including respective random processes is depicted in Figure 5.22.

C2X Communication Model For the analysis of the advocated privacy protocol two characteristics of the C2X communication are of major interest. First, it has to be analyzed how the protocol deals with message losses of the channel. A sender node generally cannot expect that messages, which are sent only once, are received by all recipients equally. Especially, shadowing effects may cause inconsistencies in the protocol process, in a sense that some vehicles receive a particular message and therefore may change their internal state, while others, e.g., blocked vehicles, will remain in their old state.

A further aspect of the C2X communication is related to the channel allocation on higher layers. In 802.11p communication, a station accesses the channel via the asynchronous arbitration scheme *CSMA (Carrier Sense Multiple Access)*. Accordingly, the privacy protocol has to be designed in a way that it performs well, independently from the order of the sending and receiving processes. In the following it is described how the communication part of the C2X system model is realized.

In the PROMELA language, predefined macros for channels are provided, which realize a point-to-point communication between different processes. In the past, several attempts

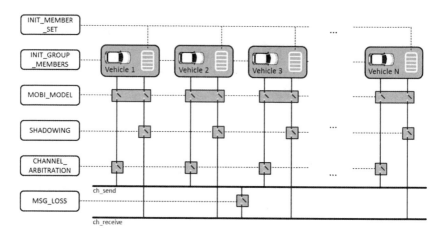

Figure 5.22: Promela model of the C2X communication scenario

have been made for extending this unicast channel for simulating also a broadcast medium. In *Renesse et al.* [138] and *Ug et al.* [139] a broadcast system is emulated using an array of unidirectional channels. In order to reduce the size of the state space and to keep the complexity for channel management low, in this thesis no separation of channels is anticipated. Instead, two single channels, one for sending and a second one for receiving of messages, are instantiated. A channel arbitration component as illustrated in Figure 5.22 arbitrary schedules one of the vehicles for sending on channel *ch_send*. The arbitration of the channel follows a uniform distribution and models the CSMA scheme (see random variable CHANNEL_ ARBITRATION). Once a message has been sent, a *ChannelBusy* flag is set which prevents other stations inside the model from sending messages. Depending on a given message loss rate (e.g., due to channel congestion), the message is either dropped or passed to the second channel *ch_receive* (see random variable MSG_LOSS). While the message loss rate affects all group members equally, shadowing effects have an impact only on some vehicles, and therefore are considered as even more critical for the synchronization process (see random variable SHADOWING). A channel monitor releases the *ChannelBusy* flag, once all receiver vehicles have been processed.

In PROMELA nondeterminism can be modeled using an *if*-statement whose guards are always true (see *Ben-Ari et al.* [140]. For the model applied in this thesis each random process assigns a *boolean* variable, which serves as a switch to trigger the successful transmission or reception of messages via the channel. Here is an exemplary realization of the PROMELA coding for the receiving part:

```
If
:: ChannelBusy \&\& !MessageLost -> C2XChannel ? <ReceiveVehicle1>;
:: ChannelBusy \&\& !MessageLost -> C2XChannel ? <ReceiveVehicle2>;
:: ChannelBusy \&\& !MessageLost -> C2XChannel ? <ReceiveVehicle3>;
Fi
```

Mobility Model Besides communicational aspects, also the mobility of group participants influences the protocol process. For instance, at starting time t_{start} the number of vehicles N, which are located inside the cell may take an arbitrary value within a predefined interval. In this thesis, an approach is followed, where the entire protocol is verified for a different number of group members, individually (see random variable INIT_GROUP_MEMBERS in Figure 5.22).

As outlined in previous sections, due to possible inconsistencies between the Neighborhood Tables of all vehicles, the determined *MemberSet* variable (see Section 5.5.5) may differ for every group member. In order to verify the advocated synchronization mechanisms, in the PROMELA model, a vehicle's initial *MemberSet* is determined by means of a random variable (see random variable INIT_MEMBER_SET).

During the group establishment phase, vehicles may suddenly leave the communication range of the group, which potentially may cause the protocol to run into a *deadlock* state. In this thesis, the sudden disappearance of a group member is modeled by a boolean random variable, which disconnects the vehicle from the overall model (see random variable MOBI_MODEL).

Verification Results

The ability to verify a certain model is bounded by the working memory available on the verification platform. In order to reduce the complexity of the stated correctness claims, in the context of this thesis, a further monitor process is introduced. The monitoring aims at consolidating the internal states of all processes into a single boolean variable. Instead of verifying the distributed processes, only the boolean variable of the monitor process is included into the LTL formula.

The SPIN Model Checker does not allow a parameterized modeling of the system. Hence, the number of concurrent processes has to be fixed at the time of the verification. In principle the group establishment protocol is not limited to a maximum number of participants. However, a possible upper bound may be found by taking into account the maximum capacity of a cell (see Figure 5.8 in Section 5.4). Assuming a cell radius of 300 meter (see Section 5.4.1) with an average number of 3 lanes and a vehicle length of 5 meters (with a minimum separation of 20 meter from each other), a maximum cell capacity may be defined by approximately 35-40 vehicles. In conclusion, the protocol has to prove correctness for a maximum number of 40 participants. For *MemberSets*, which include a higher number, it is recommended to abort the group establishment process, since correctness of the protocol cannot be guaranteed anymore. Note that the generic structure of the protocol suggests that the protocol can be well applied for an undefined number of participants. However, to prove this assumption, techniques based on a formal analysis are reaching their limits.

When performing the verification, SPIN considers all possible paths of the model execution. The high number of concurrent vehicle processes as well as the non-determinism of the mobility and channel model leads to an increasing number of states ($> 1.08 \times 10^9$). Such a high number of states requires far more memory, than available on common desktop computers, today (4 GB RAM, 2.8 GHz DualCore). Even on more powerful simulation platforms, the maximum memory capacity is exceeded (32 GB RAM, 2.8 GHz QuadCore). The author of this theses, makes use of the SPIN *supertrace/bitstate* [136] (pp. 206 – 209) mode, which prevents the re-exploration of already visited states, and by this reduces the amount of required memory considerably.

Correctness Claim	Verification Platform	State Vector Size	# States	Depth	Memory
Deadlock, Liveness	4 GB RAM, 2.8 Ghz DualCore	7320 bytes	54397040	1258936	0.35 GB
	32 GB RAM, 2.8 Ghz QuadCore	7344 bytes	$1,43 \times 10^9$	9999999	30 GB
Satisfiability 1	4 GB RAM, 2.8 Ghz DualCore	7320 bytes	34426541	1125766	0.35 GB
	32 GB RAM, 2.8 Ghz QuadCore	7344 bytes	$1,08 \times 10^9$	9999999	30 GB
Satisfiability 2	4 GB RAM, 2.8 Ghz DualCore	7324 bytes	34559095	1137806	0.35 GB
	32 GB RAM, 2.8 Ghz QuadCore	7344 bytes	$1,17 \times 10^9$	9999999	30 GB

Table 5.3: SPIN verification report for two different hardware setups

For the advocated group establishment protocol a *supertrace* verification as well as an exhaustive search is performed. Thereby the state space exploration for the exhaustive search is limited by an upper bound of 32 GByte of available memory for state storage. Verification results for both hardware setups are summarized in Table 5.3. Note that for the exhaustive search, the simulation time takes about 15 minutes, while the supertrace could be complete in less that 5 minutes.

Deadlock Freedom and Liveness Property According to [136] (page 561), deadlock freedom is a property which cannot be denoted directly in terms of LTL formula. Instead the deadlock freedom as well as the liveness property has to be verified implicitly, by defining a valid end state, which has to be finally reached by all processes. In this thesis, this end state is reflected by the status of a boolean variable *protocol_terminated* which is assigned within the previously introduced monitor process. Following this approach, both properties, i.e., deadlock freedom and liveness may be verified by means of the same LTL formula:

<>([]protocol_terminated)

Satisfiability 1 As an initial setting, vehicles are supposed to establish a group if at least a minimum number of 2 members are included. In order to verify the feasibility of the protocol for this case, a member counter is instantiated within the monitor process. At protocol termination (*protocol_terminated == true*) the number of group members are evaluated and the *min_group_numb* variable is assigned. Expressed in LTL, this refers to the following formula:

<>min_group_numb

By means of the SPIN model checker it is shown that the defined minimum number may be achieved in principle.

Satisfiability 2 Apart from proving satisfiability for a minimum number of participants, the protocol should generally be also capable of creating a common group key for a defined maximum of 40 vehicles. This leads to the following LTL formula:

<>max_group_numb

In conclusion, by means of the SPIN model checker it could be shown that the advocated protocol is free of common design flaws, such as deadlocks or livelocks. Given a minimum and maximum possible number of group participants, it could be verified that the protocol is capable of creating a common group key.

5.8.2 Protocol Comparison

Before presenting the evaluation results, in this section, an analytical comparison of different group establishment protocols with respect to their applicability for Car-to-X communication is performed. Following the requirements stated in Section 5.3, only very few approaches come into further consideration. During the analysis of related work in Section 5.2 it has been identified that none of these protocols fully applies to all stated requirements. Especially the requirement for decentralization is not fulfilled by any of the known solutions. In the introduction of Chapter 5.6 furthermore several n-party Diffie-Hellman protocols have been reviewed, which in principle are appropriate for the purpose of a decentralized key establishment. In the following, the proposed protocols C2CGE.1 and C2CGE.2 are compared with respective approaches according to *Steiner et al.* [141], *Ingemarsson et al.* [129] and *Burmester/Desmedt* [130]. For the comparison in Table 5.4 the following three criteria are applied:

1. **Number of serial rounds**
   Referring to the definition applied by *Steiner et al.* [131], a *round* is defined as the number of messages on the critical path. Thereby the critical path consists of all operations, which have to be performed sequentially. Rounds are dependent on each other and therefore cannot be executed in parallel. Since for C2X scenarios, the channel is unreliable and group participants are highly dynamic, different rounds would need synchronization among participants, to ensure that exchanged messages are received appropriately (see Section 5.5.5). Hence, for the purpose of C2X communication a low number of rounds is clearly anticipated. By defining such a metric, one can give an analytical measure on the a priori communication delay for each protocol.

2. **Total number of messages**
   The total number of messages, exchanged inside the network during the group establishment, represents a further indicator for the effectiveness of a certain group protocol regarding bandwidth consumption. In this thesis, the performed analysis is further detailed by dividing the exchanged messages into the messages a participant has to send and to receive, respectively. Note that for reasons of comparison, zero message loss is assumed for every analyzed protocol. Obviously, in real world scenarios, this is not the case, since the C2X channel is rather unreliable and consequently messages have to be repeated several times. For implementation some redundancy and synchronization messages need to be exchanged additionally, like described in Chapter 5.5.5. However, these effects apply to all protocols similarly and therefore can be fairly omitted for this type of comparison.

3. **Computational complexity**
   The third applied measure acquires the computational complexity in terms of cryptographic operations performed by every vehicle. Note that computational complexity plays a significant role in the vehicular domain, since computational resources repre-

	INGE-MARSSON ET AL.	BUR-MESTER/ DESMEDT	STEINER ET AL.	C2CGE.1	C2CGE.2
Rounds	$N-1$	2	N	1	2
Total number of messages	$N \cdot (N-1)$	$2N$	N	N	$N+1$
Messages sent for each M_i	$(N-1)$	2	1	1	2 for $i=1$ 1 for $2 < i < N$
Messages to be received for each M_i	$(N-1)$	$N+1$	2 for $1 < i < N$ 1 for $i=1,N$	$N-1$	$N-1$ for $i=1,2$ $1+N-i$ for $2 < i < N$
Calculation complexity for each M_i	N exponentiations	$N+1$ exponentiations	$(i+1)$ for $i < N$ N for M_N	$N-1$ encryptions $+\ N-1$ decryptions	$2(N-1)$ for $i=$ $1,2$, $2+2(N-i) >$ for $2 < i < N$ exponentiations

Table 5.4: Group establishment protocol comparison

sent a cost driver and are therefore not available in all vehicle categories to the full extend.

A similar comparison of DH protocols may be also found in [131], [127] or [126], respectively. Additionally in this thesis, the comparison is further extended by the proposed privacy protocols in this thesis, i.e., C2CGE.1 and C2CGE.2. In the following the different approaches are discussed with their feasibility for the C2X scenario. Thereby, the total number of group participants is denoted by N and the i-th group member by M_i.

As already discussed in previous sections, the protocol proposed by *Ingemarsson et al.* [129] requires a relatively high number of rounds. A single round implies that every node simultaneously unicasts a message, leading to a significant amount of overall messages. Furthermore, because the communication ring has to be maintained during each round, this approach is considered as rather inappropriate for fault-prone environments like C2X networks.

Instead, *Burmester/Desmedt* [130] requires a constant number of 2 rounds for key establishment. Also the total number of exchanged messages scales only linear with the number of participants N. Compared to *Ingemarsson et al.*, the performed exponentiations are rather light-weighted, since for the final calculation step the order of the exponent is for every factor except one, smaller than $N-1$. Note that for *Ingemarson et al.* the exponent is always the (large) prime number k_i.

Although the proposed approach according to *Steiner et al.* [141] does not foresee a cyclic ring structure like *Ingemarsson et al.*, each communication step consists of a unicast message between two adjacent nodes. Accordingly, a certain node cannot continue the forwarding until it has received intermediate values from the predecessor node. It can be argued, that such a chain structure shows only little improvement compared to a ring structure, since any malfunctioning of intermediate nodes, could still add a significant delay to the overall key establishment. A significant advantage of *GDH.2* compared to previous protocols lies within the reduced channel load, caused by only $N-1$ unicasts followed by a single broadcast message. Due to the unicast nature of the protocol, nodes have to receive no more than 2 messages from other participants. The essential difference between C2CGE.2 (following the mathematical description of *Steer et al.* [100]) and *Steiner et al.* [141] lies within the reduced number of rounds. Although [141] requires one message less, every message, apart from one, are unicast messages which are dependent on each other (one message per round). Hence, a vehicle always has to wait for the previous message to be received, until it can sent a message on its own. In both proposed protocols, i.e., C2CGE.1 as well as C2CGE.2, all messages are entirely broadcast messages.

One might argue that on MAC layer, a unicast message is not at all different from a broadcast message, since the wireless channel itself is a broadcast medium, transmitting one message per time only. However, from the viewpoint of the protocol throughput, this is only partly true. A more in depth analysis taking into account the CSMA channel arbitration scheme of 802.11p networks reveals, why a higher number of rounds represents such a drawback. The following argumentation has been prepared by the author of this thesis:

The 802.11p technology follows the p-persistent CSMA scheme provided by the 802.11 standard. Accordingly a *vehicle i* senses the channel until it becomes idle and then initiates sending with a certain probability p_i. In case the channel is busy, it performs a back off for a random period of time, until it tries to re-send again. A more detailed analysis on CSMA channel arbitration can be found in [142], [143].

Thus, for the receiver *vehicle j* the probability of successfully receiving a message from a particular *vehicle i* at the next available timeslot T_0 is

$$P(X_i = T_0) = P(Y = T_0) \cdot p_i \quad \forall i \in 1, 2, \ldots, N \quad i \neq j \tag{5.12}$$

where X_i represent the point in time the receiver *vehicle j* receives usable data from *vehicle i*. With the term *usable* data, messages are denoted, which are required on receiver side for protocol completion. In contrary, *unusable* data in the context of this protocol represents all other safety related message content which is permanently sent during protocol execution. Note again, that the entire protocol is executed on top of frequently sent CAM safety messages. The term $P(Y = T_0)$ models the summed up probability for successful transmission without collisions at timeslot T_0 and depends upon several parameters like, e.g., the number of interferers, or the distance to the receiver.

For the approach according of *Steiner et al.* [141], this implies that a vehicle receives a particular unicast message in timely manner with the same probability denoted in Equation (5.12). Consequently with a probability of $1 - P(X_i = T_0)$, the receiver, and though the current protocol round, is temporary suspended for at least the duration of timeslot T_0.

In comparison, the C2CGE.1 and C2CGE.2 protocols do not require any sequential ordering of message arrivals. Though, messages received from *any* group member during the broadcast phase represent usable data for the receiver. Consequently, the probability for receiving usable data at a particular timeslot T_0 is greater for C2CGE.1 and C2CGE.2 than for the approach according to *Steiner et al.*:

$$P(\bigcup_{\substack{k=1 \\ k \neq j}}^{N} X_k) = \sum_{\substack{k=1 \\ k \neq j}}^{N} P(X_k) > P(X_i) \tag{5.13}$$

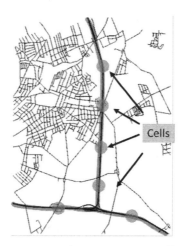

Figure 5.23: Exemplary motorway interchange scenario near Berlin, Germany

In conclusion, the likelihood for delay due to channel arbitration is greater for protocols with a high number of rounds. With respect to the previous analysis, it can be further concluded that C2CGE.1 is most appropriate for decentralized group establishment in Car-to-X communication due to its minimum number of rounds and low number of exchanged messages.

5.8.3 Simulation Setup

For the simulation of the proposed group privacy protocol, VSimRTI (V2X Simulation Runtime Infrastructure) is used, which is a flexible and light weight framework for dynamically simulating Car-to-X communication scenarios. VSimRTI enables the coupling of different simulators for simulating traffic, wireless communication as well as respective C2X applications. Some of the most common simulators are already coupled: SUMO [144] for traffic simulation and JiST/SWANS [145] for wireless communication simulations.

As an exemplary scenario, in this thesis a motorway interchange with three lanes in the area around Berlin is selected. In Figure 5.23 the related SUMO road network is illustrated and relevant road segments as well as possible cell locations are highlighted.

For the performed analysis, the protocol behavior is studied with respect to three different vehicle densities as classified by FGSV — the German research agency for roads and transport [146] (see Table 5.5).

For this evaluation, three different vehicle types with velocities of 80 km/h, 110 km/h, and 130 km/h are defined. These values represent the maximum speed a vehicle tends to drive if traffic conditions are suitable. All three vehicle types are equally likely to occur during the simulation. Vehicles are entering the scenario at a single point and then are adapting their driving behavior according to the traffic situation, e.g., they are keeping a safe distance from the vehicle ahead and are overtaking other vehicles if the fast lane is free.

Vehicle Density	Class
< 16 vehicles/km	low traffic density
16 − 32 vehicles/km	medium traffic density
32 − 45 vehicles/km	high traffic density

Table 5.5: Vehicle density classes

5.8.4 Temporal Behavior Evaluation

The entire protocol has been implemented as specified in previous sections with an initial setting of the group lifetime of about 10 seconds. Simulations of the privacy protocol have been performed at a medium traffic densities for three different cell distances, namely 1900 m (see Figure 5.24), 2600 m (see Figure 5.25), and 3200 m (see Figure 5.26). Within those diagrams, the following data is illustrated over time:

- **Generating Group Members**: This graph indicates how many vehicles are located in the cell during the starting time and are creating the group key. The number of generating vehicles is increased every time, one of the initial group members has received all necessary fragments and can start generating the group key. Based on the shape of this curve the duration of the group establishment process can be determined.

- **Joining Vehicles**: This curve shows how many vehicles are joining the group over time via the presented join protocol.

- **Disjoining Vehicles**: Vehicles spontaneously may leave the group because of the previously stated reasons. In this thesis the point in time is measured when a vehicle stops sending messages, authenticated with the group key and switches over to an own unused pseudonym.

- **Group Size**: This curve indicates the actual group size and includes all vehicles, which are currently sending anonymized messages using the group key. Together with the curves for *joins* and *disjoins* this curve essentially provides information on how stable the group formation is.

In Figure 5.24 the averaged observations of the first simulations for a cell separation of 1900 m are summarized. Accordingly, in this simulation it takes less than 1 second for the initial group members to exchange all key fragments and to create the group key. Note that the first vehicle has already generated the group key after 0.5 seconds. This short time period enables this vehicle to already reply to join requests of non-members, while other group members are still collecting key fragments. This explains the strongly increasing number of *joins* right after the group establishment phase ($d_{setup} = 1$ second). With respect to interoperability issues, this represents a desirable effect. After 2 seconds the first group members are coming into contact with another group and are disjoining the group according to the previously described protocol for group interference. From then on the entire group remains stable at a group size of about 15 vehicles until finally it is dissolved again. As a conclusion, it can be observed, that for a medium vehicle density of 23 vehicles/km and a cell separation of 1900 m the group reaches its maximum size after 2 seconds. This time interval therefore indicates the recommended *minimum group lifetime* d_{min} a group has to be maintained on that road segment.

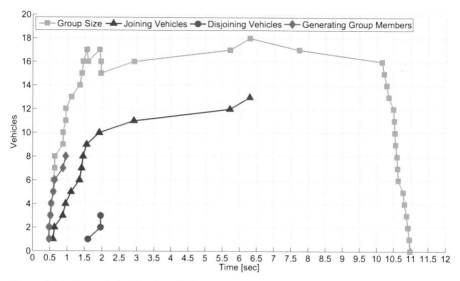

Figure 5.24: Group behavior for cell distances of 1900 m

The curves depicted in Figure 5.25 and Figure 5.26 reflect the averaged measurements taken for a *Cell-Distance* of 2600 m and 3200 m, respectively. As expected, the minimum group lifetime increases for larger cell distances. For a *Cell-Distance* of 2600 m a group lifetime d_{min} of 3 seconds, and for 3200 m a lifetime of 6 seconds is required, respectively.

Based on the previous observations the results are summarized as follows:

- The initial group establishment process is completed within a timeframe of 1 second. The duration varies only slightly for different vehicle densities
- With increasing cell distances the total number of group members is increased while the number of early disjoins is decreased.
- Vehicle densities and cell distances have the greatest impact on the minimum group lifetime. In order to include a maximum number of vehicles into the group, more join operations have to be performed.

The presented simulations give an indication on the *minimum group lifetime*. In the following, the protocol is evaluated for finding appropriate group lifetimes for which the obfuscation of an adversary has become high enough such that tracking is impeded.

5.8.5 Privacy Evaluation

In this section, the anonymity provided by the proposed privacy protocol is evaluated at the presence of an adversary. Based on the insights obtained from the performed simulations, the *recommended group lifetime* is defined with respect to the actual traffic density for a given cell distance.

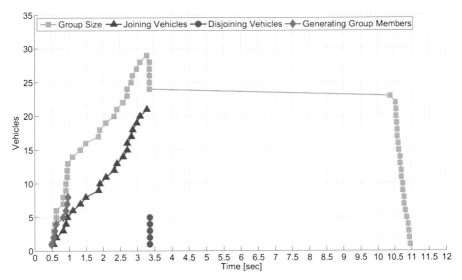

Figure 5.25: Group behavior for cell distances of 2600 m

Attacker Model

The applied attacker model is based on a global passive adversary, which has access to all exchanged messages within the network and is trying to reassemble the traces of observed vehicles. In order to resolve pseudonym changes and to track a vehicle during the group phase, a Kalman-filter based tracking system, as introduced in Section 4.3.1 is exploited. As depicted in the scheme in Figure 5.27, the adversary evaluates the CAMs serially as they are communicated over the channel. Note that the simulator framework VSimRTI in its present version does not model any GPS error, i.e., the transmitted position information within messages represents the exact positions of the vehicle. Hence, in order to make the simulations more realistic, random, normally distributed noise is added in the range of 3-5 meters to every position.

Each group is identifiable via the common *group ID*, which replaces the *vehicle ID* during the group lifetime. For every vehicle under observation, the adversary instantiates and maintains a tracker. A tracker includes several attributes like (1) the path history of the respective vehicle, (2) a Kalman filter object to predict the future mobility state, and (3) a *tracker ID* which represents the last used ID of that vehicle. The success of tracking depends upon the adversary's capability to match two subsequent messages to the correct vehicle in each of the following four scenarios:

1. The first scenario represents the most common case, in which the received message includes an already known vehicle identifier. The adversary simply selects the appropriate tracker, adds the new mobility data to his records, and continues with the evaluation of the next message ($A1 \rightarrow A2$).

2. Slightly more complicated is a scenario, where the adversary receives a message with an unknown vehicle ID. In this case the entire tracker list is iterated. If for any

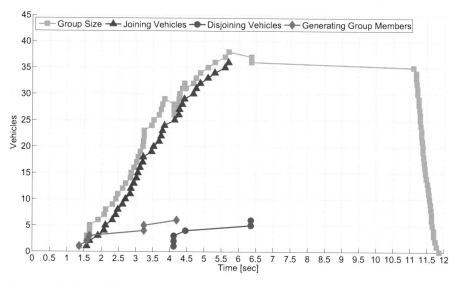

Figure 5.26: Group behavior for cell distances of 3200 m

candidate the maximum deviation between predicted and received mobility data lies within physically acceptable margins, a simple pseudonym change is supposed to be detected. Note that due to GPS errors and inevitable systematical inaccuracies in the prediction model, the matching might contain errors, i.e., the adversary accidentally may assign the message to the wrong vehicle. If a matching candidate has been found, then the adversary updates the vehicle ID of the respective tracker and adds the new mobility data ($A3 \rightarrow A4$).

3. In case a group has already been established, all messages of the group will contain an unique group identifier. Thus, like in the previous scenario, messages cannot be related to vehicles directly. Since the message originator might be any group member, the adversary has to find among all group members the one that is most likely to fit that mobility data ($A3 \rightarrow A4$). In comparison to a simple pseudonym change, the adversary has to perform the matching for every received message, which increases the likelihood of matching errors.

4. If for the previous cases 2 and 3 no matching candidate could be found, then the adversary assumes a new vehicle entering the observation area and consequently instantiates a new tracker ($A3 \rightarrow A5$).

The applied attacker model is monitored by an additional function, which has the knowledge on the true identity of all vehicles. This function is for evaluation purpose only, and detects any matching error performed by the attacker.

Privacy Metric and Evaluation

Sampigethaya et al. [108], [109] apply *maximum tracking time* to evaluate the location privacy of vehicles. In the context of this thesis, this metric is taken and further adapted

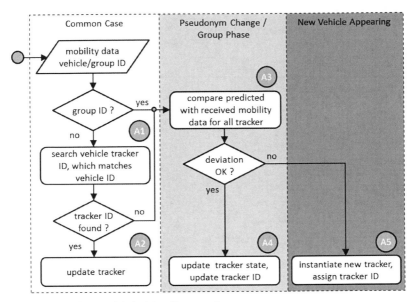

Figure 5.27: Attacker model decision flow graph

to measure the linkability for groups. Assuming a group of vehicles, whose messages are observed by an adversary, it is measured at which point in time, a certain percentage of group members is assigned to incorrect mobility data.

Simulations have been carried out with varying vehicle densities of 14, 23, and 45 vehicles/km, respectively. For each density situation, simulations were run to calculate the average tracking time. The cell distance is set to 2600 m. For reasons of comparability also the pseudonymization strategy based on simple pseudonym changes, like the one deployed within the sim^{TD} field trial [29], [9] has been evaluated, too. In order to make this approach even more effective, the pseudonym update interval is reduced to 10 seconds. Furthermore, it is assumed that all vehicles perform the pseudonym change at exactly the same point of time.

From the graph shown in Figure 5.28 it can be observed that despite the high change frequency and synchronization the adversary looses very few vehicle traces only. Hence, the performed experiments confirm the results obtained in *Wiedersheim et al.* [107]: A simple pseudonym change provides only a low level of privacy protection towards a global adversary.

The other three graphs in Figure 5.28 depict the tracking avoidance success for the proposed privacy protocol, which depends on the group lifetime. Please note that until the group has not reached a stable member size yet, the number of lost vehicles is superposed by those vehicles, which are still joining the group. Thus, in the interests of clarity, the graphs are plotted starting at the *Minimum Group Lifetime* of 3-4 seconds (see Figure 5.25 for Cell-Distances of 2600 m).

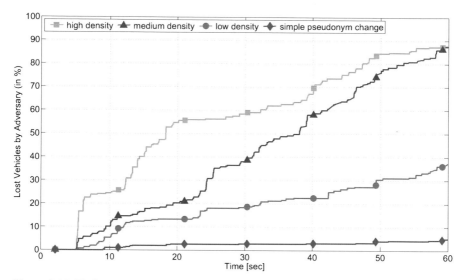

Figure 5.28: Evaluation of achieved privacy of group members

A significant drop of traceability can be observed already after the first 10-20 seconds. According to these observations, higher vehicle densities are more advantageous as the likelihood for a mismatching is being increased. For the highest vehicle density of 45 vehicles/km, almost every group member becomes anonymous within the simulation timeframe of just 60 seconds. For lower vehicle densities the obfuscation for adversaries is less significant, i.e., the group has to be maintained for a longer time period to obtain the same degree of anonymity for all group members.

However, since the complexity for group maintenance increases over time, a low overall group lifetime is generally anticipated. Consequently, a trade-off between group lifetime and overall group anonymity is envisaged. It can be argued that from statistics, the adversary only may know the overall tracking success in dependence of the vehicle density, but has no further knowledge upon which of his assembled traces are actually the correct ones. Consequently, in the following, it is assumed that for most adversaries an error rate of 50 % is already sufficient such that tracking is not worthwhile anymore.

Under these assumptions the *recommended group lifetime* d_{group} can be directly derived from the graphs in Figure 5.28 as follows:

High Vehicle Density	$d_{group} = 20$ seconds
Medium Vehicle Density	$d_{group} = 40$ seconds
Low Vehicle Density	$d_{group} > 60$ seconds

The parameters above, represent the recommended group life times for the presented motorway with a cell separation of 2600 m. These density-lifetime relations are group parameters and therefore assumed to be known by every vehicle. After group establishment, each group member constantly monitors the vehicle density via its internal Neighborhood Table and determines how long they have to stay inside the group to gain anonymity.

5.9 Conclusion

In this part of the thesis a novel approach for dynamic cryptographic Mix Zones based on group signatures has been proposed. A major aspect of the presented protocol is the decentralized group key generation using exchanged key fragments. Compared to state-of-the art centralistic approaches in C2X, a decentralized group establishment and maintenance reflects much more the cooperative nature of Car-to-X networks and avoids policy issues. A decentralized generation of the group key makes the success of a group establishment dependant on the participation of every group member. A participation of a vehicle in a group formation process is therefore considered as an implicit confirmation, that this vehicle beliefs in the trustworthiness of other group members. This property of the proposed protocol fulfills the objective for **decentralization** raised in Section 5.3.

For group establishment two possible protocols are proposed in this thesis: The first C2CGE.1 protocol is based on a confidential exchange of key fragments among all group members. Compared to other group keying protocols, this approach matches best with requirements for low latency and complexity of vehicular networks. As a further alternative, an existing n-party Diffie Hellman approach is transferred to the vehicular domain. The C2CGE.2 protocol is considered as secure, assuming the Discrete Logarithm problem is intractable. This approach gets along without the need for confidential message exchange, but results in slightly higher communication efforts. For the purpose of providing effective pseudonymization by means of the proposed privacy protocol, any of both presented group establishment protocols serve its task.

In order to achieve synchronization among all group members and in particular, to make the protocol robust against message losses, the concept of *MemberSet* variables and *VehicleReady* flags has been developed and included into the message format. This property of the proposed protocol fulfills the objective for **robustness**, raised in Section 5.3.

For group maintenance several sub protocols have been specified in order to dynamically integrate further vehicles into the group and to handle group interference with adjacent groups. The applied synchronization concepts have been verified for formal correctness by means of model checking techniques. This property of the proposed protocol fulfills the objective for **flexibility** raised in Section 5.3.

Analyzing the protocol timing yielded acceptable performance margins for group establishment. The low latency is mainly achieved by piggy-bagging the key fragments with frequently sent CAMs. This property of the proposed protocol fulfills the objective for **efficiency** raised in Section 5.3.

While being part of the group, all included vehicles sign messages instead of encrypting them. Certainly, encrypted messages have the advantage of reduced traceability as the message content is not readable by external adversaries. However, this also implies that CAM messages cannot be processed by adjacent trustworthy vehicles as long as they are not yet part of the group. Due to safety reasons this is not a preferable solution. Consequently all relevant protocol parameters are designed in a way that sufficient anonymity is provided without the need for encryption. For the same reasons of safety relevance the author of this thesis proposes to apply the group key only to CAMs and authenticate DENMs via one of the vehicles own certificates. DENMs are event-based messages and are assumed to be exchanged in scenarios where there is an urgent risk for road safety. In those cases highest priority for authenticated safety messages is considered, even if this implies to reveal the vehicles identity. So in case, a vehicle detects a hazardous situation it instantly leaves the group and switches over to the common asymmetric cryptography. This property of the proposed protocol fulfills the objective for **safety-preserving** communication raised in Section 5.3.

In order to enable lawful interception, every message is further authenticated using a symmetric CA key. This property of the proposed protocol fulfills the objective for **accountability** raised in Section 5.3.

In this thesis a powerful global adversary has been modeled and the gained privacy enhancements have been evaluated by means of simulations. The obtained results show that dynamic Mix Zones provide a significantly higher unlinkability compared to the basic pseudonym change approach. This property of the proposed protocol fulfills the objective for **privacy enhancements** raised in Section 5.3.

It can be concluded that dynamic decentralized Mix Zones represent a promising attempt for obfuscating pseudonym changes in vehicular networks.

One determining factor for effectiveness of this protocol represents the location of cells, as well as appropriate group lifetimes. A cell represents the root of the group from where the group is emerging in both directions of travel. Consequently cells have to be placed in road scenarios where vehicles follow a similar driving pattern and are expected to stay together during the group lifetime. This is the case especially for motorways and rural roads. For those scenarios, in this chapter it has been shown exemplary how simulations can be used to define those parameters in a way that the privacy protocol is supported appropriately. In order to further develop the respective protocols towards a real-world deployment more detailed evaluations by means of field operational trials will have to be carried out in the future.

6

Physical Layer Security: Secure Car-to-X Beamforming

From the previous parts of the theses, it can be already concluded that, with the exception of the *Access Technologies*, for every layer, security and privacy mechanisms have been found. Thus, to fully cover the ITS reference model as required by the standard and to further enhance the overal security of the C2X system, appropriate techniques have to be provided for the physical layer, too. This means, that privacy and security issues have to be ensured already during the sending and receiving of messages. Motivated by this lack of security within the C2X communication stack, in this part of the thesis, a novel physical protection technique called *Secure C2X Beamforming* is presented.

By means of radiation pattern control, vehicles are able to focus the transmitted energy towards a desired direction. In addition, beamforming techniques enable vehicles to improve signal reception of intended senders by rejecting those coming from unwanted directions. When applied appropriately, the adaptive beamforming method on the one hand reduces the reception of not trustable messages, and on the other hand it impedes message distribution into undesired regions. In doing so, both goals are reached at the same time: Secure C2X communication and enforced driver's privacy.

In the following, a brief history of the development of Secure C2X Beamforming in the context of this thesis is given. The basic idea for introducing radiation pattern control as a means for enhancing security and privacy in C2X communication has been presented first by *Stübing et al.* in [19]. Based on this prior work, the author of this thesis has specified an antenna system, which is modeled by two orthogonal antenna arrays and satisfies requirements of all safety relevant C2X use cases. Due to its novelty and the appropriateness of this approach, the underlying process as well as the antenna structure itself have also been filed as a patent application [147].

From the experiences made during the development of this antenna system, a generalized design flow has been derived in *Stübing et al.* [20]. Carried out design steps are presented and related simulation tools have been developed in *Stübing et al.* [21]. Within *Stübing et al.* [22], the antenna array has been applied to a representative case study.

As a further case study, the basic idea behind Secure C2X Beamforming, has been transferred to the C2X antenna system of the sim^{TD} field trial. In *Stübing et al.* [23], [24], proposals for architectural integration are given and a beamforming algorithm is defined.

These implementation aspects are considered of high relevance to automobile manufacturers for later deployment and therefore have been patented in Germany [148] and in the U.S. [149]. Furthermore, this part of the thesis also provides a novel metric for assessing the security level of different antenna patterns.

The sections of this part of the thesis are structured as follows: First, a motivation for the general potential of physical layer security in C2X communication is given in Section 6.1. In Section 6.2 some fundamentals regarding the C2X channel allocation are recalled. Related work is presented in terms of existing C2X antenna structures and physical security concepts, known from other domains than C2X. In Section 6.3 the advocated C2X Secure Beamforming design flow is outline, which sets the framework for the proceeding sections. Accordingly, in Section 6.4 and Section 6.5, two case studies with respect to that design flow are presented. The major design step consists of an evaluation of these case studies, according to a novel security metric, presented in Section 6.6. The last Section 6.7, concludes the results.

6.1 Motivation

The approach proposed in this part of the thesis is motivated by the intention to provide an enhancement to conventional methods based on cryptography and message content verification as presented in previous chapters. The idea is not just to secure the exchanged data directly, but to restrict the medium, on which an attacker can operate. In *wired-based* communication this property is inherently ensured, i.e., in order to get access to the communication data, an attacker has to physically connect to the wire. The technical difficulty associated with such an access sometimes already creates a serious barrier for many adversaries. In contrast, *wireless* C2X communication does not provide this physical barrier: An attacker may simply get access by placing his C2X communication unit anywhere in the vehicle's communication range. In C2X communication, transmission ranges up to several hundreds of meters become possible, which facilitates eavesdropping and injecting of faked messages within this field without the need of sophisticated intrusion methods. Thus, a technique is desired that enables a spatial filtering and physically excludes as many adversaries as possible from the wireless communication. Physical layer security is basically motivated by three different objectives that may be achieved at the same time: Besides privacy and security, which are the main focus of this thesis, also the channel congestion is subject to enhancement.

6.1.1 Congestion Avoidance

Currently running field operational tests, like sim^{TD} or DriveC2X, entirely rely on single pole antennas. These antennas possess a rather omnidirectional radiation pattern, distributing information into all directions uniformly. Unlike mobile cell phone communication, where such antennas are commonly used, the intended receivers in C2X communication are not arbitrarily located inside the transmission area. Vehicles always move on predefined roads and in most cases the sender is located even on the same road. Thus, a broadcast in the sense of C2X is always geographically restricted, i.e., directed to intended receivers that are located on the same road or highway. Existing C2X antenna systems do not take this fact into account. Because of their circular radiation pattern, messages sent by vehicles located on one road are also received by vehicles located on other roads.

(a) without Secure C2X Beamforming   (b) with Secure C2X Beamforming

Figure 6.1: Attacker exclusion via radiation pattern control

While being cost-effective and easily implementable, such antennas are highly dissipative concerning channel usage. Several dry-runs yielded that with a large number of vehicles on the road using an uniform radiation pattern, the channel becomes quickly congested. A particular problem may thereby arise from an excessive forwarding of DENM messages in scenarios, where several vehicles detect and broadcast the same event, like, e.g., in case of a traffic jam. In the C2X communication domain this phenomenon is colloquially referred to as the *DENM storm* problem. Currently, forwarding algorithms for C2X are being improved, to cope with such effects. In this thesis, however, novel techniques based on adaptive beamforming are presented, which intent to reduce the dispensable occupation of channel bandwidth in regions where the message shall not be distributed.

6.1.2 Privacy Enhancements

However, an omnidirectional characteristic has disadvantages not only for channel capacity reasons. Such a pattern furthermore allows adversaries to operate quite far away from the road side. This favors fundamentally the most likely attacker type, assumed in this thesis, i.e., the script kiddies. As outlined in Section 3.1.1, this kind of attacker is usually located several meters away from the road, e.g., in a residential area as depicted in Figure 6.1a.

In *Stübing et al.* [19], the author of this thesis has analyzed for the first time, that for almost all use cases, the message destinations are never omnidirectional. In fact, a message generally possesses a geographical validity, i.e., the message is either relevant for vehicles located to the front, to the rear or to the side, in case of a RSU connection. By mapping the radiation pattern for a message to its geographical validity, an attacker on the road side, as illustrated in Figure 6.1b, will have to put much more effort into his antenna system to still receive the message with a sufficient power level. The concept of Secure C2X Beamforming, which is presented in Sections 6.4 and 6.5 is thereby following the general principle of data avoidance and data economy, as demanded by European Privacy Commissionars.

6.1.3 Security Enhancements

Furthermore, adapting the antenna characteristic does not only apply for the sending of messages. Instead, a radiation pattern also defines which directions are to be focussed and which have to be suppressed in the receiving case. Jamming attacks, often performed by sending noisy signals at a high power lever, are easy to be launched and will directly cause a Denial-of-Service (DoS) of the communication channel. By orienting the receiving pattern towards relevant senders, leaving out the road sides, physical security particularly contributes to impeding attacks of radio interference; a serious class of threats. Such threats cannot be adequately addressed via conventional cryptography.

In *Xu et al.* [150] the wide of range of different jamming attack strategies is categorized into four models with respect to the effectiveness in interfering the wireless communication. According to [150], a *constant* jammer continuously emits a radio signal, which blocks the channel and prevents other stations from sending. The *deceptive* type of jammer pretends to be a regular station by jamming the channel with correctly encoded packets. These packets will be processed by the receiver, causing this station to remain in the receiving state. In contrast, a *random* jammer only sporadically performs attacks and then returns into a sleep mode again. The fourth category includes the *reactive* jammer. Instead of preventing others from sending, this jammer is targeting the successful reception of messages. Hence, it remains silent as long as there is no activity on the channel. If a station starts sending, the jammer does the same, which causes a packet collision on the channel. These types of jammers are considered as most critical, since they are much harder to detect. In this thesis, the reactive jammer is taken as reference.

For coping with reactive jamming attacks, in this thesis, a two folded approach is aspired. First, if technically feasible, the attacker shall not be noticed about the sending of packets from other stations. That way, the attacker receives no trigger for starting the jamming. Note that this objective is coherent with the motivation for privacy stated above. And, as a secondary objective: If an attacker is already jamming the channel, the effects on the C2X communication shall be reduced.

6.2 Related Work

As announced in Chapter 2, in this section, further background on the 802.11p physical layer is provided. Furthermore, the development state of currently available C2X antenna systems is summarized and further approaches from research are discussed briefly.

6.2.1 IEEE 802.11p

The IEEE 802.11p technology has its origins in the family of 802.11 standards and can be considered as a variant with several adjustments in order to fit to the vehicular domain. Most parameters like number of carriers and the modulation formats are taken directly from 802.11a. One major adjustment was to reduce the channel width from 20 MHz to 10 MHz. By doing so, only half the data rate compared to a 802.11a channel can be achieved, since each symbol becomes twice as long. For the broadcast nature of C2X Communications, however, lower data rates are preferable due to better robustness to the *BER (Bit Error Rate)* [151]. Furthermore, a lower channel width is more advantageous because of higher tolerances to multipath environments, which are likely to occur in urban environments.

Figure 6.2: European frequency allocation for Car-to-X communication

Though, a maximum of 27 Mbit/s may be achieved in principle, for safety applications the default data rate is even further reduced to 6 Mbit/s.

For safety related communication in ITS, the European Commission has decided to allocate the radio spectrum of 30 MHz in the 5875 — 5905 MHz frequency band (ITS G5A). According to the European Profile as specified by ETSI, this frequency band is divided into three channels with 10 MHz each [152]. As depicted in Figure 6.2, the lower two channels are denoted as *Service Channel 1* (SCH1) and *Service Channel 2* (SCH2), whereas the upper channel is called *Control Channel* (CCH).

Apart from the frequency allocation of the channels, the ETSI standards do not prescribe, how messages shall be assigned to each channel. Therefore, the C2C-CC is currently engaged in harmonizing the usage of these three channels. Whereas earlier discussions have centered on the usage of all three channels equally for message transmission [151], recent considerations tend to introduce a further channel seperation by leaving SCH2 unused [153]. As a proposal, the channel CCH and SCH1 are used for single and multihop communication, respectively. Hence, all single hop messages defined in Section 2.2 are going to be transmitted via the CCH. Forwarded messages are either also transmitted via the CCH, in case of a low channel load. Or, if the CCH is already congested, the station switches to the service channel SCH1, for load balancing reasons. The upper bound on the maximum antenna *EIRP (Equivalent Isotropically Radiated Power)* is defined by ETSI [152] to 33 dBm at any angular position. At the receiver side the sensitivity shall not fall below a minimum of -82 dBm. Both, the transmit power and the sensitivity shall be adjustable in steps of $0, 5$ dBm.

6.2.2 Car-to-X Antenna System Design

Within the *Working Group Communications (WG COM)* of the C2C-CC a task force has been created with the purpose of defining minimum requirements for the C2X antenna design [154]. Starting point for the link budget computation is the safety distance between two vehicles, required to stop the vehicle in case of an emergency brake. Assuming a certain path loss and the minimum specified sensitivity at the receiver (-82 dBm), the required gain, necessary to correctly receive the signal at the given distance has been determined exemplary for highway and urban intersection scenarios. Note that the C2C-CC does not recommend a particular antenna design nor does it prescribe the exact pattern of the radiation field, in order to achieve the stated requirements. This task is clearly up to C2X system developers and is not subject to joint harmonization activities.

Compared to early C2X dry-runs, recently a fundamental shift is being observable: away from antenna designs, which produce omnidirectional patterns, towards more directive radiation patterns, which are tailored to better match the actual C2X requirements. For instance, in *Emmelmann et al.* [155] (pp. 47-48) generally an elliptical or cigar-shaped beam is anticipated, for increasing the range in forward and reverse directions. The invention claims stated in [156] go into similar directions and advocate an elliptical radiation pattern, which additionally may be controlled in range by adjusting the transmission power. As relevant parameters for power control, the speed of the host vehicle and the number of neighbors in communication range are considered. Instead of a having a forward and backward beam, in [157] a method is claimed for controlling the orientation of a single main lobe in dependency on the driving direction.

In *Navda et al.* [158] [159], an off-the-shelf array antenna system has been deployed, which operates at 2.4 GHz and consists of eight elements placed in a circular arrangement. This antenna offers a great variability of different beams, which may be switched via software at a low latency. Experiments have been conducted to measure the obtained connectivity between vehicles and between vehicles and RSUs, respectively. Promising improvements in the *SNR (Signal-to-Noise Ratio)* up to 15 dB, relative to an omni-directional pattern have been measured. The results presented in [158] and [159] give further motivation to investigate in more sophisticated approaches towards a beamforming for Car-to-X communication. While *Navda et al.* have primarily focused on point-to-point beamforming between two stations, in this thesis, a more generalized approach for *all* possible C2X communication types is introduced.

Besides different antenna steering concepts, also first dedicated radios, designed for the G5A band become more and more available. Automotive suppliers, like, e.g., in *B. Gallagher* [160] have developed an antenna system, which features an oval coverage pattern with a reduced gain at the broadside of the vehicle. It could be shown through direct experimentation that such an antenna system has the potential of suppressing noise introduced by a jamming station located on the roadside. These results are particularly promising for the secure beamforming concept proposed in this thesis, since it effectively demonstrates by means of real world tests, that indeed, a sophisticated antenna design has the potential to increase robustness towards jamming attacks.

According to experts in the field, in the near future up to 20 different antenna types for different communications might be integrated into automobiles [161]. It seems likely, that most antennas, including the 802.11p antenna, will be integrated into a *shark-fin* housing on the roof of the car. In terms of manufacturing and level of integration, the antenna developed in the sim^{TD} field trial approximates best a near-series production. As outlined in Section 2.1.1, the sim^{TD} system already includes three different communication technologies, i.e., 802.11p, 802.11 b/g and cellular communication. Together with GPS, a total number of four different antenna structures are integrated into a single shark fin housing [35]. Due to its near-series alignment and profound integration into an existing C2X architecture, the sim^{TD} antenna system will be subject to further investigations in Section 6.5.

6.2.3 Physical Security with Antennas

Previously presented C2X antenna systems are mainly designed for enhancing the connectivity via directional sending and varying of the transmission power. According to the best of the author's knowledge, in this thesis, for the first time, beamforming is discussed as an approach for enhancing security and privacy in C2X networks.

In other communication domains, first approaches towards a limitation of the network access by means of beamforming have already been discussed. For instance, in [162] a method is claimed, which obstructs eavesdropping within today's home WLAN networks. Accordingly, if one WLAN-equipped station (like, e.g., PC, printer, or telephone) within the network intends to communicate to a second one, it forms a narrow beam, directed to the receiving station, only. Range control is realized by the receiver station, in reporting back whether the transmitting station shall increase the transmission power, or not.

In *Lakshmanan et al.* [163], besides directional sending, additional measures are advocated, by which different stations may cooperatively exclude an attacker from the network. Several techniques are described: *Secret Sharing* refers to a technique, used to establish a common secret among trustworthy stations. The WLAN access points are thereby pointing their beams exactly to the client postion to transmit their share of the secret information. Due to the spatially disjoint nature of the transmission, an adversary will only be able to receive some, but never all required message fragments. By means of *Information Overloading* an adversary is selectively jammed by other stations, while the intended receiver station is remained unaffected.

Presented solutions are promising for the given domains, but are only to a limited extend transferable to the C2X scenario. While [162] focuses on stationary point-to-point communication only, approaches proposed in [163] are not feasible at all, due to the broadcast nature of C2X communication.

Other approaches for secure communication using multiple antennas are based on the *secrecy capacity* of a communication channel. The term secrecy capacity originally goes back to the work done by *C. Shannon* [164] and *A. Wyner* [165], denoting a technique to communicate a confidential message between two stations in a way that a third malicious observer cannot decode the message. This approach is based on an information-theoretic view of secure communication and makes use of the different channel characteristics between each sender/receiver pair by using appropriated channel coding techniques. In particular, if the adversary's channel is degraded, the trustworthy station may increase the data rate beyond the maximum rate at which the adversary is unable to decode exchanged messages. For interested readers, recent works on this topic can be found in, e.g., in *Jeong et al.* [166] and *Li et al.* [167]. Though, the idea of using the secrecy capacity of a channel seems very interesting in general, this approach is not technical feasible for the purpose of broadcasting CAMs to a multitude of vehicles.

From the previous review of related work, it can be concluded that addressing security by means of beamforming methods may be considered as a promising novel field of research. Up to now only few, if any, solutions specific to the C2X domain have been proposed.

6.3 Secure Car-to-X Beamforming Design Flow

Secure Car-to-X Beamforming represents one of the first attempts to ensure security and privacy in C2X communication directly on the physical layer. Instead of using a single omnidirectional antenna, an assembly is selected, which enables beamforming. By this means, the advocated approach allows adjusting the transmission and reception pattern of a vehicle, which is essential for excluding undesired communication parties, trying to eavdrop exchanged messages or to distribute corrupted information (see Figure 6.1).

Currently available C2X antennas are mainly designed towards an omnidirectional coverage of the radiation pattern in the ϕ-plane. Main challenges to overcome are thereby distortions of the radiation field due to the car body shape and disadvantageous mounting positions of antennas on the rear rooftop of the car [168]. In particular for the 5.9 GHz band, observed degradations of gain caused by roof racks and panorama glass roofs are challenging [169]. In order to study these effects, and to develop respective solutions, appropriate methodologies and powerful simulation tools, like, e.g., CST Microwave Studio [170] are available for this purpose.

However, due to the novelty of Secure C2X Beamforming approach, adequate design methodologies and tools are still missing, which are aimed to support C2X system designers in specifying antenna systems, under security and privacy considerations. Therefore, in the following, a simulation-based design flow is proposed, which is aimed for defining and evaluating Secure C2X Beamforming algorithms with respect to Car-to-X security and privacy requirements. In the context of Secure C2X Beamforming, the term *algorithm* denotes a procedure for adapting the radiation pattern via an adjustment of antenna parameters (e.g., phasing, element biasing, or transmission power) depending on the observed C2X scenario (e.g., attacker position, host vehicle velocity, or message type)[1].

In order to support and deploy the advocated design flow, in Section 6.3.2 a dedicated simulator is presented, which calculates field patterns and visualizes them according to a traffic situation model and on designer settings. Based on the visual simulation results the beamforming algorithm is defined and evaluated for effectiveness by means of a complementary evaluation tool.

6.3.1 Design Flow

In this section, the advocated design flow for developing a Secure C2X Beamforming algorithm is presented. Following a top down approach, the designer starts with a definition of the application requirements (see Figure 6.3). Given a certain antenna pattern model, different radiation patterns and traffic scenarios are explored. The designer evaluates the simulation results and refines the simulation settings, until an acceptable beamforming is reached. In the final design step, the resulting beamforming algorithm is evaluated for security and privacy enhancements by means of dedicated metrics.

In more details, the following steps will be presented:

1. **Defining the C2X Use Case and Application Requirements**: As a first step a requirement analysis of all applications is performed, whose messages are going to be affected by the beamforming. At this design step, a broad description of requirements is sufficient. The messages exchanged within a use case are generally characterized by a geographical direction. In order to send a message to a RSU, for instance, the beam has to be directed to the roadside. On the contrary, a warning message to other cars causes directing the beam rearwards. Within this design step the area is defined, which has to be covered by the radiation pattern depending on the use case. Hence,

---

[1]In comparison, the often used term *MAC protocol* usually describes methods for different stations to coordinate access to a common channel (e.g., CSMA, TDMA, etc.). The author introduces the novel term of *beamforming algorithm* to emphasize that the advocated approach affects the radiation pattern and power of the antenna. Hence, the CSMA access scheme of 802.11p is not affected.

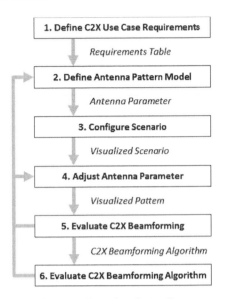

Figure 6.3: Secure C2X Beamforming algorithm design flow

this first design step results into a table, stating in plaintext the required directions of sending for each relevant use case. Note that in a later step of the design flow these rather coarse grained sending directions (e.g., front, rear, sideways) are transferred into more formalized requirements for security evaluation purposes.

2. **Defining an Antenna Pattern Model**: For the purpose of secure C2X beamforming, the antenna pattern in the horizontal- (ϕ-) plan is of further interest. Therefore, the designer has to specify an antenna pattern model that describes how the radiation pattern is formed, depending on a set of antenna parameters, adjustable by the designer. The model may either consist of a mathematical description in terms of formulas, which would allow a direct calculation of the resulting field. Or, instead, every possible pattern may be given in a graphical representation and a look-up table defining which pattern is chosen, given a set of input parameters. In this thesis, both modeling variants are explored by means of two different case studies presented in Section 6.4 and Section 6.5,respectively.

3. **Configuring the scenario**: A primary objective of the simulation flow is to adjust the antenna pattern with respect to a given scenario. The scenario is defined by the designer and is characterized by the following parameters:

   a) Road Map: Out of a database, the designer selects a road map of interest. The road map consists of real world highway and rural roads.

   b) Traffic Situation Model: In order to evaluate the antenna pattern model under different traffic conditions, the designer may adjust the vehicle density, accordingly.

c) Attacker Model: Two attacker models are supported: A static attacker model, which assumes that the attacker operates from the roadside. A more advanced model assumes that the attacker operates out of a vehicle driving on the road.

4. **Adjusting the Antenna Parameter**: The designer assesses the antenna pattern model by setting the antenna parameter (e.g., biasing, phasing, transmission power). Generally, it is recommended, to select an appropriate beamforming in a way that minimum area is covered and in contrary no safety relevant message gets lost. Note that for the case of a static attacker model, the designer explicitly has to exclude regions on the roadside where an attacker may be located.

5. **Evaluating C2X Beamforming**: For each configuration the designer compares the pattern generated by the simulator with the pattern required for the selected use case or application. In case of conformance, the corresponding configuration is recorded along with the use case for further simulations under different simulation conditions, e.g., for various traffic situation models or road maps. Otherwise, the designer repeats step 4 until an acceptable pattern is reached.

6. **Evaluating C2X Beamforming Algorithm**: As a result from previous design steps, a first version of the beamforming algorithm is obtained. Now, a more in depth security analysis of the algorithm is performed by means of dedicated beamforming metrics. A detailed description of the security analysis will be given in Section 6.6. Note that this last design step may also include a complete refinement of the antenna pattern model, in case the resulting metric values are not satisfactory to the designer.

In order to support the designer in applying the advocated design flow, two dedicated simulators have been developed, which are described in the following section.

6.3.2 Simulation and Evaluation Tool Chain

The simulation and evaluation environment consists of two separate tools. The first simulator incorporates functionalities for realizing design step 1-5, while the second evaluator allows a security and privacy evaluation, according to design step 6. Note that the deployed simulators, by no means, claim to provide a complete physical correctness of results. Instead, the applied visualization approach helps antenna designers to obtain a quick estimation of the appropriateness of their beamforming concept. In the following, a brief description of the simulator and evaluator is given. Further implementation details for both simulator architectures can be found in the student's work done by *S.Miglietta* [171] and *T.Ruppenthal* [172], supervised and instructed by the author of this thesis.

Simulator Architecture

In order to design a beamforming algorithm, a simulator has been developed, which works on the basis of MATLAB, a well-known simulation environment in the automotive domain. Many built-in routines for mathematical calculations in MATLAB were used to yield an efficient calculation of the antenna field. The developed software for calculating the appropriate antenna parameters is compatible with existing MATLAB/SIMULINK modules already used for C2X communication and read-access on the vehicle's CAN bus. This property is of importance for future implementations within a vehicle. Hence, for future work, the antenna pattern model and the visualizer may be replaced by a physical antenna, while

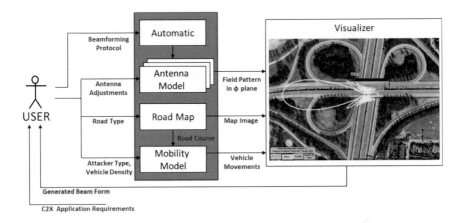

Figure 6.4: C2X Secure Beamforming simulator architecture

the MATLAB tools for antenna parameter calculation can be left unchanged. The only additional work to be done is connecting these MATLAB modules to the antennas driver interface. However, the drawback from exploiting MATLAB stems from the fact that this software offers a rather poor graphical engine, which slows down the simulator. Figure 6.4 depicts the general architecture of the C2X beamforming simulator. For clarity, the designer is included into the diagram to show its role in the simulation process. The simulator consists mainly of five modules, which are described in the following briefly.

Road Map For the utilization of realistic highway and rural roads, the *Road Map* module exploits *Google Earth*^{TM} maps. Currently, some highways in Germany are available in this simulation environment. Besides pure visualization purposes this module also provides the extracted road course to the Traffic Situation Model for simulating vehicle movements along the road.

Traffic Situation Model The *Traffic Situation Model* describes the vehicle movements on the roads with a vehicle density, as specified by the designer. The number of vehicles, their velocities, and their routes may either be chosen randomly, or in a controlled way directly by the designer. The latter case may be interesting for testing special traffic situations.

Antenna Pattern Model This module integrates the *Antenna Pattern Model*, including the related propagation model of the electromagnetic field as specified by the designer. In principle, no restrictions on the complexity of the model are made. However, in the context of this thesis, a basic modeling is applied. Hence, physical effects such as *refraction*, *reflection*, or *diffraction* of the emitted signals are not considered in the design so far. This is mainly due to missing models, which would allow an efficient calculation of these quite complex effects. Also state-of-the art network simulators like JiST/SWANS [145] rely on a simplified free space model for radio propagation, for similar reasons. Promising approaches for reducing computational complexity based on *ray tracing* algorithms are studied in *Moser et al.* [173], whereas an in-depth discussion of the topic can be found in the dissertation by *J. Maurer* [174].

Visualizer The Visualizer uses the road map data as a background picture. The host vehicles as well as other driving vehicles are displayed based on the data provided by the Traffic Situation Model. The graphical form of the current beams are generated based on the pattern produced by the Antenna Pattern Model. Vehicles driving within the host vehicles beam and, thus, having access to the sent message, are colored green. Other cars appear in red on the map. During simulation all antenna configuration parameters can be adjusted interactively. The corresponding beamforming can be immediately observed and evaluated according to predefined application requirements.

Automatic Mode Besides the described interactive mode, the simulator also provides an *automatic mode*. In this mode, the previously defined beamforming algorithm is executed, and the designer may once more observe the final behavior of the algorithm in a dynamic environment.

Evaluator Architecture

The evaluator is a stand-alone tool written in Java and possesses a similar architecture as the previously described simulator tool. Hence, a map component may be used to read in satellite images and visualize them on the screen. Instead of randomly generated vehicle movements, the designer explicitly defines scenarios on his own, by placing common vehicles and attackers with static positions directly on the map. A scenario design also includes the placement of the host vehicle, for which the beamforming is performed. Different scenarios under test may be stored in a database for later re-use.

The beamforming algorithm, running on the host vehicle's C2X communication unit, is subject of evaluation. For the purpose of modeling, the evaluator directly emulates the vehicle's internal software architecture as outlined in Section 6.5.3. Different Java libraries are offered for interfacing all relevant components inside a vehicle, which deliver the required information to the beamforming process. Among others, these are the vehicle's CAN bus for accessing data like, e.g., velocity or steering angle; the Neighborhood Table to assess positions of possible receivers; or the *Security Module*, to obtain information about suspicious stations. The emulator iterates all entries of the scenario database and evaluates the beamforming performance with respect to security metrics as specified in the following Section 6.6.

6.4 Secure C2X Beamforming Algorithm I: Antenna Array

The first case study, presented in this thesis, is related to the definition of an antenna aperture and beamforming algorithm, which matches the requirements of C2X applications defined in Section 2.2. As antenna model, an antenna array is defined, which offers a great variability of different beams. It is shown, how the simulator is employed to obtain the required patterns and to determine the respective antenna configurations. The most challenging use cases for beamforming, are those related to the initial sending and forwarding of DENMs. As an accompanying example, in this thesis, a situation-dependent beamforming algorithm is studied exemplary for the *Weather Hazard Warning* application.

Before going into detail of the first step of the design flow, i.e., the requirements analysis, the adversary model is examined: In this section, it is assumed that the adversary position is unknown, but may be restricted to the roadside [78]. Equipped with a common C2X antenna system, the adversary is trying to send corrupted data as well as to eavesdrop messages sent by passing vehicles. Based on this attacker model, the beamforming technique aims at directing both, the transmission and the reception patterns, in a way that only the intended receivers are covered and the roadsides are excluded. In contrary, due to the safety-relevance of sent messages, a restricted antenna pattern shall not impede the successful reception for intended trustworthy receivers. Note that although the defined patterns are valid for both, the transmission and the reception case, the analysis performed in this section is restricted to the transmission case for simplicity. The receiving case is subject of Section 6.4.3.

6.4.1 Use Case Requirements

The C2C-CC and ETSI have identified three different application categories, which are complemented with several use cases as summarized in Section 2.2. Ongoing field operational tests, such as sim^{TD} or DriveC2X use these scenarios as a reference. Considering the wide range of possible C2X applications and use cases, only a subset is related to messages, which are sent by the vehicle, and thus, are in the focus of this work. In Table 6.1 the *vehicle-centric* use cases are stated, along with stated requirements regarding the applied radiation pattern.

Use Case	Required Radiation Pattern
UC1: Emergency vehicle warning	Fore-beam on all lanes
UC2: Slow vehicle indication	Rear-beam and fore-beam on same road
UC3: Intersection collision warning	Rear-beam and fore-beam on same road
UC4: Motorcycle approaching indication	Rear-beam and fore-beam on same road
UC5: Emergency electronic brake lights	Rear-beam on same lane
UC6: Stationary vehicle	Rear-beam on same road
UC7: Traffic condition warning	Rear-beam on same road
UC8: Collision risk warning	Rear-beam and fore-beam on same road
UC9: Decentralized floating car data	Event Detection: Rear-beam and fore-beam on all roads. Event Forwarding: Rear-beam or fore-beam on same road

Table 6.1: Cooperative road safety: Use cases and required radiation patterns

Messages, which are indicating an approaching emergency vehicle (UC1) are highly relevant to all vehicles driving in front of it. Thus, these special cars should send their warning messages within a fore-beam, which covers a wide range. Even though ambulance cars on duty may have rather low privacy requirements, the situation is completely different for police cars. For them, the message dissemination shall be minimized in order not to give an advantage to criminal organizations, which might be able to track the trajectories of approaching police cars. Note that for similar reasons the unauthorized interception of conventional police radio is prohibited by law. The basic privacy scheme based on changing pseudonyms (see Section 3.4) is inefficient in this case. In fact, the physical restriction of the message distribution by means of beamforming represents the so far only approach to that issue.

Use Case	Required Radiation Pattern
UC10: Automatic access control and parking management	Narrow beam towards receiver position
UC11: ITS local electronic commerce	Narrow beam towards receiver position
UC12: Media downloading	Narrow beam towards receiver position

Table 6.2: Cooperative local services: Use cases and required radiation patterns

The use cases UC2-UC4 as well as UC8 are triggered via CAMs, which are regularly broadcasted by all the vehicles, to inform about their mobility status (see Table 2.1 in Section 2.2.1). As these messages are highly interesting for an adversary on the road side, they should be disseminated in narrow beams covering the same road only.

Messages signalizing an EEBL (UC5), are only relevant to vehicles on the same lane, located behind the sender. Thus, these messages should be sent in rear-beams, which are possibly as wide as the lane. The same applies for use case UC6 and UC7. However, for these use cases, the sent messages are relevant to *all* following vehicles on the same road.

Decentralized environmental notification messages (UC9) contain geographical information on safety-related events like, e.g., weather hazards or traffic jams and, thus, have a corresponding local validity. For their distribution, a differentiation has to be made between the detection and forwarding of an event. In case the host car is the originator of the warning message, all vehicles in proximity shall be noticed using a pattern, which covers all roads leading to that event. For the directed forwarding of DENMs by vehicles driving into the same direction, however, rear-beams are more adequate, which cover the road width.

For the second category of Cooperative Traffic Efficiency, exchanged messages are almost entirely directed from the infrastructure to the vehicle (see Table 2.2 in Section 2.2.2), and are therefore not in the primary scope of this thesis.

The third category may include confidential communication between a single vehicle and a RSU. UC10 - UC12 relate to the exchange of unicast messages, which demands dynamic beamforming with a high directivity (see Table 6.2).

The first conclusion that can be stated already is that apart from one use case, the required radiation pattern is never omnidirectional. In fact, message dissemination can be reduced to the area in front, behind or to the side of a vehicle.

6.4.2 Antenna Pattern Model

The assumed anntenna model is based on a linear antenna array with a variable antenna number, distance, and adjustable phasing. In the following, the basic theory behind antenna arrays is explained and possible parameters for adjusting the radiation pattern are identified. Then, the final antenna model is derived, which satisfies the requirements stated in the previous section.

Antenna Array Theory

An antenna array is an arrangement of single antenna elements, aimed to direct radiation energy to a desired area in contrast to a uniform distribution obtained when applying omnidirectional antennas. According to antenna theory, the far-field approximation for an array pattern is given by the pattern of an individual array element multiplied by the array factor AF [175] (pp.283-333):

$$ArrayPattern = ElementPattern \times AF \tag{6.1}$$

The array factor AF describes the resulting radiation field in the ϕ-plane and is a function of the geometry of the array and of the excitation (amplitude, phase) of its elements only. The pattern described by AF denotes the 3 dB drop of power, i.e, the distance from the sender, at which the signal has lost 50% of its power. For common C2X communication units, as deployed by the assumed attacker model, the 3 dB margin is considered as critical for correct reception of the signal. With N identical elements the normalized array factor is given as:

$$AF = \frac{1}{N} \left[\frac{\sin(\frac{N}{2}\psi)}{\sin(\frac{\psi}{2})} \right] \tag{6.2}$$

For a linear array, the *progressive angle* ψ is a function of the element separation d, the phase shift α between the elements, the wave number $k = \frac{2\pi}{\lambda}$, and the elevation angle θ:

$$\psi = \alpha + kd\cos\theta \tag{6.3}$$

Note that when choosing the distance d between two antenna elements as a multiple of the wavelength λ the expression $k \cdot d = \frac{2\pi}{\lambda} \cdot d$ becomes independent of the frequency, and so the overall array factor.

Antenna Model Specification

A linear antenna array may be phased, such that the main beam is formed either along (end-fire array) or normal to the array axis (broadside array). In C2X communication, on the one hand, a high flexibility is required in directing the main beam both, along the road to communicate with other cars, and normal to the road direction to communicate with road side units. On the other hand, grating lobes are highly undesired as they increase the system vulnerability. In order to combine these two requirements of high flexibility and directivity, the usage of two crossed antenna arrays is proposed, i.e., an X-array and a Y-array (see Figure 6.5). The following set of parameters may be adjusted in order to explore different pattern alternatives, achievable with that antenna model:

- Array type X or Y
- Number of elements of each array, N_x and N_y
- Element separation in each array, d_x and d_y
- Phase shift in each array, α_x and α_y
- Transmission Power P_x and P_y

Apparently, finding the optimal array form and configuration for each traffic and road situation is a non-trivial task. In the following, different beams are explored, which build the basis for the beamforming algorithm presented in subsequent sections.

A crucial system prerequisite for performing beamforming on ITS stations, is a communication system, which may perform *per packet* power control and *per packet* beamforming control. The latter term is introduced in this thesis, to denote the capability of a communication system for adjusting the antenna pattern for each C2X message individually. In

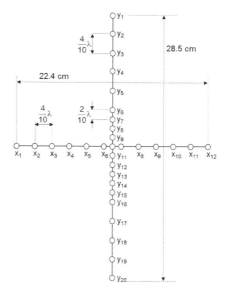

Figure 6.5: X-Y antenna array model

the context of this case study, the antenna parameters are set depending on the following scenario properties:

- The communication situation, i.e., the requirements of the currently sent message, as specified in Table 6.1 and Table 6.2 .

- The current traffic situation including geographical positions of all the vehicles in the specific communication range of about 600-1000 m.

- The current road properties such as curves and road widths.

The communication situation is selected by the designer, who adjusts the array configuration affecting the radiation pattern. Recall that the array configuration determines the array factor AF according to Equations (6.2) and (6.3).

Based on the data obtained from the Traffic Situation Model of the simulator in Figure 6.4, each vehicle sets up and maintains the Neighborhood Table, which contains current information on all the vehicles in the reception field. This information is used to determine the distance of two kind of vehicles: the vehicles driving in front of and behind the host vehicle, respectively. These distances are essential to determine the range of the generated fore-beam, rear-beam, or both depending on the use case. This range will later be used by a real-world implementation, to determine the transmission power, necessary to reach the intended receivers.

A major purpose of the Road Map module in Figure 6.4 is to consider the road course for the beamforming process. A static road-oriented fore- and rear- beam, for instance, would not serve its purpose when driving in a curve, as this beam is directed beyond the road. In particular, scenarios with sharp curves, like, e.g., motorway exits demand a dynamic

Use Case	Antenna Configuration				Example
	Array	**N**	**d**	**α**	
UC2-4,8	X	12	$4/10\lambda$	α_c	Fig. 6.6a, Fig. 6.6b
UC6-7,9	Y	15	$4/10\lambda$	207	Fig. 6.6c
UC5*	X	20	λ	5	-
UC1	Y	10	$2/10\lambda$	60	Fig. 6.6d
UC9	X	2	$4/10\lambda$	0	Fig. 6.6e
UC10-12	X	9	$4/10\lambda$	Linear	Fig. 6.6f

Table 6.3: Simulation results: Antenna configurations

alignment towards the actual driving direction. In [148] a method has been patented by the author of this thesis, by which the actual course angle α_c is directly transferred into the *phase shift* α, used to calculate the progressive angle ψ in Equation (6.3). In a real-world implementation, the course angle may either be derived from the current angle of the steering wheel, or, if available, from a digital map. This method may be used to direct the fore- and rear- beam so that it is kept on the road as far as possible.

Table 6.3 summarizes the antenna configurations, required to create the beams for the different use cases. For all simulation processes a wave length λ of 5.09 cm was selected, which corresponds to the C2X center frequency of 5.890 GHz. In Figure 6.6 related patterns are visualized. Note that for reasons of enhanced visibility, in this thesis, the author refrains to directly show satellite images, used within the simulator, and instead, include a more schematic view of the road topology.

Apparently, the different antenna array characteristics, i.e., *broadside, endfire* or *road-aligned* pattern fulfill the requirements stated in the previous Section 6.4.1. The number of elements in the X-array and Y-arrays and the dimensioning of these arrays appear to have a high technical feasibility. The only exception relates to UC5, where the X-array should contain 20 antennas with a separation of λ. This results from the necessity of producing a beam, which is as narrow as a single lane (approx. 3.5 m). Thus, to support this use case, the X-array should have a length of $20 * \lambda = 101.8$ cm, which may cause technical difficulties. For this use case, therefore, it is recommended using the same configuration as for UC6 and UC7 due to the high similarity in the required beams. For the DENM distribution within UC9, two beamforms are required, i.e., a broad pattern on all roads for initial distribution of the message (see Figure 6.6e), and a more directive pattern, applied by intermediate stations for forwarding the message to relevant recipients (see Figure 6.6c)

Figure 6.5 depicts the layout of the proposed antenna array according the simulation results. The tables embedded in Figure 6.7 give the active antennas for some exemplary use cases. Note that UC2 is treated as UC5 and UC6 to keep the array dimension in an acceptable range. A total of 12 antennas in the X-array and 20 antennas in the Y-array are required, respectively. Note that the 20 antennas of the Y-array are never activated at the same time for any of the analyzed use cases. Moreover,the requirement of 20 antennas in this array is attributed to the different element separations needed by the set of use cases.

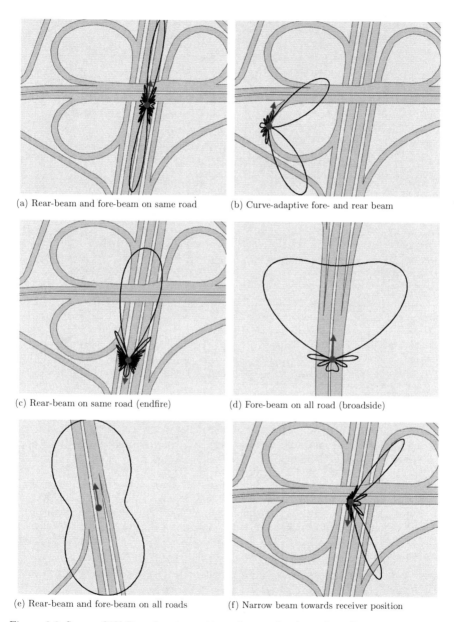

(a) Rear-beam and fore-beam on same road   (b) Curve-adaptive fore- and rear beam

(c) Rear-beam on same road (endfire)   (d) Fore-beam on all road (broadside)

(e) Rear-beam and fore-beam on all roads   (f) Narrow beam towards receiver position

Figure 6.6: Secure C2X Beamforming patterns for weather hazard application

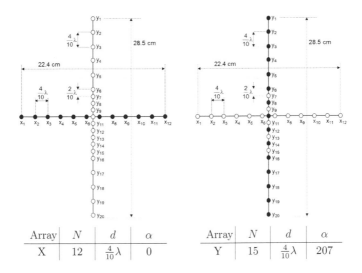

Array	N	d	α
X	12	$\frac{4}{10}\lambda$	0

Array	N	d	α
Y	15	$\frac{4}{10}\lambda$	207

(a) Rear-beam and fore-beam on same road

(b) Rear-beam on same road (endfire)

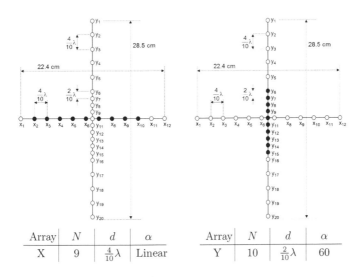

Array	N	d	α
X	9	$\frac{4}{10}\lambda$	Linear

Array	N	d	α
Y	10	$\frac{2}{10}\lambda$	60

(c) Narrow beam towards receiver position (d) Fore-beam on all roads (broadside)

Figure 6.7: Antenna array configurations

6.4.3 Beamforming Algorithm

In this section, an appropriate pattern steering of the presented X-Y antenna array model is derived for each of the communication types occurring inside the Weather Hazard Warning application. In the following a brief introduction into the different communication scenarios of the C2X weather application is given. Within the sim^{TD} field trial, this application has been developed in detail and fully implemented by *Jaeger et al.* [73]. In this thesis, the specification and terminology as defined in [73] and [22] are taken as reference.

Weather Hazard Warning Application

Especially for use cases such as Weather Hazard Warnings, the driver may greatly benefit from the exchange of this foresighted traffic information like, e.g., heavy rains, fog, strong cross winds, or slippery roads due to ice or snow. The message distribution thereby may include the forwarding via several intermediate stations using Car-to-Car and Car-to-Infrastructure communication links. Besides enhancing safety on the road, collecting weather relevant data via a vehicle's local sensors and forwarding of this information via C2X communication is also of high interest for meteorological institutions. For them, vehicles on the road may be regarded as a network of sensor nodes, providing valuable information about the current weather or climate in a specified region. Actually, today's vehicles are equipped with a bundle of sophisticated sensors such as temperature sensors, light sensors, or rain sensors. How to derive certain weather conditions out of the information obtained from the these sensors is further detailed by *Jaeger et al.* [73]. By distributing sensor probes of all vehicles, a central infrastructure facility may aggregate this data to derive weather relevant information. Including weather information from conventional sources like satellite observations or weather measurement stations, helps metrological institutions to create a more accurate weather view, and thus, enhance their forecasts significantly.

From the description of the Weather Hazard Warning application according to [73], the following three basic communication scenarios may be identified in this application type: *Weather Hazard Notification*, *Weather Hazard Forwarding*, and *Probe Vehicle Data Distribution*. Before starting the definition of the beamforming algorithm, the required radiation patterns have to be defined for each of these three communication scenarios. In the following, this is done by means of argumentative reasoning.

If a vehicle detects a whether hazard such as black ice, heavy rain or fog by its local sensors it instantly distributes a corresponding warning message to all surrounding vehicles. By nature, weather hazards are not limited to the vehicle's positions only, but rather have an effect on the entire area around the vehicle. Hence, since these messages are relevant for all vehicles in communication range, no a priori dissemination direction is anticipated for the Weather Hazard Notification communication scenario. Nevertheless, a beamforming adaption according to the position of vehicles in communication range is intended.

Via forwarding techniques as outlined in Section 2.1.2, hazard warning messages are forwarded over longer distances to warn approaching traffic in time. Besides adapting the field to surrounding vehicles, for Weather Hazard Forwarding, further refinements may be applied according to the intended dissemination direction of the message. Assuming that messages sent by the originator have also been received by all surrounding vehicles, the next forwarder may adapt its radiation pattern in a way that already notified vehicles are left out.

The distribution of *Probe Vehicle Data* (see PVD in Table 2.1) requires unicast communication to RSUs, and therefore possesses similar requirements concerning the pattern steering as for UC10-12. Note that the exchanged data does not only include probes of all sensors, relevant for weather identification, but further may include related information for other applications, such as congestion warning. This requires the exchange of large sets of data when passing by a RSU. In order to support the secure transmission of these packets, a mutual beamforming of both, sender and receiver is anticipated.

In the following section, a pseudo-code description of the beamforming algorithm for each communication scenario is determined. Again, the beamforming is designed primary for the transmission case. Reducing the pattern also for the reception is not anticipated for this type of application, but may be a possible approach in case of severe interferers.

Secure Transmission

Selecting and steering the different beams is a task, performed on lower abstraction layers within the C2X architecture. The exact architectural integration of that beamforming component will be subject of Section 6.5.3. In Algorithm 6 the basic beamforming algorithm for the Weather Hazard Warning application is described.

Accordingly, if a DENM is handed over from the application layer for sending, a beamforming component on MAC layer analyses the message header to determine the communication scenario associated to that message. In case the *originator* field equals the own vehicle ID, a new event has been detected by the host vehicle, which relates to the scenario of *Weather Hazard Notification*. For sending, the antenna elements x_6 and x_7 are biased to obtain an almost omnidirectional pattern which covers all receivers in the proximity (see Figure 6.6e). In contrary, for forwarding of a DENM, an endfire pattern is created by biasing respective elements of the Y-antenna array and applying an electronic phase shift of 207 degrees (see Figure 6.6c). By adjusting the power level of the feeding signal, the communication range is scaled to the most distant vehicle, for both cases respectively. In the context of his bachelor thesis, *Y. Berghöfer* [176] has performed several tests, for finding a relation between signal level (in dBm) on the one hand and the obtained range (in meters) on the other. As expected, a generally valid rule, which would apply to all scenarios in the same way can hardly be found due to the high dependency on the particular surroundings which affect the channel. However, for line-of-sight conditions with only few obstacles on the road, a logarithmic dependency could be observed for a single monopole antenna (at sender and receiver).

Probe Vehicle Data is sent every time the vehicle passes a RSU. For that purpose, the position-based pattern is deployed to produce a very narrow beam towards the position of the RSU (see Figure 6.8). In order to steer that beam according to the dynamic driving behavior of the vehicle, the relative geometric angle between both stations is calculated and transferred to an electrical phase shift of the feeding signal. Mutual beamforming between both stations leads to an enhancement of the directivity, and by this, also impedes unauthorized eavesdropping of exchanged messages.

Secure Reception

The proposed secure beamforming algorithm serves the purpose of enhanced driver's privacy by minimizing the dissemination area of messages. In order to enhance also security,

---

Algorithm 6 determineWeatherHazardWarningBeamforming()

In: Message Msg, Neighborhood Table N_{Table}
Out: Biasing X$[1; 12]$ Y$[1; 20]$, Phasing α_x α_y, Transmission Power P_x P_y
1:   Pos {Position to most distant receiver}
2: **if** Msg.getType() $= DENM$ **then**
3:    **if** Msg.getOriginator() $=$ getVehicleID() **then**
4:      $X[6] =$ true
5:      $X[7] =$ true
6:      $\alpha_x = 0$
7:      $Pos = N_{Table}$.getMostDistantVehicle()
8:      $P_x =$ calcTransmissionPower(Pos)
9:    **else**
10:      $Y[1 - 6] =$ true
11:      $Y[8] =$ true
12:      $Y[10] =$ true
13:      $Y[12] =$ true
14:      $Y[14] =$ true
15:      $Y[16 - 20] =$ true
16:      $\alpha_y = 207$
17:      $Pos = N_{Table}$.getMostDistantVehicleToRear()
18:      $P_y =$ calcTransmissionPower(Pos)
19:    **end if**
20: **else if** Msg.getType() $= PVD$ **then**
21:    $X[2 - 10] =$ true
22:    $Pos = N_{Table}$.getPosition(RSU)
23:    $RelAngle =$ calcRelAngle(Pos, getPosition())
24:    $\alpha_x =$ calcPhaseShift($RelAngle$)
25:    $P_x =$ calcTransmissionPower(Pos)
26: **end if**

---

respective algorithms have to be found for the receiving case. Whereas the beamforming for sending is bounded to a single message, the pattern for receiving has a large impact on all kinds of messages received. A dynamic arbitration of the channel, depending on the requirements of the different applications is a highly complex task and subject to future work. However, some beamforming concepts for impeding jamming attacks can be stated.

Assuming a vehicle is capable of detecting and localizing jammers or Sybil nodes via one of the methods described in *Hamieh et al.* [177] or *Bin et al.* [178]. Then, to impede the reception of messages from such a severe interferer, the antenna system may create a *Null* into the respective direction. Such a *Null* leads to a severely reduced connectivity inside that region. These techniques are known to be efficient for suppressing noise from unwanted directions and have been also applied in other communication domains, as discussed in Section 6.2.

Considering the previously discussed antenna array model, a *Null* may be obtained with an antenna configuration of 19 antennas, spaced 5 λ from each other and a phase shift of 164 degrees. Knowing the approximate geographical position of the interferer, allows scaling the pattern in range, in a way that the reception pattern is maximized, while the host vehicle is

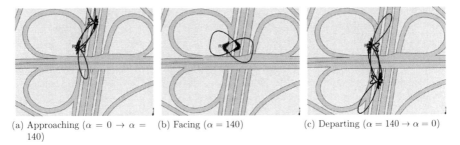

(a) Approaching ($\alpha = 0 \rightarrow \alpha = 140$)   (b) Facing ($\alpha = 140$)   (c) Departing ($\alpha = 140 \rightarrow \alpha = 0$)

Figure 6.8: Mutual position-based beamforming for unicast communication with a RSU

Figure 6.9: Attacker shielding by forming a *Null* into the direction of the attacker

"shielded" from the jamming signals (see Figure 6.9). Hence, in the following, this technique is referred to as *Attacker Shielding*.

Although, *Attacker Shielding* may be considered as a still emerging and, thus, not yet fully matured concept, it still represents the only known intend for increasing robustness towards Denial-of-Service attacks in C2X communication so far. It aims at keeping C2X communication running even in the presence of strong disturbance and therefore, may have the potential for increasing the robustness of the entire technology.

6.5 Secure C2X Beamforming Algorithm II: sim^{TD} Antenna

While the previous case study of an antenna array, was based on a generic model, in the second case study, presented in this section, the author is exploring the feasibility of an already existing antenna structure with respect to Secure C2X Beamforming. Due to its near-series alignment the antenna system, developed within the sim^{TD} field trial is subject of this analysis. Possible antenna parameters for adjusting the pattern are identified and a beamforming algorithm for one exemplary application is defined. Besides providing a basic steering concept of the sim^{TD} antenna system, in this chapter, the essential question on how to integrate the beamforming concept into already existing C2X architectures is discussed, in the context of the sim^{TD} system.

6.5.1 Use Case Requirements

The sim^{TD} architecture incorporates most of the applications stated in Section 2.2. For these applications, the same requirements as already elaborated in Section 6.4.1 apply. For direct evaluation of the sim^{TD} antenna performance against the presented X-Y Antenna array model, presented in Section 6.4, the same Wheather Hazard Warning Application according to *Jaeger et al.* [73] is taken as reference.

6.5.2 Antenna Pattern Model

The effectiveness of Secure C2X Beamforming depends highly on the degree of freedom, the MAC layer offers for producing situation-based patterns. While for the previous case study in Section 6.4, a generic antenna aperture was assumed, in sim^{TD} only a limited number of different patterns are available in practice. The sim^{TD} antennas as addressed in Section 6.2.2 is constituted by two software controlled antennas. Each consists of a $\lambda/4$ monopole and produces a semi-circular radiation pattern to the front and to the rear of the vehicle, respectively[2]. A per-packet power control is possible in steps of 0.5 dB granularity ranging from 0 dBm to 20 dBm [35]. The possibilities for Secure C2X Beamforming within the sim^{TD} architecture are limited to the given parameter:

- Antenna type A_{fore} or A_{rear},
- Transmission Power P_{fore} and P_{rear}

Note that these parameters originally had not been intended to be used for beamforming purposes, but for switching between control and service channels (see Section 6.2.1). The presented beamforming concept is also not part of the official sim^{TD} architecture and has been integrated for testing purposes only. To some extent, the sim^{TD} antenna structure can be considered as a sub-variant of the ideal X-Y antenna array presented in Section 6.4.2. Hence, by biasing only a set of two antennas within the array, a similar pattern as for the sim^{TD} antenna may be achieved. This corresponds to the configuration of UC9 in Table 6.3 and results into a pattern as illustrated in Figure 6.6e.

6.5.3 Beamforming Algorithm

Due to the limited number of parameters for antenna adjustment, no beamforming in the conventional sense can be performed. Hence, the radiation pattern control for the sim^{TD} system is reduced to a selection of antenna type and related transmission power. However, as shown in the following sections, by means of this, the requirements of the reference application may be satisfied to a great extent. Furthermore, the architectural integration of the beamforming algorithm shows the way forward towards a first deployment of this concept in future FOTs.

---

[2]Please note that the exact shape of each antenna pattern is accessible only to sim^{TD} consortium members for the time being. Therefore, in the following the antenna pattern is approximated by a schematic illustration.

Architectural Integration

In Figure 6.10 the architectural composition in terms of components and interfaces is given. Note that the presentation in this section refers to the sim^{TD} system architecture as already outlined in Section 4.4.1. Besides already described components, this illustration is further complemented by components relevant for realizing the Secure C2X Beamforming concept.

Applications running on a vehicle's AU basically perform two consecutive tasks: event detection and event notification. Event detection may thereby include information from local sensors as well as from received C2X messages. After processing and aggregation of the events, the application is encapsulating all relevant information into DENMs. Besides DENMs, in this case study, also the sending of CAMs and PVD messages is of further interest. In the sim^{TD} implementation, PVD messages consist of sets of probe values, which a vehicle takes while driving (e.g., geographical traces as well as local temperature values). These messages are sent via unicast to a RSU and then forwarded to backend facilities (see Figure 2.2). The *AU Communication Client* represents an interface for all incoming and outgoing messages to the CCU. Before passing incoming messages to the applications, the mobility data contained in the messages is verified by the *Mobility Data Verification* framework as presented in Chapter 4 of this thesis.

A major task of the facility component on the vehicle's CCU is the creation of CAMs. In sim^{TD} a sophisticated network layer is deployed, which supports most of the forwarding protocols described in Section 2.1.2 (e.g., contention-based forwarding). For position-based routing a Neighborhood Table is maintained and constantly updated upon newly received messages. Via location services, the network layer furthermore may directly query a node position within the network. The *C2X Dispatcher* obtains the host vehicle's mobility data via a *Vehicle Data Provider*, which offers access to the CAN bus and GPS module. It assembles the payload with network header and hands over the entire packet to the security component. A signature is created and the corresponding certificate is added before the message is sent via the *ITS Access* component. In contrary, incoming messages are handled by the *Ingress Handler*. Upon message reception the correctness of the signature and the validity of the certificate are verified. The Neighborhood Table is updated and the forwarding type is evaluated.

In the context of this thesis, it is proposed to realize Secure C2X Beamforming as a central component, located on the network layer. In Figure 6.10 solid lines represent already existent communication interfaces, while dotted lines indicate links to be established for integration. The *Secure C2X Beamforming* component implements the interface of (1) the Vehicle Data Provider, to determine the host vehicles mobility data, (2) the Neighborhood Table, to determine the position of relevant receivers and (3) the *Security* component, to evaluate the trustworthiness of certain receivers. It offers an interface, which is integrated by the C2X Dispatcher. Interfacing these components allows precise assessment of the current C2X scenario. With the objective of enhancing security and privacy, this component determines dynamically the appropriate beamforming for sending and receiving messages. In the following sections a description of the evaluation scheme executed by the subcomponents *Secure Receive* and *Secure Transmit* are given in terms of related beamforming algorithms.

Concepts of trust are not foreseen within the sim^{TD} security architecture (see Section 3.5.3). A very basic approach is anticipated, where possible attackers are categorized into two classes: *light* and *severe* attacker. Having received multiple incorrectly signed messages

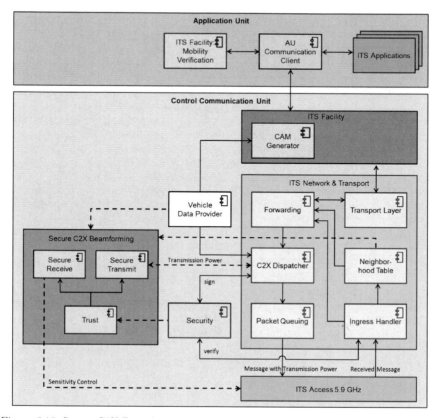

Figure 6.10: Secure C2X Beamforming architectural integration

from a certain node, indicates a light attacker. In particular, the mobility verification approach, as presented in Chapter 4 may be applied for detecting this type of attacker. In contrast, a severe attacker is a node, which is jamming the channel, i.e., sending messages with a frequency that exceeds the maximum allowed CAM frequency (refers to message frequency check as deployed in Section 4.3.1). An attacker classification allows for a more appropriate alignment of respective security countermeasures. More detailed work on attacker classification can be found, e.g., in [150], [179], [178] and will be subject of ongoing research in the C2X security community. For the purpose of detecting the different attacker classes a *Trust* subcomponent needs to be provided, which interfaces the *Security* component. It receives the results from the security evaluation and monitors the message interval of neighboring nodes.

Note that due to limited project funding and the tight time scheduling of the sim^{TD} project, these concepts could not have been integrated directly into the final architecture for the field trial. Instead, as a proof of concept, within several student's projects carried out in [180], [181] and [182] (supervised by the author of this thesis), the essential parts of the sim^{TD}

network and physical layer have been fully reconstructed, based on the detailed documen-
tation given in [8], [35], and [10]. This includes in particular the implementation of relevant
components such as a Neighborhood Table, Forwarding, Vehicle Data Provider, or a facility
layer for standard compliant CAM generation. Several tests, performed together with real
sim^{TD} vehicles, yielded that the reconstructed C2X architecture is completely interoperable.

Secure Transmission

Since every C2X message, which is produced by the application and facility layer is further
processed by the C2X Dispatcher component, this is considered to be a good entry point
for performing the transmission power calculation for each antenna. Besides message payload, the application layer also specifies a destination address. This destination address,
mainly provided by DENM applications, specifies the intended receivers, i.e., either a single
receiver via unicast or an entire geographical area via geocast. In contrast, a CAM is addressed to all communication nodes via broadcast. Based on this data, the Secure Transmit
subcomponent is determining the transmission energy for both antennas in a way that only
a minimum area is covered, including all relevant receivers. By taking into account, the
trustworthiness of certain receivers, an even more secure adaption can be achieved. In the
following, different secure beamforming algorithms are proposed for sending of CAMs and
unicast/geocast DENMs for the given sim^{TD} antenna system.

As described by the decision flow graph in Figure 6.11, the relevant parameters including the
C2X message, the intended communication range and all attacker IDs are delivered serially
to the Secure C2X Beamforming component, which evaluates the destination address (see
D1 in Figure 6.11). In this thesis, a further parameter, called *Dissemination Area (DA)*,
is introduced, which features an oval shape and is defined to the front and to the rear of a
vehicle, respectively. The DA is used for internal relevance determination and specifies the
area around a vehicle, which has to be covered by the antenna pattern.

In case of periodically broadcasted CAMs, the Secure Transmit subcomponent queries the
current vehicle speed from the Vehicle Data Provider. For reasons of safety, in this thesis,
it is proposed to emit CAMs in the movement direction with a transmission energy proportional to the vehicles current speed. For the antenna to the rear a scaling of the transmission
energy inversely proportional to the speed is anticipated. Thus, at higher speeds the relevance of CAM messages is shifted from the rear to the front of the transmission range.
In Figure 6.12 a three-lane motorway is illustrated, where *vehicle A* is moving at higher
speeds than *vehicle B* and therefore is sending messages with a higher transmission energy
to the front. *Vehicle X* is changing the lanes and getting notified about the presence of the
approaching *vehicle A* in a timely manner. Compared to an uncontrolled omnidirectional
message dissemination, this approach achieves safety requirements with respect to privacy
needs.

While the initial setting of the *DA* is focused towards a restricted message transmission
in general, further refinements consist in a more aligned adaption, in presence of a known
attacker. Based on identified insecure IDs, provided by the Trust subcomponent, the current position of the attacker is queried from the Neighborhood Table. If the attacker is
not located in the intended *DA*, no further adaptations have to be performed (see D3 in
Figure 6.11). In contrast, if the *DA* is including the attacker's position, the area has to
be redefined in order to exclude this position. This approach follows the paradigm that
privacy of a driver has to be ensured by all means, even if message transmission has to be

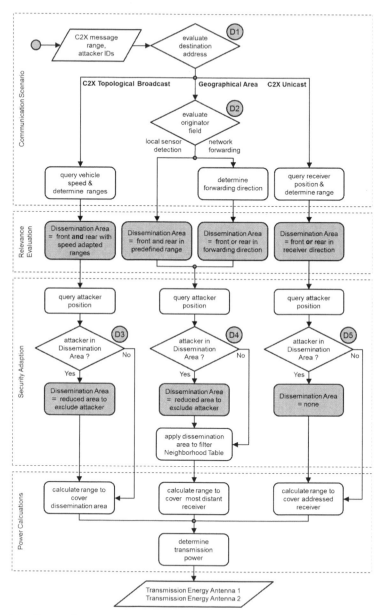

Figure 6.11: Secure C2X Beamforming Transmit subcomponent: Decision flow graph for the sim^{TD} algorithm for sending C2X messages

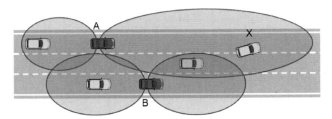

Figure 6.12: Speed dependant CAM sending

intermitted. However, further investigations have to be carried out, concerning the privacy protection in safety-critical situations. After the security adaptations have been performed, the ranges related to both directions are calculated in order to cover the DA. These ranges are then mapped to respective transmission energies for both antennas and returned back to the C2X Dispatcher, which performs the appropriate MAC Layer adjustments.

In comparison to a CAM, a DENM allows a more directive beamforming, because relevant receivers can either be derived directly from the destination address (unicast), or can be determined from the specified geographical area (geocast) (see D2 in Figure 6.11). For a geocast, the originator field inside the network header indicates whether the message is created by the application or has been received from surrounding vehicles for forwarding in the network. In Figure 6.13a and Figure 6.13b the different beamforming approaches for the example application Weather Hazard Warning are illustrated. For the Weather Hazard Notification communication scenario, the transmitted C2X messages are relevant for all vehicles in communication range. Hence, no a priori dissemination direction is anticipated. However, adapting the transmission power according to the position of vehicles in the communication range is intended. Thus, the DA defines an ellipsoid in both directions with ranges as predefined by the traffic class. During the security analysis this area can further be restricted to exclude insecure receivers. That way, the DA for DENMs can be considered as a filter, which is applied to the Neighborhood Table in order to extract all relevant vehicles. For transmission energy calculation the most distant vehicle present in the DA is crucial.

If the originator field does not coincide with the host vehicle ID, the message was received from neighboring nodes and is being forwarded towards the specified destination area (see D2 in Figure 6.11). Assuming that messages sent by the originator have also been received by all surrounding vehicles, the next forwarder may adapt his radiation pattern in a way that already notified vehicles are excluded. Depending on the geographical destination area the forwarding direction is calculated and the parameter value for DA is set accordingly. After the security analysis and attacker exclusion (see D4 in Figure 6.11), the DA is applied to the Neighborhood Table to filter relevant vehicles in forwarding direction as illustrated in Figure 6.13b.

The third branch of the decision flow graph in Figure 6.11 is related to the sending of PVD to RSUs via unicast messages. The RSU position can be directly queried from the Neighborhood Table based on the destination address encoded within the message. Depending on the relative position either the front or rear antenna is selected. Because PVD messages consist of large sets of data, the beamforming evaluation is executed repetitively to adapt

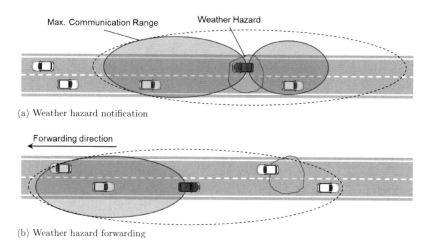

(a) Weather hazard notification

(b) Weather hazard forwarding

Figure 6.13: Secure C2X Beamforming patterns for weather hazard application

to the changing position. In Figure 6.14 a sequence is shown, where a vehicle is passing by a RSU and is either radiating to the front or to the rear, depending on the relative position to the RSU. If an attacker is located in the direct LoS between the vehicle and the RSU (see D5 in Figure 6.11), it is recommended to stop the message transmission. Accordingly, the DA is set idle, which leads to a zero transmission energy calculation.

Secure Reception

The *Secure Receive* subcomponent performs calculations of antenna sensitivity based on frequently updated attacker IDs provided by the Trust subcomponent. The beamforming protocol as described by the decision flow graph in Figure 6.16 is constantly running and polling the Trust subcomponent for identified attackers. The position of the attacker is queried and the affected antenna (fore or rear) is identified. It is proposed to linearly decrease the antenna sensitivity in 0.5 dB steps. After every adjustment, the Secure Receive subcomponent returns to its initial state and further refines the sensitivity until no messages are received anymore. After having successfully excluded the attacker, the component starts to increase the sensitivity again until the maximum value has been reached (see Figure 6.16).

6.6 Evaluation Results

In order to efficiently support a designer in defining an antenna system for C2X, appropriate measures are required, which allow for a quantitative comparison of different radiation patterns. In *Lakshmanan et al.* [163] first attempts can be found for quantifying the achieved security against eaves-dropping when applying smart antennas in indoor environments. In the following section a novel security metric is introduced, which applies to the C2X domain and takes into account application requirements and attacker positions, particularly. The presented case studies in Section 5.5 and 5.6 are evaluated with respect to this metric for some representative traffic scenarios.

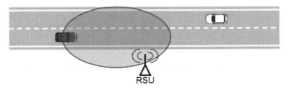

(a) Biasing antenna A_{fore} when approaching a RSU

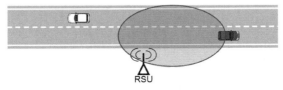

(b) Biasing antenna A_{rear} when departing a RSU

Figure 6.14: Radiation pattern steering for sending Probe Vehicle Data (PVD) via unicast communication to a RSU.

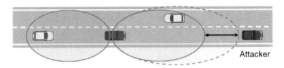

Figure 6.15: Sensitivity adjustment of the antenna A_{fore} to exclude an attacker

6.6.1 SCBM Metric

For the purpose of defining an adequate metric for physical security, a comparison to already existing antenna measures is considered as beneficial. For instance, the *gain* of a certain antenna is defined according to *C. Balanis* [175] (pp. 65 -67) as "the ratio of the intensity, in a given direction, to the radiation intensity that would be obtained if the power accepted by the antenna were radiated isotropically". Note that an *isotropic* radiator represents a purely theoretical antenna with no dimensions, no mass, and an uniform radiation pattern in all directions. It therefore represents an ideal model of an omnidirectional antenna, which may be used to compare different antenna patterns. In the context of Secure C2X Beamforming a similar approach for defining a security metric is aspired.

Hence, in order to define the reference (optimum) radiation pattern, the area around a vehicle is modelled by a circle with a radius R, which corresponds to the average expected communication range of ITS stations ($\approx 600m$). This circle is furthermore divided into a set of different sectors, denoted by the set of S_{all}. In order to serve as a reference, each sector within the set of S_{all} shall be dimensioned to cover exactly the width of a single highway lane. By this definition, a sector represents the minimal measurement unit, used to evaluate a particular pattern against the ideal reference. Assuming an average lane width of $W = 3.5m$ on German highways [146], the total number of sectors $|S_{all}|$ is determined as follows:

$$|S_{all}| \equiv \frac{R \times 2 \times \pi}{W} = \frac{600m \times 2 \times \pi}{3.5m} \approx 1024 \qquad (6.4)$$

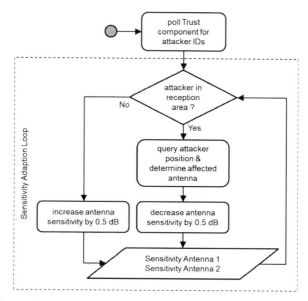

Figure 6.16: Secure C2X Beamforming Receive subcomponent: Decision flow graph for performing power control to exclude attacker

Within the set S_{all} further subsets are defined, as summarized in Table 6.4.

NOTATION	DESCRIPTION
S_{all}	set of all sectors
S_{nom}	nominal sectors, to be covered by radiation pattern
S_{init}	initial sectors, defined by respective C2X use case
S_{attack}	sectors, including the position of an attacker
S_{cov}	actual covered sectors, given by produced radiation pattern

Table 6.4: Secure C2X Beamforming metric notations overview

Accordingly, the subset S_{nom} includes all sectors, which ideally have to be covered by the actual radiation pattern. Of further importance are thereby all those sectors, which are regarded as *insecure*, e.g., due to the presence of an adversary, and consequently have to be omitted (denoted by S_{attack}).

Taking up the introductory example, of an antenna gain, the subset S_{nom} is therefore very well comparable to the notion of an isotropic radiator. Hence, S_{nom} represents an ideal reference, which physically is hard to be achieved by an antenna system, but is useful as a theoretical model for comparing different beamforming concepts against each other. In the following the advocated algorithm for determining the nominal sectors is presented.

Nominal Sectors

Determining the optimum beamforming represents a non-trivial task, due to the dependency on various factors, like, e.g., the message type, road course, or the location of adversaries. In this thesis, a first concept for determining the nominal sectors of a radiation pattern in C2X is described in Algorithm 7. The algorithm is designed in a way that in principle it may also run on a vehicle's local C2X unit. Several data is required as input:

- *Use Case UC*: For every given C2X use case, a subset of sectors have been predefined. These initial sectors are denoted by the set of S_{init} and can be considered as a refined and more formalized notion of the pattern requirements already stated in Section 6.4.1.

- *Sectors Path History S_{PH}*: In order to include a vehicle's current trajectory, the path history is matched to respective sectors. Inside the vehicle, this data may be obtained by recording the past geographical positions.

- *Sectors Path Prediction S_{PP}*: For similar reasons also the future path is mapped to related sectors. Depending on the available components inside a vehicle, the future path may be predicted using vehicle data like, e.g., the current steering angle or the yaw rate.

- *Neighborhood Table N_{Table}*: The Neighborhood Table containes the position of all adjacent vehicles and is used within the algorithm to assess occupied sectors.

- *Security Module SEC*: The security module evaluates the trustworthiness of surrounding vehicles. Related information is considered in the calculation of the set of S_{nom} to explicitly mark insecure attacker sectors.

Each calculation step of the algorithm is illustrated in Figure 6.17 by means of an accompanying example for use cases UC2-UC5, i.e., applications, which rely on CAM messages. Note that for reasons of clarity, the illustration in this figure is reduced to 16 sectors instead of 1024. As a first step the nominal sectors S_{nom} are initialized with the sectors given by the current use case. Hence, for the example in Figure 6.17a this includes the front and rear sector in driving direction. If the path history or the future path (see *red* and *blue* coloring in Figure 6.17a) are not entirely included in the subset of nominal sectors yet, then S_{nom} is expanded by all sectors defined within S_{PH} and S_{PP}, respectively. In Figure 6.17b and 6.17c the trajectory adaptions are illustrated for a vehicle driving a sharp curve.

In the subsequent steps, the set of S_{nom} is adapted to the traffic scenario given by adjacent vehicles. For each activated sector ($S_{nom}[i] = 1$), N_{Table} is polled to determine, whether a potential receiver is located inside that sector. If not, this sector does not necessarily have to be covered. Hence, for privacy reasons, these sectors are removed from the set of nominal sectors ($S_{nom}[i] = 0$) as illustrated in Figure 6.17d. However, for malicious neighbors, a simple removal of the respective sector is considered as insufficient. Therefore, if the security module identifies the location of potential adversaries, these sectors are explicitly marked as untrustworthy ($S_{attack}[i] = 1$). This means that for the created pattern these attacker sectors, denoted by the set of S_{attack}, must not be included into the communication. In Figure 6.17e the final subset of nominal sectors is illustrated for a vehicle, which is sending CAMs in the given example traffic scenario.

Algorithm 7 determineNominalSectors

In: Use Case UC, Sectors Path History S_{PH}, Sectors Path Prediction S_{PP}, Neighborhood
    Table N_{Table}, Security Module SEC,
Out: Nominal Sectors S_{nom}, Attacker Sectors S_{attack} {each 1024 bit vector}
  1: $S_{nom} = UC.S_{init}$
  2: **if** $S_{PH} \nsubseteq S_{nom}$ **then**
  3:     $S_{nom} = S_{nom} \cup S_{PH}$
  4: **end if**
  5: **if** $S_{PP} \nsubseteq S_{nom}$ **then**
  6:     $S_{nom} = S_{nom} \cup S_{PP}$
  7: **end if**
  8: **while** $i < |S_{all}|$ **do**
  9:     **if** $S_{nom}[i] = 1$ **then**
 10:         **for all** $n \in N_{Table}$ **do**
 11:             **if** $n.\text{getPosition}() \in S_{nom}[i].\text{getArea}()$ **then**
 12:                 $S_{nom}[i] = 1$ **break**
 13:             **else**
 14:                 $S_{nom}[i] = 0$
 15:             **end if**
 16:         **end for**
 17:     **end if**
 18: **end while**
 19: **while** $i < |S_{all}|$ **do**
 20:     **if** $SEC.\text{getAttacker}().\text{getPosition}() \in S_{nom}[i].\text{getArea}()$ **then**
 21:         $S_{nom}[i] = 0$
 22:         $S_{attack}[i] = 1$
 23:     **end if**
 24: **end while**
 25: **return** S_{nom}, S_{attack}

Any Secure C2X Beamforming algorithm aims at achieving a pattern as close as possible to
the sector assignment defined by the set of S_{nom}. For instance, by means of the beamforming
concept presented in Section 6.4, an almost ideal pattern can be created for this particular
scenario (see Figure 6.17f). Due to the coupling of the steering angle with the electronic
phase shift of the antenna array, the main lobes may be oriented to cover the vehicles
current trajectory. Except for one node, all relevant neighbors are covered, while the overall
coverage is kept to a minimum. The notch created towards the position of the adversary,
impedes message dissemination into that direction.

Sector Ratios

Based on the notion of nominal set of sectors S_{nom}, in the following, metrics are derived,
which allow for a comparison of different antenna patterns. For this purpose the terminology
of sectors as introduced in previous sections, is further extended by means of S_{cov}, which
denotes all sectors, which are actually covered by the current radiation pattern. Note that
in general the subset S_{cov}, i.e., the area, where a message can be received with a sufficient
power level, is also a function of the receiver's (or adversary's) antenna gain. For a better

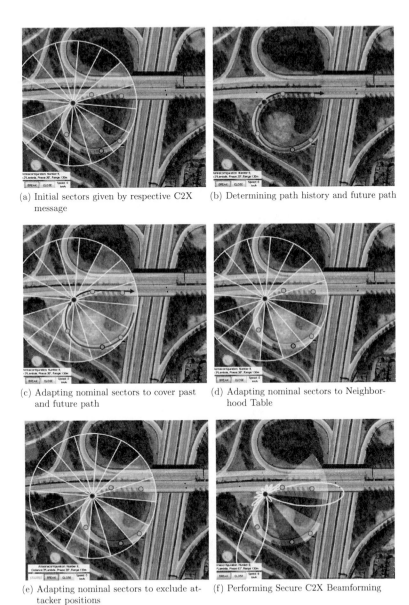

(a) Initial sectors given by respective C2X message

(b) Determining path history and future path

(c) Adapting nominal sectors to cover past and future path

(d) Adapting nominal sectors to Neighborhood Table

(e) Adapting nominal sectors to exclude attacker positions

(f) Performing Secure C2X Beamforming

Figure 6.17: Determining the nominal sectors for the Secure C2X Beamforming

comparison, within the following definitions, all references to S_{nom} are determined for a fixed receiver antenna capability and it is assumed, that beyond the -3 dB margin, message cannot be decoded anymore due to an insufficient power level. The secure beamforming metric proposed in this thesis is composed of three separate expressions, each describing the different aspects of the system.

The first *Secure C2X Beamforming Metric (SCBM1)* assesses the satisfiability of the actual antenna system. As a prior target of any beamforming concept, at least all determined nominal sectors shall be covered by the actual radiation pattern for safety reasons. This property is captured by Definition (1), where the term $|S_{nom} \cap S_{cov}|$ denotes how many nominal sectors are covered by S_{cov}.

Definition 1 (SCBM1 Metric)

$$SCBM1 := \frac{|S_{nom} \cap S_{cov}|}{|S_{nom}|}$$

The second *Secure C2X Beamforming Metric (SCBM2)* described in Definition (2) aims at measuring the composite property, i.e., the number of sectors that are unnecessarily covered by the actual radiation pattern. Thereby, unnecessary covered sectors are defined as sectors, which do not belong to the subset of nominal or attacker sectors (see Table 6.4). This number is considered in relation to all other sectors, which are not nominal or attacker sectors.

Definition 2 (SCBM2 Metric)

$$SCBM2 := \frac{|S_{cov} \backslash (S_{nom} \cup S_{attack})|}{|S_{all} \backslash (S_{nom} \cup S_{attack})|}$$

The third *Secure C2X Beamforming Metric (SCBM3)* in Definition (3) takes into account how many covered sectors are actually attacker sectors, and, thus, must not be covered by the radiation pattern.

Definition 3 (SCBM3 Metric)

$$SCBM3 := \frac{|S_{cov} \cap S_{attack}|}{|S_{cov}|}$$

Considering, that each metric only covers a certain aspect of the system, a linear combination of all three metrics is advocated in order to yield a compact expression for the overall performance of a certain beamforming concept:

Definition 4 (SCBM Metric)

$$SCBM := (a \cdot SCBM1) - (b \cdot SCBM2) - (c \cdot SCBM3)$$

Use Case	Antenna System	SCBM1	SCBM2	SCBM3	SCBM
UC2-4,8	Antenna Array	1.0	0,0076	0,0918	0,8126
	sim^{TD}	1.0	0,0232	0,1028	0,7828
UC5-7,9	Antenna Array	1.0	0,0072	0,1102	0,776
	sim^{TD}	1.0	0,0178	0,1152	0,7607
UC1	Antenna Array	1.0	0,0064	0,0888	0,8192
	sim^{TD}	1.0	0,0208	0,09	0,8096
UC10-12	Antenna Array	1.0	0,0014	0,0334	0,9325
	sim^{TD}	1.0	0,0068	0,1442	0,7082

Table 6.5: Evaluation of Secure C2X Beamforming Algorithms

Within the Definition (4) of $SCBM$, the parameters a, b and c are applied to weight the different components against each other, depending on the designer's preferences. For instance, for a highly confidential communication, a designer might prioritize the direct exclusion of an adversary (SCBM3) over the unnecessary channel dissipation (SCBM2), and therefore may assign higher values to parameter c than to parameter b.

6.6.2 Beamforming Evaluation

During the last step of the design flow (see Section 6.3), the evaluation tool presented in Section 6.3.2 is deployed. As example scenarios, highway maps of the sim^{TD} test area around the city of Frankfurt are taken as example. For more detailed description of the example scenarios, including a visualization of the field patterns, please refer to the bachelor's thesis of T. Ruppenthal [172]. For each scenario, the two antenna systems, presented in Section 5.5 and 5.6 are evaluated with varying traffic densities between 10 and a maximum of 70 vehicles within the communication range. In order to explore the capability for excluding attackers, 3-5 different attacker vehicles are placed on the map. In this example evaluation, the designer assigns great importance to the satisfiability of the radiation pattern ($a = 1$), a medium weight on unnecessary channel occupation ($b = 0.5$), and a very high impact on the exclusion of adversaries ($c = 2$). In Table 6.5 the results for relevant use cases are summarized, averaged over a set of 5 different scenarios.

Remarkably, but not really surprising, for the given parameterization and scenario configuration, the antenna array is more appropriate with respect to $SCBM$. In particular, for a communication towards the roadside (UC 10-12), the high dynamic and directive beamforming, possible with the antenna array, clearly outweighs the static switching of front and back patterns of the sim^{TD} antenna. For other use cases, like, e.g., emergency vehicle warnings (UC1), both antenna systems perform equally well.

6.7 Conclusion

Wireless ad-hoc communication, such as Car-to-X networks, are highly susceptible to threats on the physical layer. Within this part of the thesis, for the first time, a technique for reducing these vulnerabilities is proposed for the C2X domain. The approach of Secure C2X Beamforming aims at reducing the opportunities for adversaries to illegitimately eavesdrop messages within the Car-to-X network by significantly reducing the coverage area of this network.

The Secure C2X Beamforming concept is based on a reconsideration of the geographical destination of messages and its implication on the physical layer. Whereas most antenna designs aim at maximizing the gain into all directions equally, this concept introduces space filtering to reach two objectives at the same time: a reduced channel occupation and by this, an enhanced privacy of the driver. A tool chain, consisting of a basic beamforming simulator and evaluator has been developed, and a dedicated design flow has been presented for defining appropriate Secure C2X Beamforming algorithms. Though, the presented tools do not consider physical effects, due to the heavy computational complexity, these may serve well for fast prototyping purposes.

As a use case study, two different antenna systems are evaluated. The first antenna model consists of two orthogonal arrays. By proper biasing a subset of the available antennas, the number of radiating elements is adjusted and the distance between them. By applying a successive phase shift to the feed current, the main beam may be steered into the desired direction. Furthermore the communication range is scaled by varying the power feed. With an appropriate setting of these parameters almost any desired field pattern can be produced. The second case study is based on a real world antenna implementation from the sim^{TD} field trial. The sim^{TD} architecture is taken as a reference, for showing how this concept may be embedded into an existing C2X vehicle architecture.

A major contribution of this part of the thesis furthermore consists in the definition of a metric by which different Secure C2X Beamforming algorithms may be compared against each other. The metric is composed of three components, to assess the capability for covering the intended area, impeding radiation into undesired regions and third, excluding suspicious positions. Both case studies have been evaluated with respect to that metric.

The next step towards a deployment within the vehicle consists of implementing a first prototype for the proposed antenna array and to perform field tests. By means of this, physical side effects, such as multipath or reflections may be evaluated in more detail, with the purpose of refining the antenna specification accordingly.

7

Conclusions and Perspectives

'The age of privacy is over' - this statement, assigned to Mark Zuckerberg, the founder and CEO of Facebook has received great amount of public attention. Though, it turned out later, that this statement has been slightly taken out of the context, however, the reaction of society demonstrates quite well, how sensitive this topic has become recently. In fact, the great amount of collected data, in general, should be not a concern to users of social networks only. Technologies like, e.g., mobile internet or electronic passports are only the latest technological achievements, which have implications on its user's privacy. Furthermore, smart metering for power supply, electronic voting, or vehicular networks based on C2X communication are the next technologies on the horizon, by which personal data will be collected and processed in a large scale.

Surprisingly, with respect to upcoming communication technologies, it seems that people are often more concerned of associated security risks, rather than worrying about their loss of privacy. Actually, for C2X communication, the community does not question the need for strong security measures anymore. It seems that experiences made with current threats in the internet, as well as published attacks on a vehicle's internal network [49] have led to a fundamental rethinking, especially in the automotive industry. Today, security measures are designed into novel systems from the start, and higher costs in terms of additional hardware and protocol overhead have become acceptable for the sake of safety.

However, the situation seems to be slightly different for the common awareness of privacy in C2X communication: 1) Often heard opinions either tend to underestimate the true value of privacy in general. 2) Or, people are principally aware of privacy, but doubt that C2X communication provides enough information, for seriously infringing their own privacy. Both attitudes are highly questionable and are briefly discussed in the following:

People adopting the first attitude are often under the mistaken belief that as long as they behave honestly, they do not have to put too much attention on privacy. Driven by the formula, 'If I dont have something to hide, I dont have to fear surveillance neither', privacy preserving techniques are often regarded as a nuisance. This attitude oversees that already small personal details, combined together may be sufficient to draw certain conclusions. Right or wrong, these conclusions might be used to blackmail or expose individuals. The risk of misuse is high and may affect especially the honest citizen. In general, the loss of control over a person's own data represents a fundamental shift in power, away from the individual, towards the authority assessing the data. If every interaction with new media or other technologies is subject to surveillance via some higher instance, people will be inhibited in using it, which considerably restricts their freedom to act in a digitalized world.

Regarding the second attitude, one has to consider that the privacy relevance of C2X messages is directly related to the evidence of the included position information. A comparison to other communication domains shows, which conclusions may be already drawn, if only few data like, e.g., position information is assessed. In context of a lawsuit against the retention of the connection data in mobile telephony networks for law enforcement purposes in Germany, the Chaos Computer Club (CCC) has analyzed the entropy, which is contained in this type of data [183]. The dataset thereby included connection data of mobile telephony calls in terms of time, dialog partners and the associated cell locations in the area around Berlin. For the studied example, the calls between a female, a politician, a counseling center and a hospital, including the movements between the cells have been analyzed. Without having any knowledge on the actual content of each conversation, this data provided sufficient entropy for reconstructing the concrete life situation of involved callers. Whatever the conclusions are, this example shows quite well how single pieces of information may be combined to actually create evidence. Considering a vehicle as inseparable from the person driving the vehicle, the position information included in C2X messages is indeed, highly privacy relevant.

This thesis was motivated by the ambitious goal of providing comprehensive coverage of the ITS architecture model with respective security and privacy solutions for each layer. Towards this objective, different approaches were presented and evaluated. Regarding market maturity and the related timeframe for deployment, some estimation can be made, based on discussions together with experts in the field:

Very likely, the advocated Public Key Infrastructure will be an integral part of the baseline security solution of the *day-one* system. The general decision for deploying asymmetric cryptography is settled by standards and the required infrastructure is currently developed within the C2C-CC. Also the developed mobility verification framework, installed on facility layer, is expected to be a promising candidate for early deployment. The prototypical implementation proves low computational complexity at a high accuracy. Furthermore, this approach does not require a time-consuming harmonization and standardization process, which may fasten its deployment. In contrary, the advocated privacy protocols on network layer require to be harmonized among all station providers. Hence, this approach is expected to be deployed during a later second phase of the C2X roll out. In particular, if privacy protection becomes legally binding, more sophisticated measures will be required, and though the advocated approach may become a potential candidate for deployment. On the physical layer, the Secure C2X Beamforming concept may be realized by each system provider individually. Even though, for early systems a fine grained beamforming via an antenna array will be likely too expensive, the basic idea can be well applied to common C2X antennas, as shown in the use case study presented in this thesis.

Taking up again the somewhat provocative statement at the beginning of this conclusion chapter, one has to clearly object. According to the opinion of the author of this thesis, the age of privacy is definitely **not** over yet. Actually, it might have just begun, since with new technologies finding their way into our everyday lives, more and more data will be acquired, and thus, society might start to appreciate the true value of privacy. Car-to-X communication promises to make driving safer, more efficient and by this, more enjoyable. This thesis intends to make its modest contribution towards a privacy preserving usage of this novel and exciting communication technology.

Network Layer Security: Situational Mix Zone Detection

In this section, an approach for detecting situational Mix Zones in Car-to-X networks as defined in Section 5.2.1 is presented. According to the simulations performed by *Wiedersheim et al.* [107], a simple pseudonym change strategy, which does not take into account additional traffic parameters, provides only low privacy protection against a global passive adversary. However, despite the high success rate for resolving pseudonym changes, real world experiments performed in [12] and [14] yielded, that if the trajectory of several vehicles coincide in a temporal and spatial manner, even a sophisticated tracking algorithm may perform matching errors. The presented protocol takes advantage of this observation. Hence, it aims at obfuscating a pseudonym change by detecting traffic situations, which may serve as a situational Mix Zone for changing a pseudonym in an efficient way (see Section 5.2.2). Due to its novelty and appropriateness of the approach, a patent has been assigned to this approach, too [184].

A.1 Mix Zone Detection Protocol

Approaches like proposed by *Gerlach et al.* [116] take the number of nodes in proximity as a criteria for defining Mix Zones. Instead, for this protocol, the adversary's tracking capabilities are taken as a measure for defining an appropriate point in time for changing pseudonyms. This approach is based on the assumption, that an adversary is equipped with a state-of the art tracking algorithm like the one deployed in [7] or [107]. Accordingly, in case a pseudonym change is detected, the adversary associates the unknown ID to the trace, which matches best the given mobility data, i.e., position, speed and heading.

The basic idea behind this protocol is to integrate the described attacker model as a reference into every vehicle station. In case a pseudonym change is pending, the reference model is evaluating the trajectories of adjacent vehicles and estimates their future paths. The purpose of this is to identify, whether at some point in time, the host vehicle's future trajectory interferes with the ones from other vehicles, such that the tracking algorithm could not tell them apart. If this is the case, then both vehicles are changing their pseudonym simultaneously at the specified point in time.

In Figure A.1 the concept is illustrated by means of a common traffic scenario, where a *vehicle A* is about to enter a highway and meanwhile on the right lane a second *vehicle B* is approaching. By evaluating the emitted CAMs of both vehicles via the deployed prediction

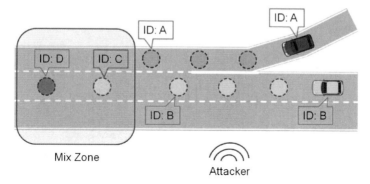

Figure A.1: Situational Mix Zone at a highway access

model, the future path may be determined, in order to evaluate, whether both trajectories are intersecting at some point in time. Changing pseudonyms at this location, turns the marked region into a Mix Zone. Note that for creating the Mix Zone no prior synchronization among respective participants becomes necessary. Instead, it is required that the protocol is running on vehicles, which are supposed to create the Mix Zone. Hence, assuming a similar data basis, vehicles will implicitly calculate the same Mix Zone.

By means of the pseudo-code description in Algorithm 8, 9 and 10, the situational Mix Zone detection is described. Within the C2X communication stack, the top routine described by Algorithm 8 is called for starting the pseudonym change. A pseudonym change is triggered every time the pseudonym change interval, denoted by PCI in line 1 in Algorithm 8 has expired. Depending on the respective implementation, the pseudonym change interval may be in the order of seconds or minutes [6],[5]. The time interval defined by MCL in line 2 denotes the maximum latency for finding a Mix Zone. If this latency is exceeded, a pseudonym change is performed directly.

Finding appropriate situational Mix Zones is the task of Algorithm 9. Possible timeslots are evaluated by iterating over the latest entries of the Neighborhood Table. For each entry the future path is predicted for a given interval (see line 1 in Algorithm 9). Per default, the prediction range, defined in line 2, is set to 100 ms, which corresponds to the minimum CAM sending interval according to ETSI specification [36]. If for a future point in time, the prediction of any neighbor matches the mobility data of the host vehicle, a Mix Zone is considered to be detected. The respective timestamp is returned and the pseudonym change is triggered.

In order to ensure the effectiveness towards an adversary, a monitoring function is advocated, which verifies, if at the specified timestamp the predicted Mix Zone was created successfully. In this thesis, the verification is done by Algorithm 10, following a straight forward approach. Hence, a Mix Zone is considered to be created successfully, if at the determined *Pseudonym Change Time (PCT)* the Neighborhood Table has registered a new vehicle, with similar mobility data as the host vehicle. The presented approach may be further enhanced by extending the Mix Zone via a silent period according to *Sampigethaya et al.* [109].

Algorithm 8 doPseudonymChanges

1: $PCI = 30min$ {Pseudonym Change Interval}
2: $MCL = 5min$ {Maximum Change Latency}
3: PCT {Pseudonym Change Time}
4: **while** $true$ **do**
5:   **if** getUTCTime() $= NextPseudonymChange$ **then**
6:     **while** getUTCTime() $< NextPseudonymChange + MCL$ **do**
7:       $PCT = $ determinePseudonymChangeTime()
8:       **if** $PCT \neq -1$ **then**
9:         changePseudonym(PCT)
10:         **if** verifyPseudonymChangeSuccess(PCT) **then**
11:           **break**
12:         **end if**
13:       **end if**
14:     **end while**
15:     **if** $PCT = -1$ **then**
16:       changePseudonym(PCT)
17:     **end if**
18:   **end if**
19:   $NextPseudonymChange = $ getUTCTime() $+PCI$
20: **end while**

Algorithm 9 determinePseudonymChangeTime

In: Neighborhood Table N_{Table}, Last sent message of host $LastHostMsg$
Out: Pseudonym Change Time PCT

1: $PI = 3000ms$ {Predict Interval}
2: $PS = 100ms$ {Predict Step}
3: $PCT = -1$ {Pseudonym Change Time}
4: **for all** $n \in N_{Table}$ **do**
5:   **for** $i = 0$ to PI **by** PS **do**
6:     $HostPredict = $ doPrediction($LastHostMsg$.getPosition(), i);
7:     $NeighborPredict = $ doPrediction(n.getPosition(), i);
8:     **if** $HostPredict = NeighborPredict$ **then**
9:       **if** $-1 \leq PCT > LastHostMsg$.getTimestamp()$+i$ **then**
10:         $PCT = LastHostMsg$.getTimestamp()$+i$
11:       **end if**
12:     **end if**
13:   **end for**
14: **end for**
15: **return** PCT

A.2 Evaluation

The presented protocol has been implemented and evaluated using VSimRTI (V2X Simulation Runtime Infrastructure) (see Section 5.8.3). In the context of the Master's thesis, done by *Y. Wang* [185] simulations have been carried out for road scenarios, which support

---

Algorithm 10 verifyPseudonymChangeSuccess(PCT)

In: Neighborhood Table N_{Table}, Pseudonym Change Time PCT
Out: Boolean, *True* for successful, *False* for unsuccessful Mix Zone creation

 1: **wait until** getUTCTime() = PCT
 2: **if** N_{Table}.hasNewEntry() **then**
 3:   $NeighborPos = N_{Table}$.getNewEntry().getPosition()
 4:   **if** $NeighborPos \approx$ getPosition() **then**
 5:     **return** true
 6:   **else**
 7:     **return** false
 8:   **end if**
 9: **else**
10:   **return** false
11: **end if**

---

the creation of situational Mix Zones. These are in particular highway slip roads, junctions, confluences, or narrowing lanes. Simulations yielded, that the likelihood for creating a Mix Zone scales best with increasing traffic densities. At the highest traffic density category of approximately 32-45 vehicles/km (see Table 5.5 in Section 5.8.3) a Mix Zone could be created by 30% of all passing vehicles.

A.3 Conclusion

In this section a novel approach for creating situational Mix Zones has been presented, which is characterized by its low complexity. Compared to other privacy protocols, no prior synchronization has to take place among respective participants. This means, that no additional overhead is imposed on the channel load. The protocol works in a decentralized manner and therefore does not require infrastructural support.

A further key property of this approach is that it has no implications on the C2X safety functionality. This represents an important but often underestimated aspect, which is not taken care enough by most C2X privacy protocols so far. Besides aforementioned advantages regarding low communication costs, this protocol imposes also a low computational complexity. Several required functionalities like, e.g., the monitoring of adjacent vehicles is implicitly realized by the Neighborhood Table, a component already present inside every C2X communication stack.

The presented algorithms are lightweighted and easily executable on today's automotive processors. Due to its low communicational, computational, and organizational overhead in conjunction with an acceptable efficiency this privacy protocol represents a good candidate for early deployment of the C2X technology.

Side View to Privacy

Privacy International (PI) [186] has identified four major models for privacy protection. These are the namely:

1. Comprehensive Laws
2. Sectoral Laws
3. Self-Regulation
4. Technologies of Privacy

The first model of *Comprehensive Laws* foresees a consolidation of privacy rights by means of comprehensive laws (e.g., the federal constitutions), which every individual, amenable to the law, can refer to, to claim his right to privacy. In contrast, the second model of *Sectoral Laws* describes a rather distributed legal privacy framework, where dedicated laws exist only, to protect some specific sections of personal data. The model for *Self-regulation* assumes that authorities and individuals act responsible when treating with personal data, such that no observation or regulation becomes necessary. *Technologies of Privacy* can be used to impede privacy violations from the start and therefore is especially important for areas where law enforcement is hardly achievable. Depending on the country, several models may be applied simultaneously to ensure privacy of individuals. In the following, a brief survey over the legal frameworks of data protection in European Union, Germany, and the United States is given and possible implications to the Car-to-X technology are identified.

B.1 Comprehensive Laws

The United Nations have identified the protection of *personal data* as a fundamental right, which has been manifested in *Article 12* [187] of the *Universal Declaration of Human Rights*. An informal definition of the term personal data, sometimes also referred as *sensitive* data can be found [101](pp. 12 -15). Accordingly personal data does not only include data, which can be associated directly to an individual. Also secondary data, which can be associated to individuals using additional information is regarded as relevant for privacy protection. For instance, a network IP address might become personal data if the individual enters her/his name into an email account and both information parts become available to an observer. Whether or not, messages exchanged within Car-to-Car and Car-to-Infrastructure Communication are considered as personal data, has to be evaluated by lawyers and goes beyond the scope of this work.

B.1.1 European Union

In 1995, the European Parliament and the European Council defined minimum standards for data protection inside member states of the European Union (EU). The *Directive 95/46/EC* (protection of personal data) [188] represents a regulatory framework, which is aimed to balance the individuals privacy on the one hand and the free movement of personal data within the EU on the other. The directive is aimed towards automated processing of data and includes guidelines for lawful processing. Accordingly, processing of data is considered as lawful, if it follows the stated guidelines. For Car-to-X Communication it has to be evaluated to what extend *Directive 95/46/EC* applies for scenarios, where for instance, a citizen of one EU member state is driving with a C2X equipped vehicle into a neighboring EU state and the broadcasted C2X data is processed at this state. If broadcasted location information is interpreted as personal data, it must not be processed together with the individual's identity without her or his confirmation.

Especially for areas of electronics and telecommunication, the EU has enacted the *Directive 2002/58/EC* (Directive on privacy and electronic communications) in 2002 [189]. According to this Directive, EU member states are obliged to establish a telecommunication specific regulation, which impedes overhearing of telephonic communications as well as eavesdropping and interception of emails. Transferring this directive to the Car-to-X Communication domain might not be so straight forward, as communication modes differ considerably. Compared to existing telecommunication standards, ETSI deploys messages, whose content is fixed. A CAM for example delivers predefined data contents (i.e., position, speed, heading) and cannot be compared to the message contents exchanged, e.g., in mobile telephony, where message content is completely generic.

B.1.2 Germany

According to the jurisdiction of the Federal Constitutional Court, data protection is regarded as a fundamental right. The so called "right to informational self-determination", is a personal right based on the Basic Law of the Federal Republic of Germany, the so called *Volkszählungsurteil* from 1983, as well as the *German Federal Data Protection Act (FDPA)*. Accordingly, every individual has the right to determine the usage and publication of his personal data. In consequence, every kind of gathering, processing or utilization of personal data is prohibited, unless it is demanded by other laws or the individual has given his confirmation. Motivated by the European mandate, Germany has changed the FDPA to implement the *Directive 95/46/EC* in 2004. Data protection regulations can be found in many other complementary German laws such as the Telecommunications Act (*German*: Telekommunikationsgesetz) and the Telemedia Act (*German*: Telemediengesetz). According to the latest study carried out by Privacy International Organization [186] in 2007, Germany has one of the strictest privacy laws in the world.

B.2 Sectoral Laws

Although not explicitly stated within the federal constitution, legal privacy concepts are contained in most of the recently passed laws, which regulate the affairs of new technologies and media, such as emailing, digital payment or eCommerce. Privacy International criticizes that relying privacy only on sectoral laws is not sufficient, as it requires new legislation to be introduced by lawmakers every time a new technology comes up in the market. Consequently, legal privacy protection frequently lags behind the technological process. In the following, the legal privacy framework of the United States is briefly discussed as one of the largest market for a potential roll-out of the Car-to-X technology.

B.2.1 USA

In the U.S. no comprehensive act for privacy protection is foreseen and concepts of privacy are not reflected within the U.S. constitution [190]. Several provisions in the *Bill of Rights* include a right to privacy from state surveillance into an area, where a person has a "reasonable expectation of privacy". However, the constitution only protects against surveillance of the state, leaving out the protection of privacy against invasions of individuals. Also the *Privacy Act of 1974* [191] is limited to the treatment of an individual's records held by the state government and requires them to apply fair information practices. Instead of a comprehensive framework, a patchwork of laws embodies some specific areas of personal data.

B.2.2 California

Some U.S. states, such as California [192] or Montana [193] have explicitly incorporated privacy as an inalienable right within their constitutions. Of special interest for Car-to-X system designers might be the *Californian Vehicle Code Section 9951* [194] of the *General Privacy Law*, which relates to the installing of event data recorders in vehicles. Such a black box is commonly used, to retrieve data after an accident and records steering and braking activities, and even more problematic, the entire driving history for certain time period before the accident. The *Section 9951* requires automobile manufacturers to ask the vehicle owner for permission, every time they want to access and process the stored data. Furthermore, the data retrieved from such a device must not be used for any other purpose than improving vehicle safety, servicing or repairing issues. Forwarding of stored information to other vehicle safety organizations must not reveal the owners identity. Obviously, type and quality of the data stored within that device is very comparable to the information broadcasted within frequently sent CAMs in Car-to-X communication. As access to CAM messages is public, a strong need to obfuscate the driver's identity in order to still comply with that law, can be identified.

Of further importance for Car-to-X might be the *Government Code Section (11000-11019.10)* [195], which consolidates, that if a government agency is collecting information electronically, the individual has to be informed. If the data is forwarded to third parties, the individual has to give her/his consent. Based on the system architecture described in Chapter 2.1, several analogies can be drawn to Car-to-Infrastructure communication scenarios. The majority of RSUs are likely to be operated by governmental institutions. Besides traffic assessment and message aggregation, a RSU might also forward collected C2X data to non-governmental organizations (e.g., for forwarding of weather hazard messages to meteorological service by means of PVD data). How far this law applies to Car-to-X messages has to be evaluated in the future.

B.3 Self-Regulation

Self-Regulation foresees no central privacy policy and relies data protection upon the responsibility of every individual, governmental or industry body. Self-policing is endorsed in areas, which are not covered by law or technological solutions, yet. However, self-regulation is considered as too unreliable and in contrast, Car-to-X as too sensitive towards privacy violations, to entirely rely on that model, only.

Bibliography

[1] H. Zimmermann, "OSI Reference Model - The ISO Model of Architecture for Open Systems Interconnection," *IEEE Transactions on Communications*, vol. 28, no. 4, pp. 425–432, April 1980.

[2] *Intelligent Transport Systems (ITS); Communications Architecture*, European Telecommunications Standards Institute ETSI Technical Specification TS 102 665, 2009.

[3] *IEEE Trial-Use Standard for Wireless Access in Vehicular Environments - Security Services for Applications and Management Messages*, Intelligent Transportation Systems Committee Std. 1609.2-2006, 2006.

[4] PreDrive C2X Consortium, "Deliverable D1.3 - Security Architecture," Tech. Rep., February 2009.

[5] Car2Car Communication Consortium, "Public Key Infrastructure Memo," Task Force PKI, Report, October 2011.

[6] N. Bißmeyer, H. Stübing, E. Schoch, S. Goetz, J. P. Stotz, and B. Lonc, "A generic Public Key Infrastructure for securing Car-to-X Communication," in *Proceedings of the 18th World Congress on Intelligent Transportation Systems*, Oct. 2011.

[7] H. Stübing, A. Jaeger, N. Bißmeyer, C. Schmidt, and S. A. Huss, "Verifying Mobility Data under Privacy Considerations in Car-to-X Communication," in *Proceedings of the 17th World Congress on Intelligent Transportation Systems*, Oct. 2010.

[8] simTD Consortium, "Deliverable D21.2 Konsolidierter Systemarchitekturentwurf," Tech. Rep., September 2009.

[9] ——, "Deliverable D21.5 Spezifikation der IT - Sicherheitslösung," Tech. Rep., August 2009.

[10] ——, "Deliverable D22.1 - Spezifikation der IVS," Tech. Rep., October 2010.

[11] ——, "Deliverable D22.3 Fahrzeugseitiges IT - Sicherheitssystem," Tech. Rep., January 2010.

[12] A. Jaeger, N. Bißmeyer, H. Stübing, and S. A. Huss, "A Novel Framework for Efficient Mobility Data Verification in Vehicular Ad-hoc Networks," *International Journal of Intelligent Transportation Systems Research (IJIR)*, 2011.

[13] J. Firl and Q. Tran, "Probabilistic Maneuver Prediction in Traffic Scenarios," in *Proceedings of the European Conference on Mobile Robots - ECMR 2011*, September 2011.

[14] H. Stübing, J. Firl, and S. A. Huss, "A Two-Stage Verification Process for Car-to-X Mobility Data based on Path Prediction and Probabilistic Maneuver Recognition," in *Proceedings of the 3rd IEEE Vehicular Networking Conference VNC 2011*, Amsterdam, The Netherlands, November 2011.

[15] ——, "Ein Konzept zur Plausibilitätsprüfung von Car-to-X Mobilitätsdaten basierend auf Pfadprädiktionen und Hidden Markov Models," in *Proceedings of the 3rd VDE GMM-Fachtagung AmE Automotive meets Electronics*, May 2012.

[16] J. Firl, H. Stübing, S. A. Huss, and C. Stiller, "Predictive Maneuver Evaluation for Enhancement of Car-to-X Mobility Data," in *Proceedings of the 2012 IEEE Intelligent Vehicles Symposium, Alcalá de Henare, Spain*, May 2012.

[17] H. Stübing, M. Pfalzgraf, and S. A. Huss, "A Decentralized Group Privacy Protocol for Vehicular Networks ," in *Proceedings of the 3th IEEE International Conference on Information Privacy, Security, Risk and Trust (PASSAT 2011)*, October 2011.

[18] H. Stübing, M. Ceven, and S. A. Huss, "A Diffie-Hellman based Privacy Protocol for Car-to-X Communication," in *Proceedings of the 9th IEEE Conference on Privacy, Security and Trust (PST 2011)*, Montreal, Canada, Jul. 2011.

[19] H. Stübing, A. Shoufan, and S. A. Huss, "Secure C2X Communication based on Adaptive Beamforming," in *Proceedings of the 14th VDI International Conference on Electronic for Vehicles*, Oct. 2009.

[20] ——, "Enhancing Security and Privacy in C2X Communication by Radiation Pattern Control," in *Proceedings of the 3rd IEEE International Symposium on Wireless Vehicular Communications (WIVEC 2010)*, May 2010.

[21] ——, "A Demonstrator for Beamforming in C2X Communication," in *Proceedings of the 3rd IEEE International Symposium on Wireless Vehicular Communications (WIVEC 2010)*, May 2010.

[22] H. Stübing and A. Jaeger, *Secure Beamforming for Weather Hazard Warning Application in Car-to-X Communication*, ser. Lecture Notes in Electrical Engineering. Berlin: Springer, Nov. 2010, vol. 78., pp. 187–206.

[23] H. Stübing, A. Jaeger, N. Wagner, and S. A. Huss, "Integrating Secure Beamforming into Car-to-X Architectures," in *Proceedings of the SAE 2011 World Congress & Exhibition, Detroit, USA*, Apr. 2011.

[24] ——, "Integrating Secure Beamforming into Car-to-X Architectures," *SAE International Journal of Passenger Cars- Electronic and Electrical Systems*, vol. 4., pp. 88–96, Jun. 2011.

[25] *Intelligent Transport Systems (ITS); European profile standard for the physical and medium access control layer of Intelligent Transport Systems operating in the 5 GHz frequency band*, European Telecommunications Standards Institute ETSI ETSI Standard ES 202 663, 2009.

[26] "simTD: Sichere Intelligente Mobilität Testfeld Deutschland." [Online]. Available: www.simtd.de

[27] Car2Car Communication Consortium, "CAR 2 CAR Communication Consortium Manifesto," Tech. Rep., August 2007. [Online]. Available: www.car-to-car.org

[28] simTD Consortium, "Deliverable D21.1 - Bewertende Übersicht existierender Systemarchitekturen," Tech. Rep., June 2009.

[29] N. Bißmeyer, H. Stübing, M. Matthess, J. P. Stotz, J. Schütte, M. Gerlach, and F. Friederici, "simTD Security Architecture:Deployment of a Security and Privacy Architecture in Field Operational Tests," in *Proceedings of the 7th ESCAR Embedded Security in Cars Conference, Germany, Düsseldorf* , Nov. 2009.

[30] H. Stübing, M. Bechler, D. Heussner, T. May, I. Radusch, H. Rechner, and P. Vogel, "simTD: A Car-To-X System Architecture for Field Operational Tests," *IEEE Communications Magazine*, May 2010.

[31] European Commission Road Safety. EU Road Safety Policy. [Online]. Available: http://ec. europa.eu/transport/road_safety/specialist/policy/index_en.htm

[32] ——. (2001, September) White Paper European transport policy for 2010: time to decide. [Online]. Available: http://ec.europa.eu/transport/strategies/2001_white_paper_en.htm

[33] ——. White Paper Roadmap to a single European transport area - Towards a competitive and resource-efficient transport system. [Online]. Available: http://ec.europa.eu/transport/ strategies/2011_white_paper_en.htm

[34] *Intelligent Transport Systems (ITS); Vehicular Communications; GeoNetworking; Part 1: Requirements*, European Telecommunications Standards Institute ETSI Technical Specification TS 102 636-1, 2010.

[35] simTD Consortium, "Deliverable D21.4 - Spezifikation der Kommunikationsprotokolle," Tech. Rep., August 2009.

[36] *Intelligent Transport Systems (ITS); Vehicular Communications; Basic Set of Applications; Part 2: Specification of Cooperative Awareness Basic Service*, European Telecommunications Standards Institute ETSI Technical Specification TS 102 637-2, 2010.

[37] *Intelligent Transport Systems (ITS); Vehicular Communications; Basic Set of Applications; Part 3: Specifications of Decentralized Environmental Notification Basic Service*, European Telecommunications Standards Institute ETSI Technical Specification TS 102 637-3, 2010.

[38] *SAE International; Dedicated Short Range Communications (DSRC) Message Set Dictionary*, SAE International Std. J2735, 2009.

[39] PreDrive C2X Consortium, "Deliverable D4.1 - Detailed description of selected use-cases and corresponding technical requirements," Tech. Rep., October 2008.

[40] Drive C2X Consortium, "DeliverableD23.1 - EnhancedSystemSpecification," Tech. Rep., December 2011.

[41] simTD Consortium, "Deliverable D11.1 Beschreibung der Funktionen," Tech. Rep., June 2009.

[42] *Intelligent Transport Systems (ITS); Vehicular Communications; Basic Set of Applications; Definitions*, European Telecommunications Standards Institute ETSI Technical Report TR 102 638, 2009.

[43] K. Pudenz, "Forschungsprojekt Diamant: Opel präsentiert erste Ergebnisse des Telematik-Feldtests," *ATZ - Automobiltechnische Zeitschrift*, June 2011.

[44] A. Aijaz, B. Bochow, F. Dtzer, A. Festag, M. Gerlach, R. Kroh, and T. Leinmller, "Attacks on Inter Vehicle Communication Systems - an Analysis," in *Proceedings of the 3rd International Workshop on Intelligent Transportation (WIT)*, March 2006, pp. 189–194.

[45] *Intelligent Transport Systems (ITS); Threat, Vulnerability and Risk Analysis (TVRA)*, ITS WG5 Technical Report, 2010.

[46] (2012, April) HPP Project Overview, Basic Presentation. Hackers Profiling Project (HPP). [Online]. Available: http://www.isecom.org/hpp/

[47] R. Chiesa, S. Ducci, and S. Ciappi, *Profiling Hackers: The Science of Criminal Profiling as Applied to the World of Hacking*, 1st ed. Boston, MA, USA: Auerbach Publications, 2008.

[48] H. G. Molter, K. Ogata, E. Tews, and R.-P. Weinmann, "An Efficient FPGA Implementation for an DECT Brute-Force Attacking Scenario," in *Proceedings of the 5th IEEE International Conference on Wireless and Mobile Communications (ICWMC 2009)*. Los Alamitos, CA, USA: IEEE Computer Society, Aug. 2009, pp. 82–86.

[49] K. Koscher, A. Czeskis, F. Roesner, S. Patel, T. Kohno, S. Checkoway, D. McCoy, B. Kantor, D. Anderson, H. Shacham, and S. Savage, "Experimental Security Analysis of a Modern Automobile," in *Proceedings of the IEEE Symposium on Security and Privacy 2010*, ser. SP '10. Washington, DC, USA: IEEE Computer Society, May 2010, pp. 447–462.

[50] L. Buttyan and J.-P. Hubaux, *Security and Cooperation in Wireless Networks*. Cambridge: Cambridge University Press, 2008.

[51] C. Eckert, *IT-Sicherheit - Konzepte, Verfahren, Protokolle*. Oldenbourg, 2009.

[52] Kraftfahrt-Bundesamt (KBA). (2011, January) Jahresbilanz des Fahrzeugbestandes am 1. Januar 2011. [Online]. Available: http://www.kba.de/nn_124584/DE/Statistik/Fahrzeuge/ Bestand/bestand_node.html?__nnn=true

[53] (2011, December) Fahrerlaubnisbesitz in deutschland. webside. Bundesanstalt fr Straenwesen (BASt). [Online]. Available: http://www.bast.de/nn_40694/DE/Publikationen/Infos/ 2007-2006/16-2007.html

[54] H. Stübing, H. Berninger, and S. A. Huss, "Security and Privacy in Car-to-X Communication: Legislation, Standardization and Field Operational Trials," in *Proceedings of the VDE AmE "Automotive meets Electronics", 2. GMM-Fachtagung, Dortmund*, May 2011.

[55] P. Papadimitratos, L. Buttyan, T. Holczer, E. Schoch, J. Freudiger, M. Raya, Z. Ma, F. Kargl, A. Kung, and J.-P. Hubaux, "Secure Vehicular Communication Systems: Design and Architecture," *IEEE Communications Magazine*, vol. 46, no. 11, pp. 100–109, November 2008.

[56] T. Leinmüller, R. K. Schmidt, E. Schoch, A. Held, and G. Schäfer, "Modeling Roadside Attacker Behavior in VANETs," in *Proceedings of the 3rd IEEE Workshop on Automotive Networking and Applications (AutoNet 2008)*, December 2008.

[57] F. Schaub, Z. Ma, and F. Kargl, "Privacy Requirements in Vehicular Communication Systems," in *Proceedings of the International Conference on Computational Science and Engineering, 2009. CSE '09*, vol. 3, August 2009, pp. 139–145.

[58] VSC-A Consortium, "Vehicle Safety Communications Applications (VSC-A) Project Final Report," Research and Innovative Technology Administration (RITA), National Highway Traffic Safety Administration (NHTSA), Intelligent Transportation Systems (ITS), Project Final Report, May 2010.

[59] "NOW: Network on Wheels Project." [Online]. Available: www.network-on-wheels.de

[60] A. Festag, G. Noecker, M. Strassberger, A. Lübke, B. Bochow, M. Torrent-Moreno, S. Schnaufer, R. Eigner, C. Catrinescu, and J. Kunisch, "NoW-Network on Wheels: Project Objectives, Technology and Achievements," in *Proceedings of the 6th International Workshop on Wireless Intelligent Transportation (WIT)*, March 2008.

[61] "SeVeCom (Secure Vehicular Communication) Project." [Online]. Available: http://www. sevecom.org/index.html

[62] "Drive C2X Accelerate Cooperative Mobility," 2011. [Online]. Available: http://www.drive-c2x.eu/project

[63] Car2Car Communication Consortium, "In-Vehicle Security and Assurance Levels," Task Force Secure Hardware, Tech. Rep., April 2012.

[64] J. J. Haas, Y.-C. Hu, and K. P. Laberteaux, "Design and Analysis of a lightweight Certificate Revocation Mechanism for VANET," in *Proceedings of the 6th ACM international Workshop on VehiculAr Internetworking*, ser. VANET '09. New York, NY, USA: ACM, September 2009, pp. 89–98. [Online]. Available: http://doi.acm.org/10.1145/1614269.1614285

[65] P. P. Papadimitratos, G. Mezzour, and J.-P. Hubaux, "Certificate Revocation List Distribution in Vehicular Communication Systems," in *Proceedings of the 5th ACM International Workshop on Vehicular Inter-networking*, ser. VANET '08. New York, USA: ACM, September 2008, pp. 86–87.

[66] M. Raya, P. Papadimitratos, I. Aad, D. Jungels, and J. Hubaux, "Eviction of Misbehaving and Faulty Nodes in Vehicular Networks," *IEEE Journal on Selected Areas in Communications*, vol. 25, no. 8, 2007.

[67] T. Leinmüller, E. Schoch, and F. Kargl, "Position Verification Approaches for Vehicular Ad Hoc Networks," *IEEE Wireless Communications, Special Issue on Inter-Vehicular Communications*, vol. 13, no. 5, pp. 16–21, Oct. 2006.

[68] T. Z. Stan Pietrowicz and H. Shim, "Short-Lived, Unlinked Certificates for Privacy-Preserving Secure Vehicular Communications," in *Proceedings of the 17th World Congress on Intelligent Transportation Systems*, Oct. 2010.

[69] A. Jaeger, H. Stübing, and S. A. Huss, "A Dedicated Hardware Security Module for Field Operational Tests of Car-to-X Communication," in *Proceedings of the 4th ACM Conference on Wireless Network Security (WiSec '11)*, Jun. 2011.

[70] ——, "WiSec 2011 Poster: A Modular Design for a Hardware Security Module in Car-to-X Communication," *ACM SIGMOBILE Mobile Computing and Communications Review (MC2R)*, vol. 15., pp. 43–44, 2011.

[71] PRESERVE Preparing Secure Vehicle-to-X Communication Systems. [Online]. Available: http://www.preserve-project.eu

[72] M. Stöttinger, S. Malipatlolla, and Q. Tian, *Survey of Methods to Improve Side-Channel Resistance on Partial Reconfigurable Platforms*, ser. Lecture Notes in Electrical Engineering. Berlin: Springer, Nov. 2010, vol. 78.

[73] A. Jaeger and S. A. Huss, "The Weather Hazard Warning in simTD: A Design for Road Weather Related Warnings in a Large Scale Car-to-X Field Operational Test," in *Proceedings of the 11th IEEE International Conference on Telecommunications for Intelligent Transport Systems (ITST-2011)*, Aug. 2011.

[74] T. Leinmüller, E. Schoch, F. Kargl, and C. Maihöfer, "Influence of Falsified Position Data on Geographic Ad-Hoc Routing," in *2nd European Workshop on Security and Privacy in Ad Hoc and Sensor Networks (ESAS 2005)*, Springer LNCS 3812/2005. Visegrad, Hungary: Springer LNCS 3812/2005, 07/2005 2005.

[75] J.-P. Hubaux, S. Čapkun, and J. Luo, "The Security and Privacy of Smart Vehicles," *IEEE Security and Privacy*, vol. 2, pp. 49–55, May 2004.

[76] P. Golle, D. Greene, and J. Staddon, "Detecting and Correcting Malicious Data in VANETs," in *Proceedings of the 1st ACM International Workshop on Vehicular Ad Hoc Networks*, ser. VANET '04. New York, NY, USA: ACM, October 2004, pp. 29–37.

[77] S. Marti, T. J. Giuli, K. Lai, and M. Baker, "Mitigating Routing Misbehavior in Mobile Ad Hoc Networks," in *Proceedings of the 6th Annual International Conference on Mobile Computing and Networking*, ser. MobiCom '00. New York, USA: ACM, August 2000, pp. 255–265.

[78] R. Schmidt, T. Leinmüller, and A. Held, "Defending Against Roadside Attackers," in *Proceedings of the 16th World Congress on Intelligent Transport Systems*, September 2009.

[79] T. Leinmüller, C. Maihöfer, E. Schoch, and F. Kargl, "Improved Security in Geographic Ad Hoc Routing through Autonomous Position Verification," in *Proceedings of the 3rd International Workshop on Vehicular Ad Hoc Networks*, September 2006, pp. 57–66.

[80] T. Leinmüller, E. Schoch, F. Kargl, and C. Maihöfer, "Decentralized Position Verification in Geographic Ad Hoc Routing," *Wiley Security and Communication Networks Journal*, vol. 3, no. 4, July 2010.

[81] G. Yan, S. Olariu, and M. C. Weigle, "Providing VANET Security through Active Position Detection," *Journal of Computer Communications*, vol. 31, pp. 2883–2897, July 2008.

[82] R. K. Schmidt, T. Leinmüllerer, E. Schoch, A. Held, and G. Schäfer, "Vehicle Behavior Analysis to Enhance Security in VANETs," in *Proceedings of the 4th IEEE Vehicle-to-Vehicle Communications Workshop (V2VCOM2008)*, June 2008.

[83] T. Leinmüller, R. K. Schmidt, and A. Held, "Cooperative Position Verification - Defending Against Roadside Attackers 2.0," in *Proceedings of the 17th World Congres on Intelligent Transport Systems*, October 2010.

[84] M. Gerlach, "Trusted Ad Hoc Communications for Intelligent Transportation Systems," Ph.D. dissertation, Technische Universität Berlin, 2010.

[85] M. Gerlach and F. Friederici, "Towards RSSI - Based Position Plausibility Checks for Vehicular Communication," in *Proceedings of the 4th Workshop on Vehicle-to-Vehicle Communications (V2VCOM)*, Eindhoven, the Netherlands, June 2008.

[86] R. E. Kalman, "A new Approach to linear Filtering and Prediction Problems," *Transactions of the ASME–Journal of Basic Engineering*, vol. 82, no. Series D, pp. 35–45, 1960.

[87] R. P. Samuel S. Blackman, Robert Popoli, *Design and Analysis of Modern Tracking Systems*, 1st ed. Artech House Publishers, Aug 1999.

[88] E. J. Krakiwsky, C. B. Harris, and R. V. C. Wong, "A Kalman filter for integrating dead reckoning, map matching and GPS positioning," in *Proceedings of the Position Location and Navigation Symposium, 1988. Record. Navigation into the 21st Century. IEEE PLANS '88.*, Aug. 2002, pp. 39–46.

[89] D. Sutherland, Ed., *GPS Guidbook Standards and Guidelines for Land Surveying Using Global Positioning System Methods*. Natural Resources, November 2004.

[90] A. P. A. Mohinder S. Grewal, Lawrence R. Weill, *Global Positioning Systems, Inertial Navigation, and Integration*. Wiley, February 2007.

[91] SAFESPOT Consortium, "Deliverable D3.3.3 - Local dynamic map specification," Tech. Rep., 2008.

[92] Continental, *ARS 300 Long Range Radar Sensor 77 GHz Datasheet.* [Online]. Available: http://www.conti-online.com/generator/www/de/en/continental/industrial_sensors/themes/ars_300/ars_300_en.html

[93] L. R. Rabiner, "A tutorial on hidden Markov Models and selected Applications in Speech Recognition," *Proceedings of the IEEE*, vol. 77, no. 2, pp. 257–286, February 1989.

[94] M. Stanke, "Gene Prediction with a Hidden Markov Model," Ph.D. dissertation, Universitt Göttingen, 2004. [Online]. Available: http://gobics.de/mario/papers/diss.pdf

[95] U.-V. Marti and H. Bunke, *Using a statistical language model to improve the performance of an HMM-based Cursive Handwriting Recognition Systems.* River Edge, NJ, USA: World Scientific Publishing Co., Inc., 2002, pp. 65–90.

[96] C. Karlof and D. Wagner, *Hidden Markov Model Cryptanalysis.* Springer, 2003, vol. 2779, pp. 17–34.

[97] D. Quanz, "Implementierung einer Fahrzeugplausibilitätsprüfung basierend auf Kommunikations- und Sensordaten," Bachelor's Thesis, Technische Universität Darmstadt, January 2011, supervised by Norbert Bißmeyer and Attila Jaeger.

[98] T. Gundlach, "Generierung von Testdaten zur Kalibrierung eines Radars im Car-2-X Umfeld," Hochschule für Technik und Wirtschaft des Saarlandes, Internship Report, November 2011, supervised by Hagen Stübing.

[99] M. Gerlach and F. Friederici, "Implementing Trusted Vehicular Communications," in *Proceedings of the 67th IEEE Vehicular Technology Conference VTC2009-Spring*, 2009.

[100] D. G. Steer, L. Strawczynski, W. Diffie, and M. J. Wiener, "A Secure Audio Teleconference System," in *Proceedings of the 8th Annual International Cryptology Conference on Advances in Cryptology.* London, UK: Springer-Verlag, August 1990, pp. 520–528.

[101] Preciosa Consortium, "Deliverable 1 - V2X Privacy Issue Analysis," Tech. Rep., 2009.

[102] Z. Ma, F. Kargl, and M. Weber, "A Location Privacy Metric for V2X Communication Systems," in *Proceedings of the IEEE Sarnoff Symposium 2009 (SARNOFF 2009)*, ser. SARNOFF'09. Piscataway, NJ, USA: IEEE Press, March 2009, pp. 213–218.

[103] L. Fischer and C. Eckert, "506 Ways to Track Your Lover," in *Proceedings of the 68th IEEE Vehicular Technology Conference, VTC Fall 2008*, September 2008, pp. 1–5.

[104] C. E. Shannon, "A mathematical Theory of Communication," *Bell System Technical Journal*, vol. 27, pp. 379–42,623–656, July, October 1948.

[105] Preciosa Consortium, "Deliverable 11 - Guidelines for Privacy Aware Cooperative Application," Tech. Rep., 2010.

[106] M. Gruteser and B. Hoh, "On the Anonymity of Periodic Location Samples," in *Proceedings of the Second International Conference on Security in Pervasive Computing.* Springer, April 2005, pp. 179–192.

[107] B. Wiedersheim, Z. Ma, F. Kargl, and P. Papadimitratos, "Privacy in inter-vehicular Networks: Why simple Pseudonym Change is not enough," in *Proceedings of the 7th international conference on Wireless on-demand network systems and services WONS'10*, 2010.

[108] K. Sampigethaya, L. Huang, M. Li, R. Poovendran, K. Matsuura, and K. Sezaki, "CAR-AVAN: Providing Location Privacy for VANET," *International Workshop on Vehicular Ad Hoc Networks (VANET)*, 2006.

[109] K. Sampigethaya, M. Li, L. Huang, and R. Poovendran, "AMOEBA: Robust Location Privacy Scheme for VANET," *IEEE Journal on Selected Areas in Communications*, vol. 25, no. 8, pp. 1569–1589, October 2007.

[110] D. L. Chaum, "Untraceable electronic mail, return addresses, and digital pseudonyms," *ACM Magazine Communications*, vol. 24, no. 2, pp. 84–90, Feb. 1981.

[111] A. R. Beresford and F. Stajano, "Location Privacy in Pervasive Computing," *IEEE Pervasive Computing*, vol. 2, pp. 46–55, January 2003.

[112] L. Buttyán, T. Holczer, and I. Vajda, "On the effectiveness of changing pseudonyms to provide location privacy in VANETS," in *Proceedings of the 4th European conference on Security and privacy in ad-hoc and sensor networks*, ser. ESAS'07. Berlin, Heidelberg: Springer-Verlag, 2007, pp. 129–141.

[113] M. Gerlach, "Assessing and Improving Privacy in VANETs," in *Proceedings of the 4th Workshop on Embedded Security in Cars (ESCAR)*, November 2006.

[114] L. Huang, K. Matsuura, H. Yamane, and K. Sezaki, "Enhancing wireless Location Privacy using Silent Period," in *Proceedings of the IEEE Wireless Communications and Networking Conference*, vol. 2, March 2005, pp. 1187 – 1192 Vol. 2.

[115] L. Buttyán, T. Holczer, A. Weimerskirch, and W. Whyte, "SLOW: A Practical Pseudonym Changing Scheme for Location Privacy in VANETs," in *Proceedings of the IEEE Vehicular Networking Conference*, IEEE. Tokyo, Japan: IEEE, October 28-29 2009, pp. 1–8.

[116] M. Gerlach and F. Guttler, "Privacy in VANETs using Changing Pseudonyms - Ideal and Real," in *Proceedings of the 65th IEEE Vehicular Technology Conference VTC2007-Spring*, April 2007, pp. 2521–2525.

[117] L. Langer, "Privacy and Verifiability in Electronic Voting," Ph.D. dissertation, Technische Universtät Darmstadt, Oktober 2010. [Online]. Available: http://tuprints.ulb.tu-darmstadt.de/2313/

[118] J. Freudiger, M. Raya, M. Felegyhazi, P. Papadimitratos, and J.-P. Hubaux, "Mix-Zones for Location Privacy in Vehicular Networks," in *Proceedings of the ACM Workshop on Wireless Networking for Intelligent Transportation Systems (WiN-ITS)*, Vancouver, August 2007.

[119] M. Raya, A. Aziz, and J.-P. Hubaux, "Efficient Secure Aggregation in VANETs," in *Proceedings of the 3rd International Workshop on Vehicular Ad Hoc Networks*, ser. VANET '06. September: ACM, 2006, pp. 67–75.

[120] M. Dahl, S. Delaune, and G. Steel, "Formal Analysis of Privacy for Vehicular Mix-Zones," in *Proceedings of the 15th European Conference on Research in Computer Security*, ser. ESORICS'10. Berlin, Heidelberg: Springer-Verlag, 2010, pp. 55–70.

[121] K. Plößl, *Mehrseitig sichere Ad-hoc-Vernetzung von Fahrzeugen*, ser. Gabler Edition Wissenschaft: DuD-Fachbeiträge, A. Pfitzmann, H. Reimer, K. Rihaczek, and A. Roßnagel, Eds. Wiesbaden: Gabler, 2009, zugl.: Regensburg, Univ., Diss., 2008.

[122] R. Resendes, "The New Grand Challenge - Deploying Vehicle Communications," in *Keynote Address The Fifth ACM International Workshop on VehicluAr Internetworking (VANET 2008)*, September 2008.

[123] European Road Federation (ERF), "ERF 2010 European Road Statistics," Tech. Rep., 2010.

[124] P. S. M. Torrent Moreno and H. Hartenstein, "Distributed fair Transmit Power Adjustment for Vehicular Ad Hoc Networks," in *Proceedings of the 3rd IEEE Communications Society Conference on Sensor, Mesh and Ad Hoc Communications and Networks (SECON'06)*, September 2006, pp. 479–488.

[125] W. Diffie and M. E. Hellman, "New Directions in Cryptography," *IEEE Transactions on Information Theory*, vol. IT-22, no. 6, pp. 644–654, 1976.

[126] S. Zheng, D. Manz, and J. Alves-Foss, "A Communication-Computation Efficient Group Key Algorithm for Large and Dynamic Groups," *Journal of Computer Networks*, vol. 51, pp. 69–93, January 2007.

[127] K. Ren, H. Lee, K. Kim, and T. Yoo, "Efficient Authenticated Key Agreement Protocol for Dynamic Groups," in *Proceedings of the 5th International Workshop Information Security Applications (WISA)*, 2004, pp. 144–159.

[128] A. Boumso, B. A. Bensaber, and I. Biskri, "GAKAP, Multicast Key Agreement Protocol for Ad Hoc Networks Based On Group Activity Probability," in *Proceedings of the 29th Annual IEEE International Conference on Local Computer Networks*, ser. LCN '04. Washington, DC, USA: IEEE Computer Society, 2004, pp. 700–704.

[129] I. Ingemarsson, D. T. Tang, and C. K. Wong, "A Conference Key Distribution System," *IEEE Transactions on Information Theory*, vol. 28, no. 5, pp. 714–719, September 1982.

[130] M. Burmester and Y. Desmedt, "A Secure and Efficient Conference Key Distribution System," in *Proceedings of the Advances in Cryptology - Eurocrypt '94, Lecture Notes in Computer Science 950*, 1995, pp. 275–286.

[131] M. Steiner, G. Tsudik, and M. Waidner, "Diffie-Hellman Key Distribution extended to Group Communication," in *Proceedings of the 3rd ACM Conference on Computer and Communications Security*, ser. CCS '96. New York, NY, USA: ACM, 1996, pp. 31–37.

[132] J. Alves-Foss, "An Efficient Secure Authenticated Group Key Exchange Algorithm for Large And Dynamic Groups," in *Proceedings of the 23rd National Information Systems Security Conference*, October 2000, pp. 254–266.

[133] J. Buchmann, *Einführung in die Kryptographie (2. Aufl.).* Springer, 2001.

[134] M. Pfalzgraf, "Ein gruppenbasiertes Protokoll zum Schutz der Privatsphäre in der Car-to-X Kommunikation," Master's Thesis, Technische Universität Darmstadt, July 2010, supervised by Hagen Stübing.

[135] M. Ceven, "A Privacy Protocol for Car-to-X Communication based on Diffie-Hellman Group Keying," Diploma Thesis, Technische Universität Darmstadt, September 2010, supervised by Hagen Stübing.

[136] G. Holzmann, *The Spin Model Checker: Primer and Reference Manual*, 1st ed. Addison-Wesley Professional, 2003.

[137] G. J. Holzmann, "An Analysis of Bitstate Hashing," *Form. Methods Syst. Des.*, vol. 13, pp. 289–307, November 1998.

[138] R. de Renesse and A. H. Aghvami, "Formal Verification of Ad-Hoc Routing Protocols Using SPIN Model Checker," *IEEE MELECON*, vol. IEEE MELECON 2004, pp. 1177–1182, 2004.

[139] A. B. Grda Ug and M. U. a Uglayan, "A Formal Security Analysis of SAODV Using Model Checking," in *Proceedings of the 8th International Symposium on Computer Networks ISCN*, 2007.

[140] M. Ben-Ari, *Principles of the Spin Model Checker*, 1st ed. Springer-Verlag, 2008.

[141] M. Steiner, "Secure Group Key Agreement," Ph.D. dissertation, Naturwissenschaftlich-Technische Fakultät der Universität des Saarlandes, March 2002.

[142] H. Takagi and L. Kleinrock, "Correction to 'Throughput Analysis for Persistent CSMA Systems'," *Correspondence item, IEEE Transactions on Communications*, vol. COM-35, no. 2, pp. 243–245, February 1987.

[143] J. P. M. G. Linnartz, R. Hekmat, and R. J. Venema, "Near-far Effects in Land Mobile Random Access Networks with Narrow-Band Rayleigh Fading Channels," *IEEE Transactions on Vehicular Technology*, vol. 41, no. 1, pp. 77–90, February 1992.

[144] Sumo - simulation of urban mobility. webside. [Online]. Available: http://dmf.unicatt.it/~pollini/sumo_user.shtml

[145] JiST / SWANS Java in Simulation Time / Scalable Wireless Ad hoc Network Simulator. webside. [Online]. Available: http://jist.ece.cornell.edu/

[146] Forschungsgesellschaft für Straßen und Verkehrswesen, *Handbuch für die Bemessung von Straßenverkehrsanlagen (HBS)*, January 2002.

[147] H. Stübing and S. A. Huss, "Kommunikationssystem eines Fahrzeugs im Straßenverkehr und Verfahren zur Fahrzeugkommunikation," Patent DE 10 2009 011 276.6, 09, 2010. [Online]. Available: http://register.dpma.de/DPMAregister/pat/register?AKZ=1020090112766&CURSOR=0

[148] ——, "Sendevorrichtung, Empfangsvorrichtung, Kommunikationssystem sowie Verfahren zum Betreiben einer Sendevorrichtung und einer Empfangsvorrichtung," german Patent DE 10 2010 046 469.4, 03 29, 2012. [Online]. Available: http://register.dpma.de/DPMAregister/pat/register?AKZ=1020100464694&CURSOR=0

[149] ——, "Transmitting Device, Receiving Device, Communication System and Method for operating a Transmitting Device and Receiving Device," Patent 13/240 506, 03 29, 2012. [Online]. Available: http://www.freepatentsonline.com/y2012/0077430.html

[150] W. Xu, W. Trappe, Y. Zhang, and T. Wood, "The Feasibility of Launching and Detecting Jamming Attacks in Wireless Networks," in *Proceedings of the 6th ACM International Symposium on Mobile Ad Hoc Networking and Computing*, ser. MobiHoc '05. New York, NY, USA: ACM, 2005, pp. 46–57.

[151] A. F. Long Le, Wenhui Zhang and R. Baldessari, "Analysis of Approaches for Channel Allocation in Car-to-Car Communication," in *Proceedings of the 1st International Workshop on Interoperable Vehicles (IOV 2008)*, March 2008, pp. 33–38, zürich, Switzerland,.

[152] *Intelligent Transport Systems (ITS); European profile standard for the physical and medium access control layer of intelligent transport systems operating in the 5 GHz frequency band,* ITS WG4 Std. ES 202 663, Rev. Ver. 1.1.0, 2010.

[153] Car2Car Communication Consortium, "Position Paper on ETSI ITS G5 Channel Usage," Working Group Communication, Position Paper, February 2012, c2C-CC internal.

[154] ——, "TF Antenna Status Report," TaskForceAntenna, Status Report 3.0, May 2011.

[155] M. Emmelmann, B. Bochow, and C. Kellum, *Vehicular Networking: Automotive Applications and Beyond,* ser. Intelligent Transport Systems. John Wiley & Sons, 2010.

[156] P. I. . S. G. Roggero, Marco, "Method for the Transmission of Messages and a correspondingly equipped Motor Vehicle," European Patent Application Patent EP20 060 727 778, December 26th, 2007.

[157] D. Wisniowski, "Motor Vehicle for Car to Car Communication and Associated Method for Operating an Antenna Structure of a Motor Vehicle," Patent 20 090 222 173, January 30, 2009.

[158] V. Navda, A. P. Subramanian, K. Dhanasekaran, A. Timm-Giel, and S. Das, "MobiSteer: using steerable Beam directional Antenna for vehicular Network Access," in *Proceedings of the 5th International Conference on Mobile systems, Applications and Services,* ser. MobiSys '07. New York, NY, USA: ACM, 2007, pp. 192–205.

[159] A. P. Subramanian, V. Navda, P. Deshpande, and S. R. Das, "A Measurement Study of inter-vehicular Communication using steerable Beam directional Antenna," in *Proceedings of the 5th ACM International Workshop on Vehicular Inter-Networking,* ser. VANET '08. New York, NY, USA: ACM, 2008, pp. 7–16.

[160] B. Gallagher, "Wireless Vehicular Safety Systems: Car-to-Car Link Improvement in Noise," in *Proceedings of the 16th World Congres on Intelligent Transport Systems,* September 2009.

[161] F. Lorek, "Aus dem Äther ins Auto," *Automobil Produktion,* vol. 2, no. 2, pp. 48–49, February 2011.

[162] G. K. Russell John Haines, "Wireless local Area Network Security," Patent US 2005/0 059 388 A1, March 17, 2005.

[163] S. Lakshmanan, C.-L. Tsao, R. Sivakumar, and K. Sundaresan, "Securing Wireless Data Networks against Eavesdropping using Smart Antennas," in *Proceedings of the 28th International Conference on Distributed Computing Systems,* ser. ICDCS '08. Washington, DC, USA: IEEE Computer Society, June 2008, pp. 19–27.

[164] C. Shannon, "Communication Theory of Secrecy Systems," *Bell System Technical Journal,* vol. 28, p. 656715, Oktober 1949.

[165] A. D. Wyner, "The Wire-Tap Channel," *Bell System Technical Journal,* vol. 54, pp. 1355–1387, 1974.

[166] C. Jeong, I.-M. Kim, and D. I. Kim, "Joint Secure Beamforming Design at the Source and the Relay for an Amplify-and-Forward MIMO Untrusted Relay System," *IEEE Transactions on Signal Processing,* vol. 60, no. 1, pp. 310–325, 2012.

[167] Z. Li, W. Trappe, and R. Yates, "Secret Communication via Multi-antenna Transmission," in *Proceedings of the 41st Annual Conference on Information Sciences and Systems, CISS '07.* IEEE, March 2007, pp. 905–910.

[168] S. Kaul, K. Ramachandran, P. Shankar, S. Oh, M. Gruteser, I. Seskar, and T. Nadeem, "Effect of Antenna Placement and Diversity on Vehicular Network Communications," in *Proceedings of the 4th IEEE Communications Society Conference on Sensor, Mesh and Ad Hoc Communications and Networks, SECON '07* , june 2007, pp. 112 –121.

[169] A. Kwoczek, Z. Raida, J. Lacik, M. Pokorny, J. Puskely, J. Puskely, and P. Vagner, "Influence of Car Panorama Glass Roofs on Car2Car Communication," in *Proceedings of the IEEE Vehicular Networking Conference (VNC)*, O. Altintas, W. Chen, and G. J. Heijenk, Eds. IEEE, 2011, pp. 246–251.

[170] (2011, January) CST MICROWAVE STUDIO - Technical Specification. CST Computer Simulation Technology. [Online]. Available: http://www.cst.com

[171] S. Miglietta, "Entwicklung eines Simulators zur Evaluation des Adaptive Beamforming in der Car-to-X Kommunikation," Diploma Thesis, University of Applied Science Darmstadt, October 2009, supervised by Hagen Stübing.

[172] T. Ruppenthal, "Entwicklung eines Simulators zur Evaluation des Secure Beamformings in der Car-to-X Kommunikation Kommunikation," Bachelors Thesis, Technische Universität Darmstadt, June 2011, supervised by Hagen Stübing.

[173] S. Moser, F. Kargl, and A. Keller, "Interactive Realistic Simulation of Wireless Networks," in *Proceedings of the IEEE Symposium on Interactive Ray Tracing 2007*, ser. RT '07. Washington, DC, USA: IEEE Computer Society, September 2007, pp. 161–166.

[174] J. Maurer, "Strahlenoptisches Kanalmodell fr die Fahrzeug-Fahrzeug-Funkkommunikation," Ph.D. dissertation, Institut fr Höchstfrequenztechnik und Elektronik (IHE) der Universit"at Karlsruhe (TH), 2005.

[175] C. A. Balanis, *Antenna Theory: Analysis and Design*. Wiley-Interscience, 2005.

[176] Y. Berghöfer, "Implementation and Evaluation of a Car-2-X Framework on Facility Layer," Bachelor Thesis, Technische Universität Darmstadt, 2011, supervised by Hagen Stübing.

[177] A. Hamieh, J. Ben-Othman, and L. Mokdad, "Detection of Radio Interference Attacks in VANET," in *Proceedings of the 28th IEEE conference on Global telecommunications*, ser. GLOBECOM'09. Piscataway, NJ, USA: IEEE Press, 2009, pp. 5077–5081.

[178] B. Xiao, B. Yu, and C. Gao, "Detection and Localization of Sybil Nodes in VANETs," in *Proceedings of the Workshop on Dependability Issues in Wireless Ad Hoc Networks and Sensor Networks*, ser. DIWANS '06. New York, NY, USA: ACM, 2006, pp. 1–8.

[179] C. Laurendeau and M. Barbeau, "Probabilistic Localization and Tracking of Malicious Insiders using Hyperbolic Position Bounding in Vehicular Networks," *EURASIP Journal on Wireless Communications and Networking*, vol. 2009, pp. 2:1–2:13, Feb. 2009.

[180] N. S. Axel Hoffmann and J. Stein, "Praxisphasenbericht," Adam Opel AG, Praktikumsbericht, June 2011, supervised by Hagen Stübing.

[181] A. H. Joel Stein, "Entwicklung eines Car-to-X Systems," Bachelors Thesis, University of Applied Sciences Frankfurt am Main, August 2011, supervised by Hagen Stübing.

[182] N. Schweers, "Entwicklung eines "Data aquisition and distribution" Systems für Car-to-X Systeme," Bachelors Thesis, University of Applied Sciences Frankfurt am Main, November 2011, supervised by Hagen Stübing.

[183] F. Rieger, "Du kannst dich nicht mehr verstecken," *Frankfurter Allgemeine Zeitung*, pp. 33,35, Februrary 2010, newspaper article.

[184] H. Stübing and S. A. Huss, "Betriebsverfahren für einen mobilen Netzknoten (patent pending)," german Patent DE 10 2012 008 121.9., 04 25, 2012.

[185] Y. Wang, "Detektion und Evaluierung von situationsbezogenen Mix-Zonen zum Schutz der Privatsphre in der Car-to-X Kommunikation," Master's thesis, Technische Universitt Darmstadt, June 2011, supervised by Hagen Stübing.

[186] Privacy International. [Online]. Available: http://www.privacyinternational.org

[187] U. Nations, "The Universal Declaration of Human Rights," 1948. [Online]. Available: http://www.un.org/en/documents/udhr

[188] European Union Directive, "Directive 95/46/EC of the European Parliament and of the Council of 24 October 1995 on the protection of individuals with regard to the processing of personal data and on the free movement of such data," April 1995. [Online]. Available: http://europa.eu/legislation_summaries/information_society/l14012_en.htm

[189] European Union Directive 2002/58/EC, "Directive 2002/58/EC Directive on Privacy and Electronic Communications," 2002.

[190] "Charters of Freedom The Declaration of Independence, The Constitution, The Bill of Rights," 1952. [Online]. Available: http://www.archives.gov/national-archives-experience/charters/constitution_transcript.html

[191] "Privacy Act of 1974 and Amendments." [Online]. Available: http://epic.org/privacy/laws/privacy_act.html

[192] "California Constitution: Article 1 Declaration of Rights." [Online]. Available: http://www.leginfo.ca.gov/.const/.article_1

[193] "Constitution of Montana - Article II - Declaration of Rights." [Online]. Available: http://data.opi.mt.gov/bills/mca/Constition/II/10.htm

[194] "Vehicle Code Section 9950-9955," Online. [Online]. Available: http://www.leginfo.ca.gov/cgi-bin/displaycode?section=veh&group=09001-10000&file=9950-9955

[195] "Government Code Section 11000-11019.10 ." [Online]. Available: http://www.leginfo.ca.gov/cgi-bin/displaycode?section=gov&group=10001-11000&file=11000-11019.10

Printed by Publishers' Graphics LLC
LMO130605.15.16.30